To All GENERATIONS

A Study of Church History

TO ALL GENERATIONS

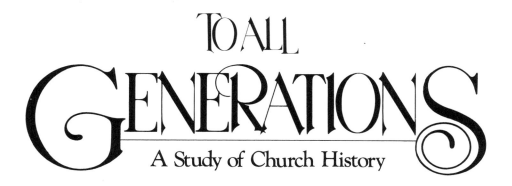

A Study of Church History

FRANK C. ROBERTS

Bible Way
Grand Rapids, Michigan

Library of Congress Cataloging in Publication Data

Roberts, Frank, 1937–
     To all generations.

     Bibliography: p.
     Includes index.
     1. Church history. I. Title.
BR145.2.R6   270   81-3832
ISBN 0-933140-17-7   AACR2

Cover Design: Chuck Spitters
Cover Photo: The Genesis Project, Inc., used by permission of the Genesis Project Photo Library.

FOR THE LORD IS GOOD;
HIS STEADFAST LOVE ENDURES FOR EVER,
AND HIS FAITHFULNESS TO ALL GENERATIONS.
Psalm 100:5

BUT THOU, O LORD, ART ENTHRONED FOR EVER;
THY NAME ENDURES TO ALL GENERATIONS.
Psalm 102:12

CONTENTS

PREFACE

To All Generations *is part of the adult education curriculum produced by the Education Department of the Christian Reformed Church. Like the two preceding courses,* A Place to Stand *and* Beyond Doubt, *this present course is offered to churches as an aid in teaching believers the fullness of the faith and in training them for mature service as members of Christ's ministering body.*

To All Generations *is a course in general church history. It does not trace the roots or relate the story of the Christian Reformed Church as a denomination—that will be done in a subsequent course. Rather it draws in broad, sweeping strokes the picture of the church of Christ through all the generations of its existence on earth, from its beginning to the present. It tells of the major events and describes the major movements that shaped the church's history.*

Every history must be selective. Out of the billions of past happenings, a book of history chooses those which can be woven together into a meaningful design according to the author's purposes. To All Generations, *attempting in twenty-five brief chapters to encompass thousands of years of church history, has had to be very selective. It has concentrated on the story of the Western church, especially the Reformation churches, including information on heretical sects or churches in distant lands only when necessary to keep what happened to the main body of the church in proper perspective.*

Selections in this course were made with the following goals in mind: to enable students to identify and evaluate the historical events, movements, and persons crucial to the preservation and growth of the church of Christ; to encourage an appreciation of the various Christian traditions which shaped the church; and, above all, to deepen an awareness of God's providential actions in preserving and building his church.

The author of this book is Dr. Frank C. Roberts. A graduate of Calvin College and Seminary, he also received his Ph.D. in history and church history from Vanderbilt University. This unusual combination of theological and historical training qualifies Dr. Roberts uniquely as author of a church education text in church history. His other published works include The

8

Reformation *(Grand Rapids, CSI, 1976) and "German Protestants Face the Social Question: Social Protestantism in Germany, 1850-1900" in* Case Studies in the History of Socialism *(Warner Lerner, ed., forthcoming). He was also coeditor with Dr. George Marsden of* A Christian View of History? *(Grand Rapids, Eerdmans, 1975). Since 1969 he has been professor of history at Calvin College.*

Accompanying this book are a teacher's manual and a series of session guides called Postscripts. These are intended to direct church school classes to a profitable study of the materials in this book. They were written by the staff of the Education Department.

A study of the history of the Christian church can be very valuable to sincere believers. We who live in Canada and the United States dwell in nations with relatively brief histories. Like most of those in the New World, for us the future has, for many years, seemed rosy with the glow of unlimited possibilities and bright hopes. We have tended to be optimistic peoples, trusting in promising futures for our countries.

Such naive faith in the future has been shaken by recent developments, the economic conundrums and depleted resources of our modern world. Suddenly it seems the future has darkened, altered from dawn to dusk.

It is a good time for us, as Christians, to look to the past history of God's people. We need to remember the long line of fellow pilgrims who lived through even darker days of frightful persecution, through eras of barbarism, through times when the church itself seemed shriveled and dead. We need to see the faith that sustained these fellow believers through the years of their lives, a faith based on deep trust in the Lord who promised never to desert his church.

From such a study of the past, we can learn again to face the future in the confidence that the God who was with his people in the past centuries will be with them also today, for he is faithful to all generations.

Harvey A. Smit
Director of Education

CHAPTER 1
HISTORY AND SALVATION HISTORY

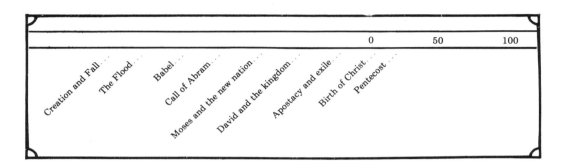

Church history is the story of what happened in the past to Christ's followers and to the religious organization that embodies them, the Christian church. That story properly begins, as many historians have pointed out, at Pentecost, the church's birthday and birth event.

Still, we will begin this study earlier; for it should be obvious we must precede it with another story—the account of the birth, life, death, resurrection, and ascension of Jesus Christ. After all, the church is *his* church, Christians are *his* followers, and the Spirit that animates them is *his* Holy Spirit. To interpret Christianity without Christ is like bathing without water; we hear of people doing it, but it seems an unlikely, even an in-herently contradictory, project.

Besides, if we consider how the earliest Christians themselves viewed the origins of their faith, we find them relating the work of Christ (and their own resultant activities) closely to the history of God's people in even earlier times. To them Jesus was clearly and importantly a descendant of Abraham and David (Matt. 1:1-17). He stood in their line. It was their God, "the God of our Father," who raised up Jesus (Acts 5:30). They themselves were, in their thinking, part of the people God was already gathering in Old Testament times. Abraham was rightly "the father of all who believe" (Rom. 4:11), and the Old Testament was rightly a book for the instruction of Christians (2 Tim. 3:16).

So for them, and for us, the roots of the living, historical phenomenon we call the Christian church reach back before Pentecost, before the ascension, before Christ's death and birth, before Israel's beginnings, to God's very first dealings with the human race. The Christian church, like a tulip from a bulb, stems directly from that long salvation history. To truly grasp the nature of Christ's redeemed people and the character of their odyssey through the ages, we need to view them in this way. We may not cut the stem at Pentecost and consider the church as just another historical phenomenon, explainable by ordinary historical causes and trends. The church, God's chosen people, is always more than that.

As in all Christian understandings of our world and human life, so too in church history, the biblical account shines like a beacon down the centuries illumining our perceptions and guiding our insights. By it we read in church history God's faithfulness—that his steadfast love endures to all generations, that he will surely keep his word and accomplish his promised purposes, that he will build his church and protect his people.

Not that we may carelessly merge salvation history and church history or presume to detect with inspired insight where God acted and where the devil did, why God destroyed the Spanish Armada, or who of the church leaders was fully faithful and who utterly faithless. We see "through a glass, darkly," we know "in part" (1 Cor. 13:12, KJV). We must evaluate and judge, but with care and caution. For this is a historical study of the church, not a series of easy pronouncements or careless moralizations about our Christian past.

To help guide us in this task, we will review in this first chapter some Old Testament roots of Christianity.

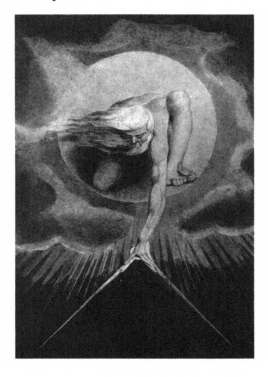

WILLIAM BLAKE, The Ancient of Days

Creation and Fall

"In the beginning God made the heavens and the earth." So the story opens. God created the world, and what he made, he found very good. His benediction rested also on his image-bearers, the ministers over his kingdom, Adam and Eve. But we are told that these first human beings, created to be God's trusted servants, rebelled against their natural lord. They sought to serve themselves and so fell, coming to serve an evil master. That crashing fall sounds down the halls of time. It is the start and source of the disharmonies of sin and death, war and weeping, hatred and hunger for the human race.

Yet God did not permit his good harmonies to be permanently disrupted. He refused to abandon these "god-players" to their unnatural alliance with his enemy. He promised to redeem his servants and save his world. Through a man of his choosing, one of Eve's children, he would turn Satan's initial victory into final defeat. "Just as a man destroyed the world in the beginning, another man will rebuild it."[1]

Carefully read, these first chapters of Genesis correct some common, misguided notions as to what history is all about. They teach us history is not just a human story. God is acting here. To read it only in terms of human deeds is like trying to discover a book's contents by touch alone. No one can, in such a self-limiting way, truly discern what has been happening. By ruling God out of the picture, we get a lopsided, misguided story of events.

Genesis (and the rest of the Bible) tells us more than *that* God acts. It portrays for us *how* God acts. He doesn't merely create the stage of history to watch passively from the mezzanine each "poor player that struts and frets his hour upon the stage."[2] Neither is God merely the author of the play who plots the action and then settles into his seat to watch the drama unfold. Nor is he simply the director, coaching the actors in their roles, establishing the play's mood. Certainly he is more than the stage manager, raising and lowering the curtain and arranging the special effects. God is all of these—Creator, author, director, and stage manager—but he is also far more. He is first of all the main actor in the drama called human history. The main role, the key part, is God's.

We, as Christians, believe and know that God is active in every contingency of an unstable history. He controls the fates that appear to rule so powerfully over history.[3] Yet though never absent, he is often very inconspicuous. It takes eyes of faith to detect his presence and understand his workings.

But there is more in these Genesis chapters for our understanding of history. The man and woman are responsible participants in the drama. What they do alters history's course. Humanity's sin (Act One, Scene Two) is no puppet play with God pulling strings and projecting his voice. The human players truly decide and decisively act. Not apart from God but against God, in flagrant disobedience, they act.

Because of this decisive human action, history can never be reduced to an evolutionary process—a straight line, imperceptible but steady, advancing to a better humanity. Neither can it be considered a prewritten scroll on which the fateful decisions appear as time unrolls. Rather, a view of history that begins with a genuine fall requires us to recognize humanity's serious responsibility in history's events.

Finally, these chapters picture a God who regards sin not as an excuse to write the responsible humans out of the scene, nor as a perplexing problem to be solved; rather they show a God who accepts human sin as a terrible impairment to be overcome by his own goodness and love. It is his intent to deal intimately with men and women—not to abandon them to their own devices, but to win them to his good purposes.

To the believer then, looking out of eyes of faith, history appears neither as an endlessly repeating cycle of events, nor as a flat march into infinite and unknown distance. History moves to a goal. God has set a purpose which he will accomplish in the historical happenings. Even though we cannot label the particular steps or mark how God is doing this, we know by faith and his Word that it is being done.

Therefore, in our study of church history we believe that God is active in what occurs and we try, though gropingly, to detect his presence and discern his hand. We believe that our own human actions help form and direct the course of events. But more than anything else it is the interplay between God and his human creatures, his patient molding of them to his purposes and turning them to his directions, that forms the very stuff of church history.

The Flood, Babel, and the Calling of Abraham

Of all the events from the ejection out of paradise until Israel became a nation, three stand out for what they tell us about history and God's working in history: the flood, Babel, and the calling of Abraham.

The flood stands out because that account of God's action to erase sin from the world and his everlasting promise never again to halt the pulse of natural existence (Gen. 9:8-17) guarantees the continuing stage on which history is played. More importantly, it teaches that God's covenantal dealings with the human race include "every living thing of all flesh." God deals in history not just with human beings, but through them with the whole of his creation.

Babel is important because that account of how God confused language and scattered humanity over the face of the earth (Gen. 11:1-9) tells us of the disintegration of the human clan. The one language, bond of unity, and vehicle of human communication was shattered into a multitude of tongues. Humanity was divided. Inevitably there followed contentions and wars between nations, tribes, and races. History became a struggle between diverse clans of humankind and a divisive tension entered the scene, a tension resolved only in Christ and, to a degree, in his church.

The calling of Abraham stands out as the event that marked a new

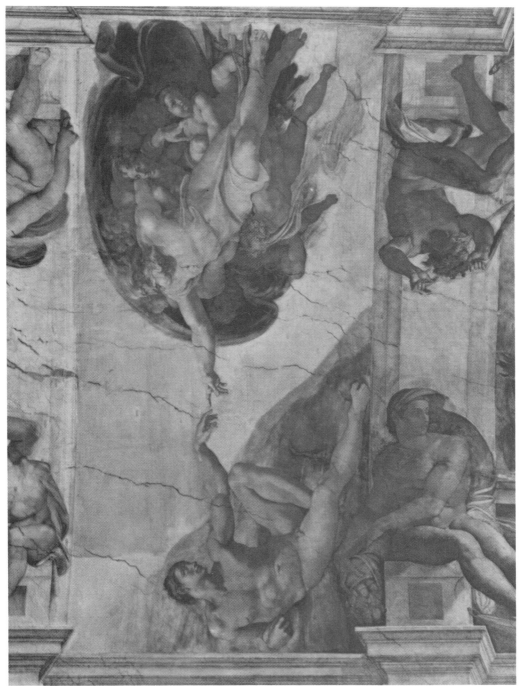

MICHELANGELO, The Creation of Adam

epoch in the history of redemption. From this point on God's saving activity, still intended for the world and all humanity, was concentrated through one clan. One land, Canaan, became special, and one nation, the children of Abraham, became God's own separate people (Gen. 12). One language, Hebrew, became the vehicle of God's speech to humankind. Not that God abandoned the other millions; rather he dealt with them indirectly. "Through Abraham and his seed" they would be blessed. God's purpose and strategy in history remained the same, but his dealings narrowed in a concentration that led through Israel to Jesus Christ.

Abraham responded to God's call. That was necessary. This new key figure had to go where he was sent and trust God when in danger. Like Adam and Noah before him, he had to learn to believe God's promise. As Paul says in Romans, by faith Abraham became righteous. By faith he became father of all believers, of all God's obedient people, in all times and places.

We cannot begin to grasp the nature of Israel or begin to comprehend the imprint of their history unless we apprehend this pattern of God's working with Abraham. It is the key to understanding the true significance of these stories. God contracted, he covenanted, to work with a segment of humanity, that through them he might accomplish his continuing purpose for all humanity and the entire world.

There are, in human terms, risks in this approach. God limited his own range of actions by requiring a human response—faith. God did not work *on*, but *with* his chosen people. They were capable of resisting his call and rejecting his leading. God placed, as it were, all his eggs in one basket, and Abraham was holding it—not too securely.

Still God is the Lord. He will do what he sets out to do. His plans will not be thwarted by his people's disobedience or lack of trust. The story of Joseph beautifully illustrates this.

Joseph experienced a series of misfortunes. His father's favoritism incited his brothers' jealousy. His own ambitious dreams fanned their hatred. So when the opportunity came, they sold him as a slave and returned to Jacob with a concocted tale of death by misadventure. In Egypt, Joseph's virtue earned only the vengeful hatred of Potiphar's seductive wife. He ended up in prison.

But then things changed dramatically. His dream interpretations won a hearing from Pharaoh and a position as a minister in charge of Egypt's granaries. Famine brought his brothers into his land. But instead of avenging himself, Joseph provided a refuge for his whole family. He said to his brothers, "Do not be distressed or angry with yourselves, because you sold me here; for God sent me before you to preserve life. . . . So it was not you who sent me here, but God" (Gen. 45:5, 8).

The lesson of Joseph's story is not a moralistic, good-will-triumph assurance. Rather it tells us that God works, mysteriously but surely, using evil to bring good. God acts both through human obedience and disobedience to accomplish his purpose. He uses even our faithless acts to accomplish his ends.

Therefore, these stories of redemption history teach us as believers to see that God covenants in history with human beings and with all flesh, a covenant that both promises and demands, a covenant that patterns the interplay between God and humanity. That covenant involves a commitment on God's part. He will accomplish his ends and keep his word even though it means sacrificing himself in history. So God has bound himself to act toward us and with us.

Moses and the New Nation

Moses is called "the redeemer of the Old Testament."[4] By his hand, God delivered the children of Israel out of bondage and formed them into a free nation. The law, God's word through Moses, gave cohesion to a motley, disunified band of ex-slaves. It provided their code of values, pattern of worship, and way of living. Israel the clan became a nation.

This story teaches us that at certain crucial points in our history, God acts with dramatic directness. He shows himself and his salvation openly. Even Pharaoh and the Egyptians were forced to recognize his fearful presence.

The history following such redemptive acts is a response to them. Israel's identity as a people stems from the exodus. God had delivered them. He formed them there as a nation. He became their God and Father. Therefore they had to serve him, obey his law, and follow his leading. Because of what God had done for them, they had to become his distinct and special people.

MICHELANGELO, The Fall of Man and the Expulsion from the Garden of Eden

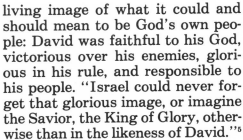

Through such examples we come to understand that all history is a dialogue between God and creation. And church history especially is such a speaking and reply, acting and response between God in Jesus Christ and ourselves. Apart from Christ's death and resurrection there could be no church. Christ's redemptive acts are the reason for the church's existence, and everything the church is and does must be a response to them.

David and the Kingdom

David is the symbol for an entire era of Israel's life. He was their ideal king, the leader in the golden age, a type of the Messiah to come. David and his kingdom provided a

David Composing the Psalms,
illustration from the Paris Psalter

living image of what it could and should mean to be God's own people: David was faithful to his God, victorious over his enemies, glorious in his rule, and responsible to his people. "Israel could never forget that glorious image, or imagine the Savior, the King of Glory, otherwise than in the likeness of David."[5]

In David the redemptive history narrowed and centralized even more. Now not just the tribe of Judah, but David's royal family became the line through which the Savior would come. Jerusalem emerged as the political and religious center of Israel, the great symbol of the place where God would finally restore his people to their glorious state.

David and his kingdom became formative concepts in the church's history: Christian kings and rulers attempted to redo David's deeds in their own age—to build an earthly kingdom that would embody the heavenly one. David's kingdom and its wars also became the model on which many came to see church history as warfare—a struggle between divine and satanic kingdoms, a conflict between two armies in which each skirmish is just a small part of the greater fight and in which our great captain will certainly lead us to final victory.

But David himself and the kingdom he established stand as a phase in the history of God's people. David is a type of the Messiah and his kingdom a type of that Messiah's reign. But David's role and function cannot be transposed into the New Testament church without doing violence to the tem-

18

poral separation of redemption history and church history. David stands unalterably before Christ, the church gloriously after him.

Apostasy and Exile

David's glorious kingdom was short-lived. It quickly fragmented and began to disintegrate. Politically weak and vulnerable, Israel soon became spiritually flabby and ethically dead. Worship of pagan gods and adherence to heathen practices became common. God spoke with prophetic warnings and divine judgments—and finally with the exile which seemed to undo Israel's deliverance. They were separated from the promised land and seemingly from their God's covenant promises.

Yet, it was as a captive, conquered people that Israel learned loyalty to Yahweh. It was during the exile that they developed synagogue worship and longing for the Messiah, founder of the new Israel. In exile they relearned what it meant to be God's people.

These years of Israel's captivity correct too simple an understanding of history as war between two kingdoms. During the exile that division was no longer very clear. God spoke to Nebuchadnezzar. He used Cyrus. God's kingdom somehow included these "outsiders."

The exile teaches that God can and will be ruthless in his love to his own people. The unfaithful will be disciplined. The ignorant will be taught. If they have become his people only in name, God will use others to accomplish his purposes and restore his own as his people indeed.

Therefore in reading church history we should not become disheartened by apostasy. There are unfaithful followers and disobedient servants. The two sides in the spiritual struggle are not always clear. But God will whip his forces into line, painful though that may prove. The ruthless love of God will accomplish his purposes and bring to pass in history his momentous work of salvation.

****

History has been called the longsuffering of God. It is his patient, persistent demand that the world and the beings he created good, happy, and pleasing to himself shall finally become what he intended from the beginning. God refuses to give up on his people and will not destroy them in disappointed wrath (Hos. 11:8, 9). Rather, in compassion he will bring about their redemption.

The history of the church is the tale of God's patient faith-keeping, often contrasting sharply to our human faithlessness. To all generations God's steadfast love endures. His goodness wins over human evil, his love over human hate. If we do not see this, we have not even begun to understand the church's history.

CHAPTER 2
FROM SALVATION HISTORY TO THE FIRST-CENTURY CHURCH

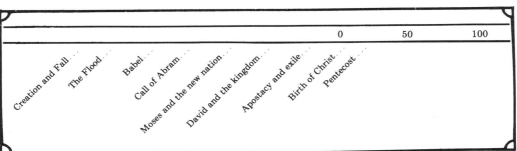

							0	50	100

Creation and Fall... The Flood... Babel... Call of Abram... Moses and the new nation... David and the kingdom... Apostacy and exile... Birth of Christ... Pentecost...

The new era of salvation history, and the new testament to God's faithfulness to all generations, commences with the story of Jesus of Nazareth. In him all the lines converge; all the strands of prophecy, all the themes of law and sacrifice, all the expectations of redemption coalesce. And from him God's redeeming work fans out beyond Israel as the good news of salvation to every nation, tongue, and tribe of the human race. Jesus is the center of history.

Almost every believer would nod approval to this last sentence. It sounds both pious and correct. We believe that Jesus is the only way to the Father, the funnel through which God's grace pours, the channel through which the stream of salvation flows. We are, I think, all convinced that the date we write on each letterhead is not merely the year of the "Christian era" or "common era" as some Jews and secularists assert—for it is profoundly proper to divide history as B.C. and A.D., making the coming of the Lord Jesus the partition point.

But the implication this truth—that Jesus is the center of history—has for our reading of the historical account may not be so clear. What does Jesus' centrality have to do with the spectacular success of early Christianity? What does it have to do with a group of motley fishermen, tax collectors, and social inferiors who took the teachings of an obscure Palestinian carpenter and within three centuries

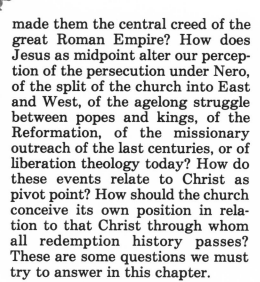

made them the central creed of the great Roman Empire? How does Jesus as midpoint alter our perception of the persecution under Nero, of the split of the church into East and West, of the agelong struggle between popes and kings, of the Reformation, of the missionary outreach of the last centuries, or of liberation theology today? How do these events relate to Christ as pivot point? How should the church conceive its own position in relation to that Christ through whom all redemption history passes? These are some questions we must try to answer in this chapter.

The Fullness of Time

Christ came in "the fullness of time" (Gal. 4:4, KJV). What does that mean? Or, better, how should we understand that?

It means, of course, that Christ came as a fulfillment of prophecy and a culmination of Israel's history. But it is also often interpreted to mean that he came at a singularly convenient point in world history. Conditions were remarkably right for a new, world religion.

The Roman Empire, first of all, had established a relatively peaceful, politically stable world. That means missionaries could travel on good, open roads protected by the soldiers of the empire and on sea lanes guarded by sailors of the empire.

Further, there was a common language. Everyone who was anyone

in the then-known world, everyone with a modicum of education, everyone who had traveled or had a trade knew Greek. And since this was the language in which the Gospels and Epistles were written, no tedious translation process was required; since this was the language evangelists knew, no time was wasted in clumsy interpreting.

Further still, Rome promoted "the idea of a common humanity which underlies all distinctions of race, society, and education."[1] Age-old barriers of culture and race were crumbling. It was a fitting time for a religion that maintained, "There is neither Jew nor Greek, there is neither slave nor free, there is neither male nor female" (Gal. 3:28).

Particularly convenient were the synagogues of the dispersed Jews, the millions who were scattered from one end of the empire to another. In these synagogues the missionaries could speak not only to the Jews but also to the local Gentiles, many of whom had converted to Judaism. Some of these Gentiles had been circumcised and accepted as full-fledged Jews, but most were halfway converts: "God fearers." It was these second-class Jews, the "God-fearers," who became the nucleus of the Gentile Christian church. The gospel of Christ completed what they had partially found in Judaism; and, as Christians, they discovered they were no longer second-class citizens of God's kingdom.

All these factors made the world ripe for the spread of Christianity. And that raises an important ques-

Mural of Triumphal Entry from the Church of St. Lazarus

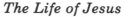

tion: does the centrality of Christ mean only that God very wisely seized his chance and sent Jesus at the most opportune time? Is God only a "smart operator" who read the market in religion well and bought when it was rising? Obviously not. That kind of thinking assumes a course of events apart from God, who sits, a deistic spectator, in the wings waiting for the best chance. For the Christian such a perception of the relation of God and the world is untenable.

We do not as Christians combine on the one hand a natural cause-and-effect view of history with, on the other hand, a pious belief in God's mysterious, behind-the-scenes operations. God does not let history run its own course, intervening only at crucial points (beginning, middle, and end). That is not what the Christian means by saying Christ is the center of history.

The Bible teaches clearly God's control at every point. A sovereign God permits no event to occur without his active participation. No Roman Empire appears, no common language spreads, no ideal of a common humanity develops without his hand. Synagogues do not merely "happen" to disperse in convenient patterns.

In Christ, God's activity in history, his dialogue with humankind, rose to a scream that forced itself on human attention. God took history so seriously he entered into it in his own Son and put himself at the mercy of sinful humanity. In Christ God was present in his world and in its history.

Many have tried to reconstruct Jesus' life, to identify his actual, "historical" words and deeds. By this, they've tried to explain how he came to be central to our history.

Most such attempts try to dig under the overlay of disciples' interpretations to find the "true Jesus." They attempt to discover how this unusual person would have appeared to a neutral observer, a modern historian.

That's no simple task. The Gospels record only a small part of Jesus' life. "For all the inestimable value of the Gospels," says Lightfoot, "they yield us little more than a whisper of [the Lord's] voice, we trace in them but outskirts of his ways."[2]

The typical life of Jesus portrays a man of ordinary family:

His father was a carpenter in Nazareth, his mother a common village girl. Although extraordinarily gifted, this Jesus was not accepted by the village people as anything more than the local carpenter's son.

He began a public ministry at age thirty or so. The stage for that was set by John the Baptist, an odd wilderness preacher. This John proclaimed judgment, repentance, water baptism, and a life of obedience to God's will. Jesus endorsed this message when he accepted baptism from John.

Jesus first gathered twelve disciples evidently as symbols of

FRA ANGELICO, *The Crucifixion*

the twelve tribes and a sign that he intended to found a new people of God. He preached and did miracles throughout Palestine so that many hailed him as the promised Messiah. But many more regarded him as an unbalanced fanatic and a threat to the true religion. His claims were extreme, maybe blasphemous.

There were attractive elements to Jesus' teaching. He preached an ethic beyond outward obedience. For him motivation and purpose were paramount in a true keeping of God's law. He taught a kingdom of God "for sinners only," closed to those who claimed any status as "the righteous."

While teaching near Jerusalem, this Jesus was betrayed by one of his own disciples, arrested, tried, and crucified. The story of his life appears, as with most humans, to end at his death.

However, his disciples unanimously affirmed that he rose from the dead, appeared to them, and ascended to God. They firmly believed the tragedy of the crucifixion was overcome by the victory of Easter. They believed this same Jesus gave them power to bring his message to the entire world.

The contrast of such a natural life of Christ and the gospel accounts is obvious. Such a "life"

25

makes the disciples' faith, not Christ's deed, the seed out of which the church sprang. It makes their convictions the true center of church history.

But the Gospels insist that it is the birth, teaching, acts, death, and resurrection of Jesus Christ which usher in the new era. These are God's great saving acts, parallel to the exodus event. These acts established God's new people. The Christ events founded the church.

Every act of faith, every deed of obedience, every movement of reform, every missionary enterprise of his people can be traced back to the central fact that God sent a Savior in Jesus and paved a way of salvation for all who believe. It's as if a new continent were created on earth, or a new dimension opened for human life. This is the key to all that follows. This is the focal event. Jesus Christ is the center of history.

But Jesus departed. He ascended to heaven, leaving the world and history. He seems no longer present, certainly not in the former bodily sense. How then can he continue to be the focus of history? Because when he left he made the apostles into his church and the church into his present body. When God in Christ entered history he did so permanently—his Word remains in our world, his presence

REMBRANDT, The Appearance of Christ to Mary Magdalen

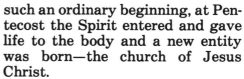

abides. And the church, the dwelling place of Christ's Spirit, is the body through which he remains within history.

Not only remains, but also works—for the work of Jesus did not stop with his death. He continues by his Spirit to work in and through his church. He told his disciples they would do greater works than he himself did because whatever they would ask in his name, he [Jesus] would do (John 14:12, 13). His Spirit would live in them. They would be the body that continues his ministry in his name.

Thus Jesus Christ remains the center of history—not as some crucial past event but as a living, contemporary presence. What happens today still centers in him. All who hear respond to him, faithfully or faithlessly. We all answer his Spirit's call, obediently or disobediently.

We may not look at the church's long history without seeing the light of Christ and feeling the breath of his Spirit. To neglect him in writing that history is like composing a biography that wholly neglects the spirit and soul of the person described. Jesus Christ is the Lord of his church and its head. His Spirit is its life. No genuine history of the church may neglect his active presence.

The New Clan

Pentecost marked the church's birth. At Pentecost a new organization began. True. But eclipsing such an ordinary beginning, at Pentecost the Spirit entered and gave life to the body and a new entity was born—the church of Jesus Christ.

By describing the church's beginning in creation's terms, we are not implying a duality of body and soul or that the church is a union of alien elements. Rather the creation of the church is parallel to the first creation of the human race: at Pentecost we witness God breathing the breath of his Spirit into a dead form he has molded. He breathed his Spirit into his band of disciples and they became a living church.

This newborn church was still immature and imperfect. The early believers carried the treasure of the Gospels "in earthen vessels." It follows that this new church is not a perfect model from a golden age, an ideal image we should emulate. It was rather the infant form of the church of Christ—young, full of potential, growing rapidly, but experiencing acute growing pains.

This new people were given a new language. Babel ended God's direct conversations with all humanity. It divided people into clans, each with a distinct tongue. But Pentecost brings a new language that includes all the diverse tongues. It marks the birth of a new clan that will encompass all people, a clan that speaks a new, spiritual tongue: the language of faith.

This new universalism was not readily understood or eagerly welcomed; in fact, it was stubbornly resisted. The history of the first-century church records a lengthy struggle by Christ's Spirit to teach the church that the gospel is for all believers and the new faith is open to people everywhere. Acts and the Epistles detail that struggle of the Spirit to form the church as something more than a Jewish sect, to make it Christ's family for all his children.

The Jerusalem Church and the Gentile Problem

Jerusalem was the "mother" church. It was Jewish. Its members still thought of themselves as Israelites, still worshiped at the

And they were all filled with the Holy Spirit.

temple, practiced circumcision, kept dietary laws, and faithfully observed the Sabbath.

These "Hebrew Christians" had added some new, distinctive practices. They gathered on resurrection day (Sunday) for prayer and praise, held fellowship meals in memory of their risen Lord, and baptized in Jesus' name. But these were additions to, not substitutions for, Jewish practices.

The first split in the body, the first question of where this new way would lead—more accurately where Christ was leading them as they followed his way—concerned this Jewish religious identity.

The church in Jerusalem had a group known as "Hellenists." These people were probably, like the Sadducees, more open to Greek (modern) influences. They were less rigid in observing the law. Because of that, some believers apparently considered them religiously inferior and excluded their widows from the food distribution. Possibly also the stricter Christians "refused table fellowship with Hellenists because they did not observe the ceremonial law in its entirety."[3]

This problem raised some vital issues. Must Christians be Jews, at least in religious observances? Was the Christian Way a Jewish sect? Was Jesus Christ King of the Jews or Lord of all people? Was God's intention a better Israel or a new heaven and earth?

When persecution struck and the church began to seed outside Palestine, the issue intensified. How was the church to treat Gentile converts? They were uncircum-

cised and unconcerned with ceremonial law. Yet they were also forgiven sinners, fellow followers of Christ's way, animated by the same Spirit that lived in Jewish Christians. How could they *not* be accepted openly and thankfully?

Paul became the champion of the Gentile believers. He worked out with the leaders of the Jerusalem church the first resolution of the "Gentile problem"—that the Gentile converts need not be circumcised or observe the ceremonial law.

Paul also framed the needed theology. The law, he said, was given by God not to achieve salvation but to make people aware of their helplessness and need of a Savior. Now that Christ, that Savior, has come, those who believe in him are redeemed from the law's bondage. In Christ there is neither Jew nor Greek, bond nor free, male nor female. People of faith are not bound by external rules or ceremonial laws; living by the Spirit of Christ within them, they are wholly free, able in love to fulfill the law.

The church, following the Spirit's urging, obediently (though reluctantly in many cases) turned in the direction which reformed it into a world religion. As Peter, staunchest of the Jewish Christians, observed: "God shows no partiality, but in every nation any one who fears him and does what is right is acceptable to him" (Acts 10:34, 35).

This first struggle of the church to discern its own destiny and follow Christ's leading teaches us much about how church history should be read. The church did not perceive these changes as natural developments that circumstances forced on them, a fight between right and left, conservative and liberal, typical of any organization.

Neither did the church discern the Gentile question as a prickly problem that could not be avoided and consequently had to be solved. Some in the church may have had that opinion, but not the church leaders, Peter, James, and Paul.

Nor did the church suppose their experience was a sort of schooling, lessons their Lord was teaching them. It was not as if Jesus were saying, "Look, this is precisely what I was trying to tell you before, but you wouldn't listen. Now I'm forcing you to hear what I say." More was involved than a sort of church education for the church.

It follows that we also should not read the history of the first-century church (and subsequent centuries) as a natural development, or as a series of problems needing to be solved, or as a library of lessons to help us avoid past errors.

The New Testament shows us that in this period Jesus was leading (not merely teaching) his church. He was taking it along a road to a destination he had in view. An active Christ, by his Spirit, was working in and with his people. His way was no static path poured in concrete or pounded into the dirt by generations who walked in his footsteps. Rather it was and is a way through new valleys and up new hills—but always a way he leads and we, his church, follow.

History is the church's training ground in being the body of Christ. In that sense it is an education—though in the world, not the classroom. But it is also an apprenticeship that involves a task. Christ is the master workman, but we also should be "doing the work of the Lord" (1 Cor. 16:10).

****

Church history instructs us in the path the church walked in past years, sometimes faithfully, sometimes faithlessly, sometimes walking with the Lord, sometimes betraying him. But we must see beyond the church's experience the enduring faithfulness of God in Christ through all the trials and byways. And church history teaches us that we, as the church in this day, must be prepared to follow the same Christ wherever he leads us by his Spirit.

CHAPTER 3
THE CHURCH SETS ITS STANDARDS

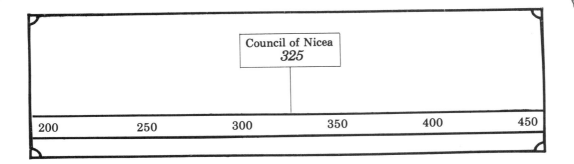

		Council of Nicea *325*			
200	250	300	350	400	450

It's a Sunday morning. Your pastor announces that the Scripture passage for the service is from *The Aquarian Gospel.* He reads:

Benares was a city rich in learning and famed for its knowledge of the healing arts. Lamaas took Jesus to Udraka, the greatest of all Hindu healers, that he might learn how to cure the sick.

Udraka taught Jesus and said: "Remember that the laws of nature are the laws of health. The human body might be likened to a harpsichord: When the strings are too lax or too taut, the instrument is out of tune—the man is sick. In nature there are many remedies for all the ills of man; but man's own will power is the greatest medicine of them all. At will a man can make a tense cord become lax, and a lax cord to become taut; and thus he can heal himself."[1]

How do you react to this? You may be intrigued; more likely you're deeply disturbed. How could anyone read such nonsense from a church pulpit as God's Word? Could your pastor have "gone round the bend"?

On another Sunday morning a guest preacher is in your pulpit. During the sermon he remarks, "Of course, Jesus was never a real flesh and blood human being! He only *seemed* to be human." Your hackles rise. This is glaring, boldfaced heresy. You'll make very sure this "minister" never ministers in your church again.

Perhaps you haven't had such experiences. But the point is that you (and a million other believers) are able, when needed, to make quick, sure judgments about which writings may properly be read in a Christian church and which teachings are orthodox. That's not surprising to you—you take it for granted—but it would have been surprising to a believer eighteen hundred years ago.

During the first centuries of the church's existence, there was no canon (measurement) that ruled decisively which books belonged in the Bible and which did not. There was no Athanasian Creed, accepted by the entire church, which stated unequivocally that "we believe and confess that our Lord Jesus Christ, the Son of God, is God and man. God of the substance of the Father, begotten before the worlds; and man of the substance of his mother, born in the world . . . . This is the catholic faith, which except a man believe faithfully, he cannot be saved."

True, believers in that period had the Jewish sacred Scriptures, the Law, the Prophets, and the Writings. They also had letters written by the apostles. But there were other writings that kept appearing, brought by visiting followers of The Way or borrowed from neighboring churches. Some of these—like the seven letters to the churches by Ignatius of Antioch, the letter of Polycarp to Philippi, or the little book called *Shepherd* by the layman Hermas—were clearly written by contemporary church leaders. But others—like the Gospel of Thomas, the Gospel of Truth, and the Preaching of Peter—were supposedly apostolic in origin.

One of these gospels of Christ told how Jesus struck dead some friends who annoyed him. Another, a letter, told how the apostle Paul had baptized lions in the desert. Were these authentic or not? How could one judge?

Besides the confusing proliferation of writings, there were a multitude of wandering prophets, going from church to church, each with his own "teaching." Some of these claimed secret knowledge, passed to them from Christ through some apostle. They offered to make you one of a special, elite group of followers, "in the know," if you'd listen to them and help them. Others taught that there were three gods: the Father, Jesus, and the Holy Spirit. Still others said that Jesus had been an ordinary man until God adopted him at his baptism. How could one be sure which prophets spoke a true gospel and which a false doctrine?

Of course, in some cases what was written and said was just too absurd. For instance, there was the story of John driving bugs out of a hotel so he could get a good night's sleep, or the tale of dogs lecturing their masters on proper morals. Such stories were too magical and superstitious to be Christian.

But others were more difficult to evaluate. The teaching that Jesus was God's adopted son and the idea of some "secret knowledge" passed on from the Lord through certain disciples were quite plausible. Such teachings had to be checked against writings you were sure came from the apostles or with

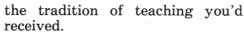

the tradition of teaching you'd received.

Still others were even more difficult. The explanation that Father, Son, and Spirit were three modes of one God or the idea that the Spirit was an impersonal force emanating from God couldn't be checked against a clear teaching on the Trinity in accepted writings. Yet these teachings concerned matters that lay at the heart of the faith. What's to be done in the face of all this confusion?

During the first centuries of its existence the church had to make some formidable, unavoidable decisions. What writings should be used in the churches? Which were false and should be ruled out of the canon? What teachings were orthodox (straight opinions) and which were heterodox (different opinions)?

The church was in a deep quandary. It needed standards by which to judge truth and error, but its decisions themselves set the standards. Heretics were probable truth-tellers until their teaching was declared heretical and they refused to conform. They were the ones who asked and tried to answer difficult questions of faith, the thinkers and teachers of the church, until their questions or answers were judged a threat to that truth.

It was the task and responsibility of the church to set the canon in terms of which the multitude of writings could be measured and to draw the straight line of doctrine against which some teachings could be judged crooked and false. This chapter tells the story of how that canon was established and that line of orthodox teaching drawn.

Gnosticism

The earliest major perversion of the gospel teaching (after the Judaizers) was spread by people within the church called Gnostics. This name came from the Greek word *gnosis,* meaning knowledge; for the Gnostics taught salvation by knowledge instead of by faith, redemption from this evil world instead of redemption from sin. Both of these teachings were basic alterations of "the way of righteousness" (1 Pet. 2:21). Yet they appealed strongly to Hellenistic Christians already deeply influenced by the Greek reverence for knowledge and disparaging of matter and the body.

Gnosticism was not an organized religious movement. If it had been, it would probably have been less of a threat. For if Gnosticism had had a creed, it might have been summarized in something like this confession:

I. I believe in an evil, Old Testament God of war and retribution, creator of this evil world.

II. I believe in a good, New Testament God of spirit and light.

III. And I believe in Jesus Christ, emanation from the good God, who appeared on earth as a phantom to re-

veal—to those people capable of understanding them—the secrets of how a human soul can escape the material world and be united with the good God.

IV. I believe in the good spirit imprisoned in the evil body of each person.

V. I believe that sex and marriage are wrong because they cause more souls to be imprisoned.

VI. And I believe in no resurrection of the body.

Compare this statement of beliefs with the Apostolic or Nicene Creed and you will wonder how any Christian could possibly be deceived by such teaching. But remember that when Gnosticism threatened, those creeds were not yet established as the unquestioned and unquestionable expression of the apostolic faith.

Furthermore, Gnosticism's attraction and threat lay precisely in its not being an organized religious movement against the Christian faith, but a way of thinking within Christianity. It used the vocabulary of faith. It spoke of Jesus as Lord and Savior. It claimed secret revelations from Jesus through the apostles. It produced writings, supposedly apostolic. It fooled many into believing this was the true teaching, the gospel of Jesus and Paul and the other apostles. It fools people still today—people who consider celibacy a higher way than marriage because it gives freedom from the evil body, people who understand the gospel as the

Christ as the Shepherd-Teacher, from an underground burial tomb in Rome (third century).

means of "saving souls" from this evil world, and people who speak of the body of a deceased person as a clump of evil matter from which the soul has escaped to its rightful, spiritual home. As a non-Christian way of thinking with a Christian face, Gnostic Christianity was a major threat to the faith.

But there were some Christian leaders who saw behind the facade to the perversion of truth. Men like Irenaeus, a bishop in France, and Tertullian, a lawyer from North Africa, wrote books explaining the Gnostic teaching, showing how it differed from true Christian doctrine.

Through their leading, the church first drew up a list of "apostolic books." That list excluded from use in Christian worship services the numerous Gnostic gospels and other writings—including Marcion's doctored-up version of the New Testament, composed only of Paul's writings and a heavily edited Gospel of Luke.

The Gnostic threat also led the church to produce creeds, like Irenaeus's Rule of Faith. This rule affirmed "one God, the Father Almighty, Maker of heaven and earth" and an historical Christ, "the Son of God, who became incarnate." It taught Jesus' "resurrection from the dead" and his "ascension into heaven in the flesh."

All in all, the threat of Gnosticism helped the church grow stronger and healthier. Because Christians were forced to define a canon and develop creeds, the church emerged from its struggle with Gnosticism with a far clearer understanding of what it believed and of the gospel it proclaimed.

A fresco depicting baptism, from the catacomb of Calixtus in Rome

The battle with Gnosticism defined the church's doctrine and solidified its teaching. But some Christians, while orthodox, protested that change. They wanted more spontaneity, more emotion, more freedom to follow the Spirit's leading. They were remarkably like today's "charismatic Christians."

One of these believers, a man called Montanus (c. 130-180), announced that he was the human instrument of God's Holy Spirit. His task, he claimed, was to prepare the church for Christ's imminent return. Two prophetesses, Maximilla and Prisca, left their husbands to join him. To prepare for Christ's return (to Phyrgia where they lived), these people and their followers practiced extreme asceticism, fasting, celibacy, and abstinence from meat.

The movement, according to opponents, became progressively more extreme. There were "gifts of revelation...converse with angels ...ecstatic visions."[2] Some "fell into a state of possession" and became "frenzied," uttering strange sounds. They prophesied "contrary to the manner which the church had received from generation to generation." They became "puffed up...and filled with no mean conceit."[3]

Because of Montanus's claim to direct revelation, the church condemned him and his movement soon after A.D. 160. They did not charge him with heretical teaching—for apart from his claim to be the Spirit's special mouthpiece, Montanus was quite orthodox. Instead they accused him of threatening—by his claims to direct revelation—the established teachings and authority of the apostolic tradition. The church feared that sooner or later this prophetic emphasis would lead to perversion of the truth.

Conflicts over the Trinity

Early Christians believed in a triune God—Father, Son, and Holy Spirit—but often did not understand the interrelationship between these three. The apostolic church made no systematic effort to explain that, and it was a mystery that "cried for elaboration."[4] Especially the question, "What do we mean when we say Jesus Christ is God?" demanded an answer.

There are those, still today, who doubt that demand, who feel that trinitarian dogma has turned a glorious mystery into a cold doctrine. But the church was forced to face that question and answer it, first by those non-Christians who accused the believers of worshiping three gods, second by Christian heretics whose speculations threatened the foundations of the faith. What finally took form as the church's fixed teaching was not cold doctrine but vital faith confession.

The development of the Trinity dogma was a complex affair spanning three centuries. We will simplify it in our sketch to two heresies, two extreme understandings of how Christ and the Holy Spirit were divine. The one, *Monarchianism*, excessively emphasized God's unity, undermining the reality of Christ's divine person. The other, *Arianism*, overemphasized the distinctions in God, turning Christ into a demigod and the Holy Spirit into an impersonal, divine force.

The Monarchian heresy sprang from the praiseworthy concern to worship one God, not three, and to teach God as one ruler (Greek, *monos* = alone, *archo* = rule). The most influential form of this teaching was called *Modalism*. It was led by Sabellius (c. 215), a Christian teacher in Rome.

Sabellius and his followers maintained that God is a single person in whom there are no distinctions of any kind. But that one God has appeared at different times in different modes. So in the Old Testament God shows himself in the Father mode, in the New Testament in the Son mode, and from Pentecost in the Holy Spirit mode.

But this means that one cannot speak today of Jesus Christ as being in heaven as a real person, our Mediator. After the resurrection God abandoned the Sonship mode for the Spirit mode. Jesus Christ is really God disguised as the Son.

The church condemned this teaching as blasphemy because it denied the reality of Jesus Christ as a person. Yet, in condemning the heresy, Dionysius of Rome, leader of the orthodox party, warned:

Sabellius blasphemously says that the Son is the Father and the Father is the Son; but

The Council of Nicea

[Sabellius's opponents] in some sort preach three Gods, [they divide God into] three substances foreign to each other and utterly separate.[5]

This opposite heresy which Dionysius feared was taught by Arius (c.300), a pastor from Alexandria in Egypt. For eighty years his teaching was a thorny threat in large areas of the church and almost took over even the largest congregations.

Arianism had three Gods in a hierarchy. On the top of the divine heap was the Father. Both Christ and the Holy Spirit were inferior, demigods. God the Father, said Arius, is "alone everlasting, alone unbegun, alone wise, alone good, alone sovereign." Jesus Christ, the Word, is "a creature of God," created before the world, higher than humans but not eternal. "There was when he was not." Christ, the Son, is of a different being than the Father. "Foreign from the Son in the essence [being] is the Father."[6]

Simply said, Arius believed Jesus was a semidivine, semihuman hero, "a pioneer of salvation" who showed us how to become good or remain good, by using our free will.[7] In Arianism, Christ is not the God-man who redeems, but a moral example for humankind.

Of the many who saw, providentially, the threat of Arius, one stood out as a "hero of the faith." Athanasius (c.320–70), bishop of Alexandria, was exiled several times, but in the face of terrible odds he steadfastly insisted Arian-

ism threatened to corrode the gospel and destroy the church. Through his leadership the church rejected the Arian doctrine, first at the Council of Nicea in A.D. 325 and again at the Council of Constantinople in A.D. 381.

How did the church leaders who attended these councils solve the riddle of the Trinity? They didn't. Rather they asserted and guarded the mystery. In rejecting various heresies they insisted that:

—God is one. The Father, Son, and Holy Spirit are "of the same essence (*homo-ousia*)." We must call each "God."

—all three persons always existed. The Son is not a mode or creation of the Father; neither is the Holy Spirit.

—the man Jesus Christ is God, just as much as the Father is God.

—the Holy Spirit is God, just as much as the Son and the Father are God.

After Nicea it was no longer possible to deny the full divinity of Father, Son, and Holy Spirit or to deny the reality of these divine persons and still call oneself a Christian. To view Jesus as an heroic man, a moral example, or a demigod was here fully rejected; for, as Athanasius recognized, to deny that Christ is truly divine, truly God, is to deny our salvation.

****

Heresy was a greater danger to the church than were external threats. The latter unified the church against a common enemy. Heresy, cloaked in Christian clothes, talking the language of faith, threatened to eat away from within and split the trunk of the body of believers like a wedge driven into its heart. It had to be identified as heresy and isolated out of the body.

One of the difficulties was that heretics were often honest truth-seekers. If they'd been mere charlatans, they would have attracted no following. This made them harder to detect and deal with.

Yet that very difficult struggle was good for the church. Through it Christ led his church to define its faith clearly, to recognize what is essential to its proper confession of him as Son of God incarnate, our Redeemer and Lord. By his Spirit God led the church through these difficult times to a clearer understanding of himself and his gospel. By what was defined then, we stand firmer in the faith today and know what we believe and where we stand.

CHAPTER 4
FROM NEW TESTAMENT CHURCH
TO CATHOLIC CHURCH

Gradual change from free, spontaneous N.T.
church to highly structured Catholic church
50–300

| 50 | 100 | 150 | 200 | 250 | 300 |

Two scenes of believers at worship may illustrate the change from apostolic to catholic church.

Scene one takes place in the Year of our Lord (Anno Domini) 50:

Ioannus (later called the Pilgrim because of his travels to Jerusalem and Rome) is a young, new convert to the Way. He heard the good news of Jesus, the Christ, from his cousin when Gaius came from the big city to visit his country relatives. Now Ioannus has come to Corinth and with Gaius attends a Christian gathering for the first time.

Entering the hall, his first impression is one of confused noise. Soon the sounds begin to filter out and he realizes several people are talking in some languages he's never heard, some strange "tongues." Before too long, however, someone else rises and in good, clear Greek begins to "interpret" what these people have been saying. It has to do with visions of the living Christ in heaven.

Suddenly a young woman begins singing. Spontaneously others join in until all who know the psalm are taking part. Ioannus hums and listens to the words telling of God's faithfulness to his people. In the lull following the song, an older man stands and begins talking about Jesus Christ—how he lived, died, and rose again. That resurrection, he assures everyone, is the guarantee of new life for all those who are "in Christ." There are

41

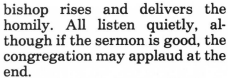

shouts of agreement and joy.

A woman is ill, so there's a short ceremony as some people anoint her with oil and pray for healing. Then someone stands up and quotes a teaching of Jesus; someone else prophesies that Jesus will return soon, warning everyone to be ready for his victorious coming. There are more shouts of joy and prayers.

Finally, it's time for supper. Everyone gathers around tables, unpacks food, and begins eating. Toward the end of the meal an older man stands up, announces the feast of love, and takes a loaf of bread and cup of wine. He recites Jesus' words: this is my body; this is my blood. They are to eat and drink in his remembrance. He invites all to share the bread and cup. Someone else speaks words of thanksgiving and benediction. The service is over.

Scene two takes place in the Year of our Lord 200:

It's Sunday, so believers come in from the surrounding towns and villages and gather in the worship hall. First the appointed reader stands, takes up the scrolls, and reads selections from the prophets and from the "memoirs" of the apostles. After the reading the choir, seated apart, begins to sing. The songs are either directly from the "memoirs" (like the Song of Mary) or from the three hundred approved hymns. The people join in, as invited, for some refrains. After the singing has ended, the bishop rises and delivers the homily. All listen quietly, although if the sermon is good, the congregation may applaud at the end.

A priest now directs all unbaptized persons to leave, for it is time for the Eucharist. Only the "initiated" may view the priestly sacrifice of Jesus' flesh and blood and partake of the Eucharist elements. Closing that solemn ceremony are prayers of thanksgiving. Then the congregation is dismissed.

The Great Change

These scenes illustrate a change in worship style so great that its like is not seen again throughout the church until the Reformation. By the end of the third century the free and spontaneous worship described in the New Testament had turned into a structured and prescribed liturgy.

Similarly the sign of admission to the church, baptism, had changed radically. From the simple ceremony conducted by any believer after a simple confession of faith, baptism became a church rite, performed only by the priest (except in emergencies), and conducted only after the instructed catechumen had affirmed an anti-Gnostic creed of faith. From a ceremony to confer the Holy Spirit, it became a rite that automatically remitted all earlier sins (some postponed baptism until just before death so as to enter heaven washed and sparklingly clean).

Christians hunted down in the catacombs

The sum of all these changes is that the New Testament fellowship of the followers of the Way had become the Catholic church. It was *catholic* in the original meaning of that word—universal, orthodox (nonheretical), and centralized in government. From A.D. 175 to 1525 the churches both in the East and the West were almost all catholic in form. (Even today the vast majority of Christians—about 75 percent—still belong to churches that are thought of as *catholic*: Roman Catholic, Eastern Orthodox, Anglican, etc.)

The questions before us in this chapter are these: What was this change? How did it take place? Why did it occur? And, more importantly, was this change good or bad? Was it, as some say, a deterioration of the New Testament's Spirit-filled body of Christ? Should contemporary churches turn their backs on their own history and try to reproduce totally the simple, free, spontaneous, loose believers' fellowship of the apostles' day? Or did God permit, even ordain, these changes in the church for his purposes and our good? Holding these questions in mind, we shall trace the change from apostolic church to catholic church.

The Early New Testament Period

The earliest churches were variously organized. Jerusalem, the mother church, had a single leader (first Peter, then James) and a sort of board of elders (the other disciples). But most other churches were more loosely ordered. Every congregation certainly had its leaders, but it's not at all clear whether these people were formally appointed to office or whether they just emerged as those who received "charisma" (gifts) of the Holy Spirit and were informally accepted by the fellowships. In Corinth, for instance, the leaders included prophets, teachers, tongue speakers, and healers—persons touched by the Spirit. Presumably there were also elders and deacons.

One thing does seem clear. In Corinth, and very likely in the rest of the churches, there was very little conscious distinction or distance between leaders and led. Paul's letters were not written to any governing body, any particular leader or board of elders. He addressed the entire congregation, calling on all to work at correcting abuses. Due honor, he urged, should be given to "every fellow worker and laborer..." who have "devoted themselves to the service of the saints" (1 Cor. 16:15, 16).

The Later New Testament Period

By the end of the New Testament period, however, the simple and fluid fellowship of the early days was already evolving into a complex and fixed organization (see 1 and 2 Tim. and Titus). Why? Partly because the church now faced enemies within as well as without.

Heresy (Gnosticism) became a menace. People who promoted false teachings claimed to be part of the fellowship. To answer such threats the church was forced to develop precisely defined offices which centered authority in properly appointed persons. They needed bishops and elders, men of high moral character who "hold firm to the sure word as taught...able to give instruction in sound doctrine and also to confute those who contradict it" (Titus 1:9). Against wandering prophets, "money grubbers," they needed deacons to guard and manage the church treasury.

Even the "charisma" from the Holy Spirit no longer seemed to be an adequate defense against the "many insubordinate men, empty talkers and deceivers" (Titus 1:10). Every heretic had his text and claimed the Spirit—thereby confusing the people. Against such false prophets the church needed officers to "test the spirits to see whether they are of God" (1 John 4:1) and to "care for God's church" (1 Tim. 3:5).

The officers were also needed to fill the gap left by the apostles (those who had seen the Lord). In the early church the apostles had enjoyed a unique status. Their authoritative teaching was a wall against error. Who could refute their words? Their presence had kept all heresy out. But the apostles died one by one. A new base of authority became essential. The church needed tighter organization, a system of officers, a long-term defense against heresies.

The period from A.D. 70 to 100 is mostly a mystery to church historians. The last New Testament record (around A.D. 70) portrays a church with bishops, elders, and deacons. When the thirty-year silence is broken (by nonbiblical documents), we find a "monarchial episcopacy," that is, churches ruled by a single, authoritative bishop.

The best description of this new church structure is given by a bishop, Ignatius of Antioch. Traveling to Rome to be executed for his faith, Ignatius wrote letters which give us a glimpse of the church of his time. He commands his readers:

Follow, all of you, the bishops, as Jesus Christ followed the Father. Moreover reverence the deacons as the commandment of God. Let no man do aught apart from the bishop. Let the Eucharist [Lord's supper] be considered valid which is under the bishop or him to whom he commits it. Wheresoever the bishop appears, there let the people be, even as wheresoever Christ Jesus is, there is the Catholic Church.[1]

Another bishop, Clement of Rome, gives a similar picture. It seems clear that most churches had one bishop and that bishop was the person who must be obeyed. Probably this officer was assisted by a board of presbyters (elders), but only the bishop could administer the sacraments (baptism and the Eu-

45

charist). The entire congregation concurred in the bishop's appointment, but he was still honored as a direct descendant of the apostles, regarded as holding their authority. It was the bishop's task, with other officers, to monitor traveling prophets and teachers, making sure they were true to the faith before allowing them to speak to the congregation. He, rather than Spirit-filled prophets, had become the guardian of the gospel truth, the bearer of the apostolic authority, the ruler in Christ's name.

The Apostolic Succession

As the second century drew the church farther from the time of the apostles, different traditions, sets of teachings, and interpretations of the gospel began to appear. Gnostics claimed a "secret tradition" going back to Christ. Other groups propounded their own special traditions and teachings. The church answered with the theory of the apostolic succession.

Clement, bishop of Rome, wrote around A.D. 96:

> Our Apostles also knew through our Lord Jesus Christ that there would be strife over the name of the bishop's office. So for this reason...they appointed the aforesaid persons (bishops) and subsequently gave them permanence, so that if they should fall asleep, other approved men should succeed to their ministry.[2]

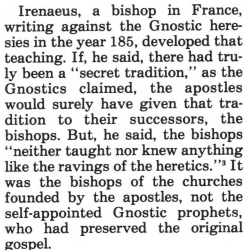

Irenaeus, a bishop in France, writing against the Gnostic heresies in the year 185, developed that teaching. If, he said, there had truly been a "secret tradition," as the Gnostics claimed, the apostles would surely have given that tradition to their successors, the bishops. But, he said, the bishops "neither taught nor knew anything like the ravings of the heretics."[3] It was the bishops of the churches founded by the apostles, not the self-appointed Gnostic prophets, who had preserved the original gospel.

Irenaeus and others began to write lists of bishops, lists which supposedly proved a continuity from the apostles to their day. Though not very accurate historically, these lists proved a marvelous weapon against heretics.

From our perspective, however, these lists only prove that Irenaeus and his fellows lacked any sense of how the church had developed historically under God's guidance. These men simply assumed that the church had always had bishops. The New Testament witness shows that assumption is false.

Third and Fourth Century Developments

In the third and fourth centuries church organization continued to change: a hierarchy of bishops appeared. Bishops in important cities began to gain authority over those in surrounding churches of smaller towns. They were called diocesan bishops. Then the five bishops of Jerusalem, Alexandria, Antioch, Constantinople, and Rome became most influential. They were called the patriarchs. Finally, centuries later, the patriarch of Constantinople emerged as dominant in the East and the patriarch of Rome in the West.

From earliest times the church in Rome had a special prestige. This was, after all, the capital of the Roman empire. Furthermore, according to Christian tradition, both Peter and Paul were martyred in this city. So the bishop of Rome had a preeminent position in the early church.

Early Christian art from the catacombs of Rome

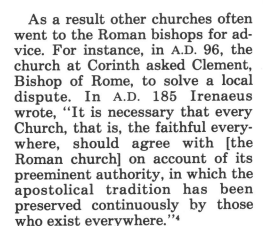

As a result other churches often went to the Roman bishops for advice. For instance, in A.D. 96, the church at Corinth asked Clement, Bishop of Rome, to solve a local dispute. In A.D. 185 Irenaeus wrote, "It is necessary that every Church, that is, the faithful everywhere, should agree with [the Roman church] on account of its preeminent authority, in which the apostolical tradition has been preserved continuously by those who exist everywhere."[4]

In Rome the first creed was formulated. In Rome the earliest orthodox New Testament canon was composed. Rome was the bastion of orthodoxy when heresy threatened. It cannot be doubted that the Roman church and the Roman bishop held a unique place.

But while the church in the first four centuries gave preeminence to Rome in status and teaching, it did not grant the bishop of Rome authority over all other bishops. Rome was rather "first among equals." There were times, as we will see in the next chapter, when the Roman church was roundly criticized by other churches.

****

In this chapter we have shown how the church changed from a simple to a complex organization—from a free, spontaneous fellowship of believers to a structured body with prescribed rituals of worship and involved sacraments. That reorganization was not just the self-entrenching of a power structure, solidifying its position, making its own continued existence the

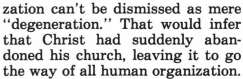

primary goal. Rather this transformation came because Jesus Christ didn't return as quickly as the church expected, because the death of the apostles left an "authority gap," and because heresy was a persistent, frightening, cancerous threat. The alteration in structure was a continual, developing, historical reaction to these factors. But if the church had faced an actual, conscious choice, it would have been in terms of the alternates—solidify or disintegrate, organize or die.

Indisputably some bad results accompanied the change. The elders of the people became the bishops above the people, the officers serving among the people became the clergy apart from the people. A gap grew between laity and clergy; laypeople became second-class citizens of the clergy-owned church. In worship, ordinary believers turned into spectators, watching the religious activities of priests. The idea of apostolic succession enhanced the bishops' authority until it came to stand with or even above the Bible's.

Intertwined with such bad developments were the growing magical conceptions of God's grace. Baptism became a sort of magic eraser, expunging all past sins. The Eucharist became "the medicine of immortality," able to restore those on the verge of death. Relics gained the supernatural power to rescue believers in dangerous situations.

Yet in spite of such bad results, the development of church organization can't be dismissed as mere "degeneration." That would infer that Christ had suddenly abandoned his church, leaving it to go the way of all human organization.

Rather we must see this period as one in which the church of God, led by his Spirit, faced an incredibly trying period of transition and threat. In the face of those trials the form of the church changed, adapting to meet the crises. But the gospel was firmly held and continued to be proclaimed to the world as the good news of salvation through Jesus Christ.

CHAPTER 5
FROM PERSECUTION TO VICTORY

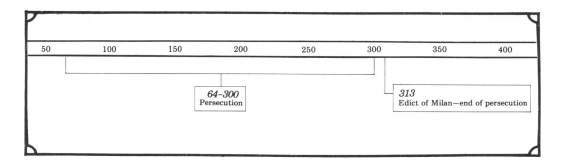

50	100	150	200	250	300	350	400

64–300
Persecution

313
Edict of Milan—end of persecution

Blessed are you when men revile you and persecute you and utter all kinds of evil against you falsely on my account. Rejoice and be glad, for your reward is great in heaven... (Matt. 5:11, 12).

These words of the Lord Jesus seem to slide past our ears with little comfort and little sting. What do we know of being reviled, persecuted, or falsely accused on Christ's account? In most of the modern West, to be a Christian is praiseworthy. Undoubtedly our brothers and sisters in China or Russia, or in other lands where believers are still a tiny minority, hear these words differently, more as the early Christians did.

Believers of the first three centuries were reviled and insulted. They were accused of sexual orgies at their evening gatherings, of cannibalism (eating the flesh and drinking the blood of a man named Jesus), of a foolish faith in a criminal who supposedly rose from the dead, of being bad citizens (since they refused to share in the sacrifice that supported the emperor and requested the favor of the gods on him), and of being atheists and haters of humanity.

They also experienced intermittent, usually localized, persecutions. These involved physical suffering and even death. There is a record of one Christian named Sanctus (the holy one) whose torturers, in trying to force him to renounce his faith, "applied red hot brazen plates to the most tender parts of his body. His poor body was a witness to what he had undergone—one whole wound and bruise. [He] lost the outward form of a man."[1] Yet his only response to his torturers was, "I am a Christian."

These were the realities of being a follower of Christ during that time.

Added to the realities of persecution were the perplexing questions it raised. Should believers rejoice at insults and persecutions? That's what Christ had commanded. Should believers then welcome or even seek such suffering, as if martyrdom were a seal of divine sanction to one's faith? That's what some thought. Others ran and hid. Was that wrong? What of those who couldn't endure the pain and escaped it by renouncing their faith and denying their Lord. Were they unalterably lost? The often-quoted phrase "the blood of the martyrs is the seed of the church," coined by Tertullian, was probably easier for later generations to repeat, those for whom the poignant memories of harsh decisions and painful divisions had long faded.

Nagging, difficult questions arise whenever the church is oppressed and persecuted. Is this of God, for our good? Must we see it so? Or is it of Satan, a war weapon meant to destroy us? What of churches that virtually disappear under persecution? Did Satan win? Did Christ desert that church, perhaps because of its unfaithfulness? And what of an end to persecution and a new favored position—is that true victory or a mixed blessing?

Many of these questions can't be answered in this chapter. But as we read of the early persecutions, Christian reactions, and the apparent victory under Constantine, we should be alert to how Christ leads his people through such experiences, how they change the church, and how each new stage of the church's life produced new challenges to its faith and loyalty, new opportunities for witness and service.

Roman Policy

Until A.D. 64 and Nero's reign, Christians were not badly treated by the Roman state. Like all local religions, they were tolerated. The Romans saw Christianity as a sect of Judaism; and the Jews, despite their refusal to sacrifice to emperors, were gently treated. This was empire policy—to allow conquered people to keep their own religions. Besides the Jews were wealthy, well-organized, and influential.

But after A.D. 64 things changed. The Jewish protective covering began to dissipate. The Jews themselves told officials, "This is no sect of ours." Besides, most members of the Christian churches were obviously gentile converts, not displaced Jews. And unlike the Jews, they were usually poor, uninfluential, lower-class citizens. All these factors placed the Christians outside the protective policy of Rome and opened the door for the persecutions that followed.

In 112 Emperor Trajan proclaimed a united policy toward the Christian faith. If someone was a Christian and refused to sacrifice to the emperor, he declared, that person was to be executed. But, and this was the one saving feature of this policy, officials were not to actively seek out such Christians. It was only when local people brought them to the officials' attention that the policy should be enforced.

Nero

An example of what could and did happen under the new policy was the persecution in Lyons, France, in 177. Mobs of angry pagans pelted Christians with stones, broke into their homes, and plundered their possessions. Many were locked in jail to await the provincial governor's arrival.

When he came, the tortures began. Those who would not renounce their faith had their bodies stretched until they broke, were thrown to wild beasts, or forced to sit in a red hot iron chair "which fried their bodies and choked them with smoke."[2] The dead were denied a Christian burial; their bodies were left to rot for six days, then burned to ashes and thrown in the Rhone River. "Now let us see if they will rise again, and if their god can help them, and deliver them out of our hands," their enemies said.[3]

Persecutions were not universal or continuous, but they were a constant threat. Christians could never be sure when the daily insults and slurs would turn into torture and death. They could never feel secure or at peace. To be a Christian was not a pleasant existence.

In the year 251, under Emperor Decius, the policy changed. An empire-wide assault on the church began. Again in 303 Emperor Diocletian inaugurated a universal persecution, the severest ever. Christians lost their citizenship. Bibles were confiscated and churches destroyed. Church leaders were imprisoned, tortured, and killed. But this was the last major persecution before the dramatic reversal of positions by which Christianity, the detested and illegal religion, became the favored faith, protected and officially proclaimed as the one true religion.

Christian Responses

During these more than two hundred years of oppression there were, of course, varieties of Christian reactions to the reviling, persecuting, and false accusing they experienced.

Thousands accepted suffering for Christ's sake "with gladness." They yearned for the promised, heavenly reward. The church even had to warn overzealous Christians not to seek persecution since some had "an earnest desire for martyrdom." For example, as a boy, Origen of Alexandria (one of the first, great theologians) was so determined to follow his martyred father that his mother had to hide his clothes to keep him home. He, like many others, was sure that a martyr's death would win a more glorious place in heaven than a natural death might merit.

Most believers didn't go to such extremes. While accepting taunts and torture and holding to the faith even when it meant death, they did not seek "the glory of martyrdom." They avoided whenever possible this final test of faith.

Between these two groups were a few select persons who neither sought death nor avoided confrontation. These individuals tried to reason with their persecutors, to "make a case" for the Christian faith that they hoped would alle-

The last prayer of the martyrs

viate persecution, answer false charges, and perhaps even win opponents into considering the possible truth of the Christian teaching.

In Rome, for instance, Justin Martyr (c.100–c.165) wrote to pagan and Jewish despisers of Christianity. He was later beheaded for his faith. Tertullian (c.160–c.220), a lawyer from Carthage, challenged those who told lies about the Christian faith and made an excellent legal "case for the defense." Origen (c.185–c.254), a brilliant thinker from Alexandria, defended the faith against attacks by the pagan, Celsus. And, of course, there were many other, though less famous, Christians who spoke and wrote, answering false charges and accusations. All these were called the Apologists.

The Apologists presented an "apology" (a defense) for the charges leveled against the Christian church. Accused of sexual immorality and cannabalism, the Apologists pointed out that Christians "commit neither adultery nor fornication; nor do they bear false witness...they honor father and mother, and love their neighbors...they comfort such as wrong them...they labor to do good to their enemies....If there is among them a man that is poor and needy...they fast two or three days that they might supply the needs with their necessary food."[4]

To the accusation that Christians are bad citizens, they replied that the opposite is true. "We, on behalf of the safety of the Emperors, invoke the eternal God, the true God, the living God....We must needs respect [the Superior] as the chosen of our Lord....Caesar's more ours than yours, appointed as he is by our God."[5] Yet, since Caesar is no divine being, they stated, Christians cannot sacrifice to him.

In response to the charge that Christians are atheists, the Apologists leveled a counter charge—that the pagan gods were demons, unworthy of worship. Justin Martyr wrote, "When Socrates endeavored by true reason...to deliver men from these demons, then the demons themselves, by means of men who rejoiced in iniquity, compassed his death, as an atheist and a profane person, and in our case they display a similar activity."[6] Since they alone worshiped the one, true God, the Christians alone were true theists.

The Apologist reply to those who scorned Christianity as a new religion was to contend that since the Old Testament was a Christian book and the patriarchs and prophets incipient Christian believers, Christianity was older than the Greek and Roman religions. All truth, they said, was Christian, for the source of all truth was the one God. Christ is the Light that enlightens all people, the eternal Logos who created the world and put ideas into the mind of Socrates and Plato. "Whatever things were rightly said [by pagans] are the property of us Christians."[7]

While at times too positive in evaluating pagan thought and too unhistorical in their claims—that Socrates was a Christian before Christ and that Plato borrowed ideas from the Old Testament—the

Apologists did remind their fellow believers and all Christians of all ages that a plausible case can be made for the Christian faith. Christians need not stand in silent embarrassment when falsely accused and taunted. Rather we can be confident enough, wise enough, and vocal enough to defend and define our faith in reasonable terms.

The Lapsed

In contrast to all those who whether eagerly, submissively, or argumentatively remained loyal to Christ, there were thousands who denied him, renounced their faith, and sacrificed to the emperor. These *lapsed* "were manifestly unready [for martyrdom] and untrained and still weak."[8]

More than a cause for regret, these lapsed Christians became the reason for a major church schism. What should be done about someone who had renounced Christ, but—when the persecution ended—repented and wished to rejoin the fellowship? Should the church readmit such people or not?

Some said we should accept them back; after all, Jesus commanded us to forgive one another seventy times seven times. Others said, "No, they've committed an unforgivable sin, the Scripture says, 'it is impossible to restore again to repentance those who have once been enlightened, who have tasted the heavenly gift, and have become partakers of the Holy Spirit . . . if they then commit apostasy, since

they crucify the Son of God on their own account and hold him up to contempt' (Heb. 6:4-6)." And some (like Tertullian) added that after baptism any major sin (fornication, adultery, apostasy) was unforgivable.

The Decian persecution in A.D. 251 brought this issue to a head. After this persecution many of the thousands who had lapsed, repented and tried to reenter the church. Cornelius, Bishop of Rome, argued that such people, after proper penance, should be readmitted: no sin, however great, is unforgivable if the sinner truly repents. Novatius, a presbyter of the same church, disagreed. Restoration was impossible, he believed, for those guilty of "sins unto death."

The issue had to be decided. The majority agreed with Bishop Cornelius. They cited Peter's denial as proof that no person is beyond God's grace in Christ, even one who renounces the Lord. In disagreement and protest, Novatius formed a new, "true" church and appointed Novatian bishops in many of the major cities.

This church lasted into the fifth century. Its unbending rigorism and discipline first appealed to many, but later, as it became clear that this self-righteous spirit and legalism was at odds with Christ's message of forgiveness, the Novatian church dwindled and died.

The result of the controversy was that the church of Christ came to understand that martyr heroes were not an ideal to be emulated nor lapsed believers an unforgivable weakness to be boldly rejected.

Their Lord led them to become a church neither feverishly seeking glorious death nor legalistically rejecting those who had failed. Instead the church came to forgive weaker believers and to assert that the grace of God is without limit and Christ's love and forgiveness without bounds.

Victory Under Constantine

Between the years 303 and 325 changes occurred that are among the most important and spectacular in all church history. From a detested, illegal religious body, seemingly on the brink of defeat, the church became a victorious organization, vehicle of the favored religion of the empire. That dramatic change from seeming defeat to apparent victory came because a pagan emperor concluded that Christianity was the true religion.

The year was 312. Emperor Diocletian, the last great persecutor of the church, was dead. On the outskirts of Rome, Constantine, Augustus of the West, was about to battle Maxentius, who also claimed that position: the winner would rule the western half of the empire.

The afternoon before the battle, Constantine decided that pagan gods couldn't help him. He decided to ask the Christian God's aid. "While he was thus praying...a marvelous sign appeared to him from heaven. He saw with his own eyes the trophy of a cross of light in the heavens, above the sun and bearing the inscription *Conquer by this.*"[9] Obediently Constantine placed the sign of the cross on his soldiers' shields. The next day he decisively defeated Maxentius and was thereby convinced that the Christian God is more powerful than the pagan gods.

Constantine converted, and both the Roman Empire and the church were irreversibly changed by that conversion.

In 313 Constantine made a treaty with one of the claimants to power in the eastern half of the empire, the pagan, Licinius. Together they issued the Edict of Milan, one of the most important documents in Roman history. This edict made Christianity a legal religion in the territories these two men ruled and restored all the confiscated church properties. For the first time in over two centuries, Christians in much of the empire did not need to fear persecution and discrimination.

When in 323 Constantine defeated Licinius and gained control of the entire empire, Christians were exuberant. "With dances and hymns, in the city and the country, [the Christians] glorified first of all God the universal King...and then the pious emperor....There was oblivion of past evils and forgetfulness of every deed of impiety; there was enjoyment of present benefits and expectation of those yet to come."[10]

Constantine was totally supportive of the church. He called councils of bishops (paying all expenses from the state treasury) to try to resolve doctrinal conflicts. He built churches and shrines to martyrs.

He financed copying of Bibles to replace those burned. He gave precedence to Christians in appointing government officers. He involved the clergy in affairs of state and gave generous gifts, especially to the church of Rome (including the Lateran palace in Rome).

Because of all he did for the church, many Christians, especially those in the Catholic tradition, feel that Constantine strengthened the church and prepared it to face its next great challenge, the barbarian invasions. Without Constantine, they believe, Christianity might not have survived that difficult situation.

Others, especially in the Baptist tradition, feel Constantine began a most unfortunate trend of state interference in church affairs. That trend led to the excesses of state and church conflict of the medieval period.

They have a point. At the Council of Nicea in 325, Constantine virtually imposed the orthodox understanding of the Trinity in opposition to the Arian heresy. He even claimed at one time to be "a bishop of the church for external affairs," believing God had called him to regulate the church's life.[11] Progressively Constantine saw Christianity as the state religion. He plundered pagan temples and forced pagan soldiers to join in Christian prayers before battles. He brought bishops, like good luck charms, along when he fought battles—to guarantee God's help. He worshiped God in the belief that he is the one "from whom all victory proceeds."[12] If the Roman Empire honored the Christian God, he believed, they would experience only uninterrupted success.

****

Was the revolutionary change of the church's condition under Constantine truly a victory? Or was the church better off as a persecuted minority, more blessed in that earlier state?

This is a difficult question to answer. On the one hand, from a mere 10 percent of the population during Constantine's reign, the number of Christians swelled to a majority of the empire's citizens. But on the other hand, many of these were at best nominal believers. A law which bequeathed to the church all property of those without heirs increased the church's wealth dramatically, but that may have been a mixed blessing. The church developed far greater influence on the state with many bishops acting as the emperor's advisors and many leading officials being Christian. The Bishop of Rome became so strong through Constantine's policies that the claims of Rome's primacy became hard to refute. Yet it was the Roman bishop who more than any other church figure successfully preserved the church when the Western Empire collapsed in 476.

Through Constantine's help the Western church became strong enough to survive the barbarian invasions, but it also developed a pattern of depending on a Christian ruler for support. Without Constantine it is unlikely the orthodox doctrine of the Trinity would have

Constantine addressing his soldiers concerning the promise of victory in the sign of the cross

been so universally accepted; still, after Constantine, Christian emperors and kings expected to have a decided say in matters of church teaching.

Many negatives and positives can be listed. But an evaluation can't be made by adding up two contrary lists to see which is longer.

Perhaps it is not a legitimate question to ask if the church were better off persecuted or favored. That's like asking if a person is better off young or old, single or married. There are different life states and experiences, each with its own goods and bads, benefits and dangers. The church is led by its Lord through different experiences which test it in different ways.

It should be recognized, however, that the change from hardship to ease, from political weakness to strength, from persecution to victory was not as sharp a contrast of dark and light as often described. For since Christ is with his church and his Spirit animates it, the dark is never so dismal as the world supposes; and while the church is in the world, under siege, still in combat, the light is never unshadowed. Its outward, political fortunes are not finally determinative for the church's inward, spiritual life.

Rather there is a faithfulness in times of persecution that is different, not less or more, than the faithfulness needed in times when the church is favored. Christ leads his people along new ways, but they must continue to follow him. The work the church is called to do may change with its varied circum-

stances, but it must continue faithfully to do the work of Christ and to testify to his enduring grace.

CHAPTER 6
AUGUSTINE
AND THE LATE ROMAN EMPIRE

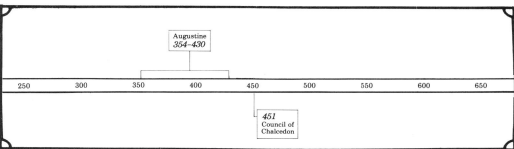

Augustine
354–430

| 250 | 300 | 350 | 400 | 450 | 500 | 550 | 600 | 650 |

451
Council of
Chalcedon

When we, from our twentieth-century perspective, look down on the ages of the church's history, it stretches out beneath us like a grand panorama seen from a descending airplane. But what we see is not a country landscape with the hills, valleys, and rivers of natural events. It's more like a city scene at night; a multitude of tiny lights shining out from the darkness of the hidden, forgotten past.

If we carry that analogy a step further, some lights are very much brighter than others. They even illumine the scene about them so we see trees and houses. These bright lights in church history are the occasional, unusual people who seem to shine out and reflect back their age. They not only write largely and reflectively, giving fascinating personal reactions to historical events but they also mirror in themselves their own society; their thinking reflects its issues, their feelings simulate its prejudices, and their life experiences reiterate what happened to thousands of others. People like Margaret of Navarre, Erasmus, and Albert Schweitzer make the past bright for us.

And when such persons are central to major movements, when they shape decisions that form or reform those about them, then church history seems to merge with biography. Then it seems the Lord of the church chose one giant agent to do his work, one focus for his light on a certain period. Martin Luther was such a light, such a mirror of the Reformation time. John

Calvin also, though in a different way, exemplified and illumined the time when he lived.

For the church in the late Roman Empire one person, Augustine of Hippo, was a gigantic beacon. His beautifully written, thoughtful *Confessions* is the first spiritual autobiograpy of a Christian person. It stands as a masterpiece of Western literature. But for the Christian student of history it is more. It is a theologically acute reflection of the spiritual life of that age. It's said of Augustine: "In his own life experience he encountered all the problems of the early church."[1] Learning of him can teach us to perceive the character of those problems.

Augustine himself was immediately involved in most of the major church controversies that occurred during his lifetime. He helped form the final decisions. In fact his influence is inescapable, not only in the Western church of his time but also in both Catholic and Protestant churches today.

So as we study the history of Christ's church from A.D. 325 to 500, it's practically unavoidable for us to join the major issues with the steps of Augustine's life (354–430), combining history and biography.

Augustine and the Manichaens

Augustine was born in North Africa of a fervently Christian mother and a stubbornly pagan father. His mother surrounded his youth with Christian training and prayer (she was later canonized as St. Monica, patron saint of motherhood). But already as a teenager studying rhetoric in Carthage, Augustine abandoned the Christian faith as too simple, too unsatisfying for an educated person. He took a freer life course. At seventeen he had a mistress (who lived with him until his conversion fourteen years later). At eighteen he had a son (by that union). At nineteen he began to "believe in the fantasies of the Manichaens."[2]

Manichaeism was the faith of Augustine's young manhood. It was a belief that permitted him to indulge the flesh for it taught that the body is a minor part of a person compared to the spirit—so minor, in fact, that the flesh cannot do harm or cause guilt. It was also a belief that appealed to Augustine's intellectual snobbery for it presented itself as reasonable and scientific in its ideas, superior to Christianity's simple faith.

Beyond that sort of personal appeal, Manichaeism had a deeper attraction. It seemed to solve better than any other philosophy or religion what Augustine perceived as a perplexing life problem: the existence of evil. It taught two opposing, eternal principles—light and darkness. These divinities, said the Manichaens, battle in the world and each human heart. Evil also is from everlasting. Thus God, who is wholly light, is in no way responsible for eternal evil. This absolute dualism provided a clean, logical solution to the problem of evil.

Another appealing Manichaen doctrine was the teaching that Christ never wore human flesh.

Augustine wrote, "It seemed to me to be a very crude and base thing to believe that [God] would have the shape of human flesh and be limited to our bodily form."[3]

After nine years, however, this "sophisticated" Manichaen form of Christianity proved dissatisfying. Augustine found the eloquent, intellectual Manichaen spokesman,

St. Augustine
(from a painting by BOTTICELLI)

Faustus, couldn't really resolve the problems he (Augustine) posed. He concluded, "just because something is expressed eloquently it is not necessarily true."[4] So finally, because of mother Monica's constant prayers (as he himself later concluded), Augustine left Manichaeism.

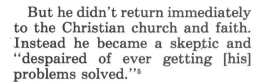

But he didn't return immediately to the Christian church and faith. Instead he became a skeptic and "despaired of ever getting [his] problems solved."[5]

Augustine's Return to Christianity

In 384 Augustine left his teaching position in Rome and took the chair of rhetoric with a school in Milan. Here began his gradual return to the Christian faith.

The first part of the bridge from skepticism to faith was a prevalent form of Plato's thought called Neoplatonism. This philosophy denied incarnation, death, and resurrection but still affirmed a world view that Augustine judged quite close to that of Christ's followers. It taught, for instance, that Christ was the Logos, God's eternal Son, Creator of the universe. This Logos is the divine source of all wisdom, the eternal Light that lightens every human, shining within each person's innermost soul.

In pointed contrast to Manichaeism, Neoplatonism taught that evil has no existence of its own. "I asked," Augustine wrote, "what is iniquity? I learned that it is not a substance, but a perversity of will that has bent and turned away from you, O God."[6]

The second part of the bridge back to Christian faith was the Old Testament. The Bishop of Milan, Ambrose, was an exceptional preacher. His sermons taught Augustine to read the Old Testament—a book he'd previously hated—in terms of

Bishop Ambrosius and Empress Justina

Jesus Christ. He learned to see the world as God's creation and to see the incarnation not as an irrational outrage, but as a possible reality. Ambrose convinced Augustine, intellectually, that Christianity is true.

But one more step was needed. Augustine had to recognize his sin. He did and "gave full vent to [his] tears" and cried out to God, "How long, how long, will you keep your anger forever?"[7] The answer came in a voice from a neighboring garden, "Take up and read." So Augustine took his Bible and read Romans 13:13, 14. "Instantly," he says, "as I finished reading . . . there was infused in my heart the light of full certainty and all the dark shadows of doubt fell away."[8]

Augustine immediately went to his mother with the news of his conversion and then to Ambrose to be baptized (in 387). In 388, with the help of some friends, he established a monastery in North Africa and remained there until his death in 430.

Augustine and the Donatists

But retreat into a monastery did not isolate Augustine from church issues and controversies. Quite the contrary.

In North Africa there was a Christian group called the Donatists. These people were similar to the Novatians of earlier centuries and to the Judaizing Christians of even earlier; that is, they were rigorists who insisted that every church member must be a certified, fully sanctified, saint.

After the last persecution under Emperor Diocletian, a new bishop was appointed in Carthage. He was one of those who had lapsed and been reinstated. Some believers found this unacceptable. They rejected him and the three bishops whom he had ordained in the area. They proceeded to elect their own bishop and formed a splinter group known to us as the Donatists (after Donatus, an early leader of theirs). They became popular in Northern Africa as the only true church with a clergy free from "deadly sins."

When Augustine was appointed bishop in 395, he had to deal with this splinter church. In writing to expose their error, he developed a number of important doctrines about the church. True, he said, only saints make up the true church. But on earth there are always some tares, hypocritical members. We can't attain a perfect church on earth. Furthermore, if we make the validity of sacraments (and ordination) depend on the moral condition of the officiating person, we end up with a salvation that depends on humans, rather than on God.

When these arguments did not prevail, Augustine urged the emperor to use force against the Donatists, to "compel [them] to come in" (Luke 14:23). This stand and his reasons for holding it later became the basis for persecuting heretics in the Middle Ages and into the Reformation period. The Donatist church, despite persecutions, survived until the Muslim conquests.

Augustine and Pelagianism

Around 380 a British monk, Pelagius, became concerned about loose morality in the church. It seemed to him that when Christians were taught that salvation was by grace alone, entirely in God's hands, that removed any valid reason for trying to live a good Christian life. After all, if nothing human beings do helps save them, why try to live up to the hard, high standards of God's law?

So to elevate morality Pelagius taught that the human person, even after the fall, retained free will. We can *will* not to sin, can become perfect like Christ, our example. We didn't inherit any original sin from Adam and Eve. Rather we are, each of us as infants, born perfect and get corrupted by the bad examples of Adam and Eve and their children. Sin, said Pelagius, is not a condition, but a choice. We are not sinners; we do sinful things. By following God's law we can storm the gates of heaven.

Augustine was appalled by this teaching. It flatly contradicted both his own experience and the Bible. He knew—and the Bible taught—that he, Augustine, was a captive of sin who only escaped that slavery through the grace of Jesus Christ.

In answer to Pelagius, Augustine taught that in Adam we all, even infants, became slaves to sin. Social flaws come from our sinful nature, not the other way around. Grace, not our own works, is the only way to be saved and the only way to stay on the road to heaven. For grace irresistibly changes us and makes us worship the Creator, not created things. That grace, Augustine continued, is by God's choice—his predestination, not ours. God saves some and leaves others in sin. And that grace comes only through the sacraments and preaching of the church.

Every age of church history has had people who, meaning well and teaching badly, reduce sin to individual "naughty acts" caused by bad environment. Such views naively deny the radical nature of human evil and lead to a moralistic Christianity—brush your teeth, be neat and respectable middle class, and God will be pleased with you.

Thanks to Augustine, Pelagianism was roundly condemned by several church councils (Carthage, 416 and Ephesus, 431). But even so the Pelagian view came back later, in less radical form, to trap many believers into putting good Christian living before reconciliation to God.

Augustine and the Collapsing Empire

In 410 Rome, the eternal city, heart of the empire, was plundered by the Visigoths led by Alaric. That exposed the empire's vulnerability and sent shock waves through the "civilized world."

Who was to blame? Pagans said the Christians were. When Rome worshiped pagan gods, they had prospered. When they began worshiping the Christian God, they had crumbled.

How was a contemporary Christian to answer that charge? It was most perplexing. The Bible seemed to agree with the pagans that prospering depends on serving the proper God: "Blessed is the nation whose God is the Lord" (Ps. 33:12). More than an argument, this was a real issue for Christian believers too. Their hearts and heads echoed the pagan's charge. How could God possibly have allowed the Roman Empire to disintegrate just when it had become Christian?

Augustine wrote his greatest work, *The City of God*, to answer both pagans and Christians. To the pagans he showed that the years of pagan gods hadn't been golden. There'd been catastrophes then also. The idea of an "eternal Rome" was an idolatrous myth. Empires are showcases of human pride, filled with seeds of self-destruction. Rome was no exception. Its crumbling was not Christianity's fault. To the Christians he pointed out that everything in the world passed away except the eternal "city of God." So all Western society may crumble, but God's city still stands.

What Augustine wrote in this book was actually a Christian theology of history. He contrasted two kingdoms or cities in this world, "the city of God" and "the city of this world." Both have a proper place in the world. (Did not Jesus say, "Render to Caesar the things that are Caesar's, and to God the things that are God's"

The vandals pillage Rome.

Mark 12:17?) Christians live in both cities. But they must clearly distinguish God's kingdom from any state. God's purpose must not be identified with any earthly kingdom.

Every city of this world will eventually pass away. Only the city of God is eternal. At the end of history, said Augustine, all states will be gone and the city of God will remain, the only society. But until that time the Christian lives and functions in two cities and must promote the peace and order of both. So Christians are good citizens and yet don't despair when the state to which they belong collapses. They know God's city will endure forever.

The Christological Debates

There was one major issue in the church of Augustine's day that

A fifteenth-century miniature of St. Augustine's City of God. The upper level represents the saints already received into heaven. The lower levels represent those preparing for heaven or excluding themselves from the heavenly kingdom by committing one of the seven deadly sins.

was not settled until after his death. He was involved in the debate, but it stretched beyond him. That's the Christological question.

In 325 the Council of Nicea had proclaimed that Christ was "of one substance with the Father," fully divine. But questions concerning the relationship of the divine and the human in Christ went unanswered. Generally there were two schools of thought. The school of Alexandria emphasized Christ's divinity at the expense of his humanity. The school of Antioch tended to divide Jesus into two parts, into two separate beings.

To show some of the different opinions in a bit more detail, we'll very briefly look at three examples.

- Apollinarius, bishop of Laodicea (d.392), asserted that the divine Logos replaced the human reason in Christ. A sort of truncated human, Jesus' divinity was assured but his true humanity "swallowed up."
- Nestorius, bishop of Constantinople from 428 to 451, had a quite different opinion. According to his critics (his own writings are lost), he taught that Jesus had two wholly distinct and separate natures. Sometimes when Jesus acted he was using his human nature; at other times he was operating through his divine nature. Nestorius denied that he was making Jesus into two persons, but his denial was not very convincing to his critics.
- Eutyches was a good monk but a poor theologian. When summoned to ecclesiastical trial in Constantinople he testified, "I confess that our Lord was of two natures before the union (i.e., the incarnation), but after the union one nature." He seemed to express another opinion—that the human and the divine are blended in Christ to form a third nature, neither fully human nor fully divine. Eutyches's trial started a lively controversy that wasn't settled until the decision of Chalcedon, three years later.

The Council of Chalcedon met in 451. It produced the definitive formula, balancing the extremes of the two opposing schools. It also rejected the errors of the three current opinions.

- Against Apollinarius, Chalcedon stated that Jesus' manhood is complete, "consisting also of a reasonable soul and body." Jesus is "of one substance with us as regards his manhood; like us in all respects, apart from sin."
- Against Nestorius, the Creed confessed the joining of the two natures in the incarnation with "one person and subsistence, not as parted or separated into two persons."
- Against Eutyches, Chalcedon held that each nature remains intact, the distinction between the human and the divine is "in no way annulled by the union."

The heart of the Creed of Chalcedon lies in the famous phrase "in two natures, without confusion, without change, without division, without separation." Those four negatives rejected the erroneous

The Council of Chalcedon

extremes and "erected a dam against speculation, or, at least, against an exaggerated form of it." Chalcedon gave "a direction in which...every attempt to speak correctly about the divinity and humanity of Jesus Christ must proceed."[9]

The Creed of Chalcedon forces us back to a biblical Jesus Christ, a real person, a unified person, fully divine and fully human. By it we confess the mystery of this Jesus Christ.

****

Surveying the church's course during the late Roman Empire, one is struck by the host of complex issues and knotty problems it faced. It solved these, but not without cost. Doctrinal precision brought schism: a Donatist church, a Nestorian church, and a Monophysite (single nature) church separated from the main body, rejecting the resolutions that satisfied the great majority. The more precise the understanding of the faith, it seems, the more splintered the body of believers.

Furthermore, those same questions or similar issues rose again. It seems in church history that questions are not answered once for all.

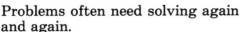

Problems often need solving again and again.

Yet as generation follows generation there is progress in understanding the faith. A creed like Chalcedon stands as a landmark to future generations. It crystallizes the church's belief so that if certain opinions reoccur, they can now be clearly labeled as errors and heresies. The church has a basis on which to judge. Its Lord has formed it a bit further into the body that he desires for his Spirit on earth.

We should notice the recurring issues, but we should also be aware of the movement in the church's history. We know the goal toward which Christ is leading his church. We should see in each stage how and where he has brought the church closer to that goal.

CHAPTER 7
MONKS AND POPES

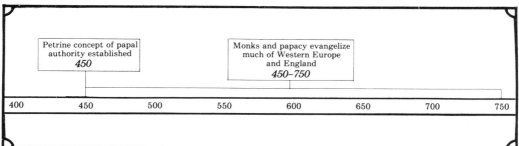

400	450	500	550	600	650	700	750

Petrine concept of papal authority established *450*

Monks and papacy evangelize much of Western Europe and England *450–750*

"Jesus Christ is the same yesterday and today and for ever" (Heb. 13:8). So reads the Bible's witness to the unchanging faithfulness of the church's head. But the body, the gathering of his disciples, dwells in this mutable continuum we call history. The church is always changing, never the same from generation to generation.

To some Christians this is regrettable. They long for a church as perfect and immovable as its Lord. To other Christians this is natural. As every living organism grows and decays and every historical institution develops and deteriorates, so too the church.

But while living in history and reacting to its changing challenges and threats, the church has a head who has ascended and is with the Father. Part of the church, its guide and leader, lives above. This means the church's changes are no blind reactions to environmental stimuli. Rather its all-seeing Lord, through his Spirit and his faithful followers, shapes his body to best carry on his work in a sinful, dangerous world.

Already in chapters 4 and 5 we've detailed some of these alterations as the New Testament church became the Catholic church and the persecuted minority became a favored majority. But by the year 450 the Western empire was in shambles, Roman authority was gone, and hordes of barbarians (some heretics) were overrunning the civilized world. As it struggled for existence in those chaotic times, the church developed two strong arms, monasticism and the papacy. These arms served both to protect the body and to reach out to the pagans beyond. But these arms also changed the shape of the body radically, so that some, especially Protestants, have viewed them as flawed and unhealthy members of the body of Christ.

Monasticism

The first shoots of monasticism appeared in the church's first centuries. Almost from the beginning some Christians considered following Jesus a call to celibacy and a life of renunciation. Jesus, they observed, had nowhere to lay his head, dwelt in the wilderness, and did not marry. Jesus urged the rich young ruler to sell all and counseled his disciples to be unconcerned about the morrow. To follow Jesus seriously, they believed, required a dramatic rejection of the world's ways. Such impulses were strengthened by the indications that the church was becoming excessively worldly: thousands of nominal Christians were joining their emperor, Constantine, in the new popular faith. Under such circumstances, a true walk with Christ seemed to lead away from the organized church into desert and wilderness places.

These Christian motives were often tainted by pagan ideas, Gnostic negativism toward the "evil," created world, Neoplatonic attempts to find God by inward contemplation, and Pelagian no-

tions of pleasing God by works of self-denial. Out of such a mixture came monasticism.

Hermit Monks

The early monks were individuals who went off alone into the wilderness areas of Egypt, Syria, Palestine, and Mesopotamia. Here each sought his, and sometimes her, own way of being a better Christian.

Living in isolation, many of these monks thought they had received divine commands to behave in quite abnormal ways. Some lay

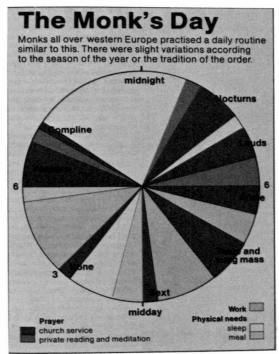

The Monk's Day

Monks all over western Europe practised a daily routine similar to this. There were slight variations according to the season of the year or the tradition of the order.

midnight

Nocturns

Lauds

6

6

and g mass

3

one

Compline

ext

midday

Prayer
church service
private reading and meditation

Work
Physical needs
sleep
meal

72

naked in the desert sunshine until they were covered with blisters. Others, the "grazing monks," ate grass like cattle. Some lived in tiny cells: Acepsimius, such a monastic, came out of his cell so bent and wild-looking that a shepherd thought he was a wolf and shot him.[1] Others tortured themselves by so-called spiritual marriages: male and female celibates slept side by side in small cells to torment their bodies by unfulfilled sexual desires. One monk, Symeon Stylites (c. 450), became famous for living thirty-seven years chained to the top of a sixty-foot pillar. People gazed with awe as this ascetic punished his body by touching feet to forehead 1244 times in succession.[2]

But the most famous of these hermits was St. Anthony (251–356). At the age of twenty, he sold his inherited country estate, gave the proceeds to the poor, and began a life of renunciation in the Egyptian desert. He subjected his body to all kinds of abuse to free his soul for God. Anthony refused to bathe. He often fasted three or four days. He slept as little as possible, since it was in his dreams, very often, that evil thoughts attacked him. When he did sleep, he did so on rocky soil, so that even when resting his body was forced to suffer.

This "athlete of God" became a hero to many who, though unable or unwilling themselves to live such an ascetic life, saw such rigorous renunciation as the highest expression of Christian faith. Athanasius, leader of the anti-Arian forces in the church, wrote a popular biography, *The Life of Anthony*. It related not only his ascetic exploits but also his active role in the trinitarian controversy, describing how he had traveled to Alexandria to promote the orthodox cause.

Both Anthony's willingness to help the institutional church in its struggle against heresy and his increased popularity signaled a change from the hermit pattern. For the first time there came into being a community of monks who made Anthony their leader, breaking into his isolation. It was monks in community, rather than monks in isolation, who set the pattern of medieval monasticism.

Communal Monks—Eastern Model

An Egyptian monk, Pachomius (285–346), first composed a "rule" to govern communal, monastic living. This structure became the model not only for his own monastery in Egypt but also for many others in the Eastern church.

The "Rule of Pachomius" united as many as three hundred monks under the leadership of one abbot. These men were divided into ten groups of about thirty, each group living in its own dormitory, with its own chief monk. Each monk was required to do some manual labor each day. This was not just a useful outlet for energy stored in hours of contemplation. It was also, for Pachomius, a form of penance which directly promoted the spiritual life.

Each monastery formed under this rule had a dining area, a

library, a kitchen, an infirmary, and a church. It was this last addition of a chapel, which seems natural to us today, that brought the most radical change. The hermit monks, usually laymen, thought they could commune with God better in lonely meditation. They usually neglected all forms of worship. But Pachomius's rule changed that: formal church services became integral to a monk's existence. This in turn meant some monks had to become priests so they could lead worship and administer sacraments. So communal monasticism naturally intertwined itself with the larger life of the church.

Communal Monks—Western Model

The father of the dominant Western form of monasticism was St. Benedict of Nursia (480–c.542). By his time, thanks not only to Athanasius's *Life of Anthony* but also to the biography of *Martin of Tours* and St. Jerome's writings on the subject, there were monks scattered through Spain, Italy, and France. But it was the "Rule of St. Benedict" which gave form to most monastic communal life.

Benedict was raised in a well-to-do Italian family of genuine faith. He went to Rome to study but found city life frivolous. So at twenty he left Rome to become a hermit. Typically he punished his own body ruthlessly, even rolling naked in thorny bushes to eliminate lustful desires and thoughts.

But Benedict came to see the dangers of such a lonely existence. He saw the pastoral need for monks to live together as families. Borrowing much from Pachomius, he developed a rule for monastic living—one geared not to a few spiritual heroes, but rather designed so that with pastoral support even the weak could follow it. Under this rule Benedict established a community at the site of an old pagan temple, Monte Cassino, between Rome and Naples.

With this deeply pastoral spirit, the Western rule differed in several ways from the Eastern. Since the monastery was to be the monks' home, the communities were smaller. Thus, as a spiritual family, the monastics could know and help each other, growing together in faith. Benedict also required a lifelong commitment to a single monastery. Monks "married" into this family. They could not even leave the monastery without the abbot's permission, and that was seldom and reluctantly granted. This rule effectively ended the era of "wandering monks" who traveled from one monastery to another.

In such a monastic home, monks were brothers. They were treated as family members, receiving adequate clothing, three meals a day, and an allotment of wine. The Pachomian rule considered sleep a necessary evil and required monks to sit up while indulging in it. Benedict's rule granted adequate, horizontal sleep. In a Pachomian monastery work was a penance, done in relative isolation. Benedict

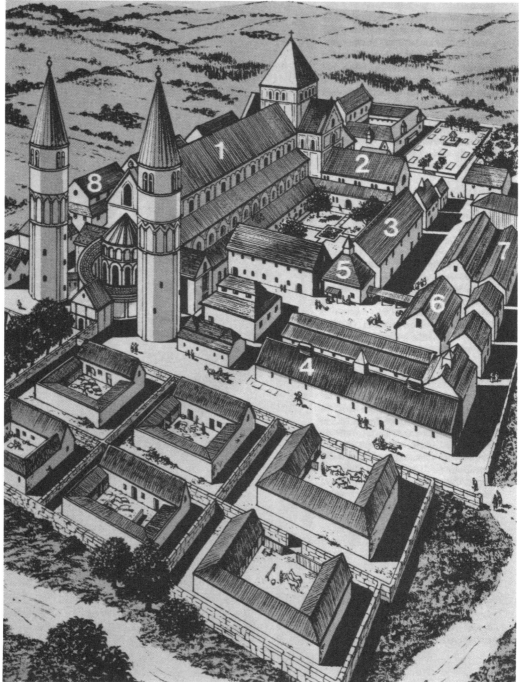

*This artist's reconstruction is based on the monastery built at St. Gall about 820. 1 Church
2 Dormitory 3 Refectory 4 Stables 5 Kitchen 6 Bakery 7 Workshops 8 Guesthouse*

regarded work as something performed for the family welfare that would enhance a loving, cooperative spirit. It was a way to Christian growth.

Benedict also made reading and study an element of monastic living. Illiterate brothers learned to read. Libraries had classical as well as Christian writings. Monks devoted themselves to copying these masterpieces of classical civilization. As a result of all this, Benedictine monasteries became centers of learning and have been called the universities of the early Middle Ages. That may be an exaggeration, but certainly these monasteries kept learning alive at a time when few had any interest in it.

The Papacy

We've already discussed in earlier chapters the rising prestige of the bishop of Rome. When Constantine moved the capital of the empire to Constantinople, he left behind a power vacuum that was progressively filled by the Roman bishop. Before long this bishop became the pope, the defender and preserver of Christianity in the West—not merely a spiritual but also a temporal power in much of Italy.

That new position and status needed to be theologically legitimized. Leo I (440–61), greatest of the fifth-century popes, first did that by formulating the petrine concept of papal authority. In simpler language this means that the authority of the Roman bishops was based on Peter's authority. Christ, Leo argued, made Peter the rock on which his church is founded when he said, "You are Peter, and on this rock I will build my church, and the powers of death shall not prevail against it" (Matt. 16:18). It was also to Peter, Leo maintained, that Christ gave the power of the keys of heaven, the right to bind on earth that held also for heaven (Matt. 16:19). As the first bishop of Rome, Leo said, Peter had passed on these keys to his successors, the Roman bishops. As Peter held absolute authority over the church of his day, so the popes rule the church in their own day.

Leo's argument was generally accepted in the Western church, but rejected in the Eastern. The bishop there argued for equality with Rome. At the Council of Chalcedon they explicitly rejected Leo's claim to absolute authority in the church.

The next step in establishing papal supremacy was taken by Pope Gelasius (492–96). He wrote, "Two there are, August emperor, by which this world is chiefly ruled, the sacred authority of the priesthood (of which the pope is the head) and the royal power. Of these, the responsibility of the priests is more weighty in so far as they will answer for the Kings of men themselves at the divine judgment"[3] Both priests and rulers, said Gelasius, should submit to the pope, who is answerable only to Christ.

With these assertions, Gelasius laid the theoretical foundations for later papal claims to authority over the secular rulers. And already in the fifth century these were more than theory. In fact the popes frequently exercised real temporal authority in many parts of Italy.

The sixth century saw that power grow remarkably. Pope Gregory I (590–604) was a highly gifted person. A Benedictine monk who held various church administrative positions, including papal secretary, he was reluctantly persuaded to accept the election to pope.

He proved a remarkably able man. He solved the previously insoluble problem of feeding the people of Rome. He administered the vast papal territories so efficiently that they produced large revenues. With this money he raised armies against the marauding Lombard tribesmen. He wrote biblical commentaries and theological works. He unified the liturgical practices of the Italian church. He developed the church music we call Gregorian chants. His energy seemed boundless, his ability measureless.

Papal-Monastic Missions

Yet Gregory's greatest achievement lay elsewhere. In a brilliant move that altered the entire situation in Europe, Gregory recruited the Benedictine monasteries into missionary service. By that move he allied these two strong arms of the church, gained the support of the monasteries, but also made sure that new converts to Christianity would be loyal to the pope.

England is a prime example. The pagan Angles and Saxons from Germany overran England in the fifth century, driving the Christian Celts into Wales and Scotland. These invaders tried to destroy any Christian remnants.

Then in 597 Gregory sent a group of emissaries—including Augustine, a Benedictine monk—to England. Fearful of the English barbarians, the monks set up an outpost near Canterbury in southeastern England. They concentrated their efforts on King Aethelbert of Kent, whose wife, Bertha, was already a Christian. After some hesitation Aethelbert converted and with him most of his nation. "Great numbers," the historian Venerable Bede relates, "gathered each day to hear the Word of God, forsaking their heathen rites, and entering the unity of Christ's holy church as believers."[4]

After the conversion of Aethelbert, Gregory named Augustine bishop of Canterbury; from that center the gospel was preached to other parts of England. By 650 most of England had converted to Christianity and because "the Anglo-Saxons owed their conversion chiefly to the direct efforts of Rome . . . they, in turn, displayed a devotion to the papacy."[5] So through the efforts of the Benedictine monks, the power of the papacy was extended.

But other "un-Roman" Christians were also working to convert England. Many years earlier (c. 389–461) St. Patrick, patron saint of Ireland and native of England, had convinced the pagan Irish that

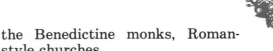

Christianity was a better religion. Although Patrick was apparently loyal to the Roman church, after his death the Celtic church of Ireland rejected Rome and refused to recognize papal authority. For a while the differences between the Irish Celtic churches and the Roman churches were pronounced. The Celtic church was structured around abbot bishops while the Roman church employed diocesan bishops. The Celtic church refused to acknowledge the Roman pope. And the Celtic church celebrated Easter on a different date than the Roman church did. So when the Celtic church and the Roman church both sent missionaries to northern and western England, tension was inevitable.

Finally because of its superior organization and the general pro-Roman sentiment of most Anglo-Saxons, the Roman church won. The Synod of Whitby in 663 provided a peaceful solution, joining the Celtic churches and monasteries in England with papal church and Benedictine order monasteries.

But even before they were united, both of these groups were sending missionaries from England back to the European continent. For even though, already in 496, Clovis—the great leader of the Franks—had converted and brought many into the church, still the progress of Christianity among the Franks was painfully slow. Europe needed the gospel, and a steady stream of missionaries from England worked on the continent. Of these, the Irish monks set up Celtic-style churches; the Benedictine monks, Roman-style churches.

Celtic missionaries first began this great work in Europe. Already fifteen years before Augustine began his efforts among Anglo-Saxons in England, Columban (543–615) was preaching in France, Switzerland, and Italy. Utterly intolerant of paganism, Columban worked by direct confrontation. He destroyed idols. He threw sacrifices offered to the Germanic god, Wodin, into the nearest stream. He challenged pagan priests face to face. These frenzied, aggressive acts led to his expulsion from territory after territory. He was also opposed by priests and monks loyal to Rome because he seemed to represent an alien form of Christianity. Still he did establish many Celtic churches and monasteries in Europe, including the famous monastery of Bobbio in Italy. He and his successors' efforts significantly weakened paganism in Europe.

The future was to be with the Roman church, however. And the greatest of medievel missionaries, Boniface (c.680–754), was an emissary of the pope. A native of England and a Benedictine monk, Boniface was too restless to be the scholar he could have become. He chose to be a missionary. His first efforts in Holland among the Frisians failed and he returned to England. But two years later (718), he returned to the Continent and began working with other Germanic tribes, destroying idols and building churches. He also reformed existing churches which had become semipagan.

Boniface was very colorful. He used dramatic methods. Before a crowd of hostile, pagan Hessians, he cut down a sacred oak tree, dedicated to Thor. They waited for Thor to strike Boniface dead. Instead a gust of wind toppled the tree, breaking it into four pieces. The deeply impressed pagans built a place of prayer dedicated to St. Peter on the very spot.

Because of his ability and loyalty to Rome, Boniface was first made bishop, then archbishop of Mainz. He remained a missionary, however, and continued to establish new outposts and centers of learning. The greatest of these was the monastery at Fulda.

As an old man, in his seventies, Boniface returned to the scene of his original efforts, the Frisians. At first he was successful on this second attempt, baptizing thousands. But in 754 a disgruntled band of pagans killed him. This great missionary, superb organizer and leader, surely died as he wished, proclaiming the gospel of Christ to a lost people.

****

During these centuries the church changed drastically. To combat worldliness within and paganism without, it developed a strong communal monasticism and a powerful, organized papacy.

To children of the Protestant Reformation, trained to understand each Christian's calling as living out the faith within the world, monasticism's attempt to escape the world is an obvious error. Yet the monks and nuns did serve as concrete reminders to all other Christians that faith demands a total commitment to Christ. The monasteries did become the evangelistic centers of the church.

Boniface fells the oak consecrated to Thor.

Likewise the papal claims to supreme authority appear to us a clear misreading of Scripture. Yet the strong, centralized organization popes gave to the church did hold it together and keep it functioning in a chaotic age.

Together these two arms of the church brough England and much of Europe within the Christian fold. Without their efforts many of our own ancestors might not have become Christian and our own heritage might be quite different.

The changes in the church should be seen both in terms of the needs of the time and in terms of the guidance of its ascended Lord. Some men and women tried to be obedient to Christ's Spirit, to follow his way. Others resisted that Spirit and followed willful ways. But through these faithful and faithless acts, Christ's Spirit continued to breathe in his church. The Lord led his church through these times of upheaval and equipped it to carry on his tasks.

CHAPTER 8
CHURCH AND STATE

The history of the Christian church is a story of conflicts. One seems to follow the other. Some are over doctrines, struggles for the truth. Others are fights for survival in the face of persecution or strong social pressures. Still others are battles for the minds and hearts of human beings. As long as there is no peace between good and evil, between the truth of Christ and the lie of Satan, it seems the church will know no perfect peace, at least not in this time frame.

But there is one agelong conflict that springs neither from heresy, nor persecutions, nor contrary world-and-life views. It appears rather to emerge from something inherent in the Christian community's own peculiar character. The church is a pilgrim and sojourner on earth; Christians are a people in the world but not of the world. From that feature, intrinsic to the church's very nature, rises the continual controversy between church and state.

Before the Christian faith appeared on the scene and began to reshape social patterns, most societies were theocratic or, to use another term, *sacral.* By these words we mean that the typical society was bound together and ordered by one common religion under a dominant priest-king or semidivine emperor.

Early Christianity, not by conscious choice perhaps but by its very nature, challenged such sacral society. It seems inherent to Christianity's character to be an independent institution and, consequently, a disturbing presence. We see this already in Jesus' clear distinction, even contrast, of the realms of Caesar and the kingdom of God (cf. Luke 20:25). Peter, in bold disobedience to his own sacral leaders, said, "We must obey God rather than men" (Acts 5:29). And Paul, while teaching that the world's leaders are God-appointed (Rom. 13), refused to submit when the Roman rulers attempted to proscribe Christianity.

It was impossible for early Christians to be true to their Lord and still become integrated parts of Roman sacral society. For by the time the new faith appeared, the pattern was already established. The Roman Empire was bound by a state religion, centering in a "divine" emperor. All were required to bow to this human god. When Christians refused and formed their own church structures, independent of state paganism, they became obvious threats to the empire's unity. In a sacral society nonconformity is treason and must be treated as such.

Under Constantine, of course, that changed. But the Christian emperors, adapting the sacral pattern, tried to unite the religious and social life of the empire through a Christian church which they themselves led. They tried to fit Christianity into the successful, religiously based structure of imperial unity. Some believers, vastly relieved that the painful persecutions were now ended, accepted the emperor's claim to religious authority in and through the church. Plain gratitude seemed to require this.

But others reacted differently. Even when threatened by Christian rulers, the church insisted on some freedom of action. So from Constantine to the Protestant Reformation there remained a constant tension, a tug of war between two powers—popes and rulers, church and state.

That conflict, the subject of this present chapter, has had an enormous impact on Western history. As one perceptive historian has observed, "The very existence of two power structures (church and state) competing for man's allegiance instead of only one compelling obedience (as in sacral society) greatly enhanced the possibilities for human freedom."[1]

East and West

Under the Christian emperors, bishops faced a difficult issue. What were the limits of imperial authority within the church? When emperors exiled bishops who disagreed with them or ruled that heretics must be readmitted (as Constantine did in the case of Arius), the church's freedom of decision and action was seriously threatened.

Generally, in the East the authority of the emperor over both church matters and political affairs wasn't seriously challenged. In fact, some have referred to the Eastern church as *caesaropapist*: the emperor (*caesar*) also acted as pope (*papa*).

But in the West the tale was different. The gradual disintegration

82

of imperial power left room for the church to assert its independence. For instance, in 390 when an army officer was killed during a riot in Thessalonika, Emperor Theodosius ordered a retaliatory slaughter of all the city's citizens. Too late he regretted that rash decision; seven thousand had already been massacred. Bishop Ambrose, when he heard of it, promptly excommunicated the emperor and demanded from him a public act of repentance. Theodosius resisted for several months, but finally stretched full length on the floor before the congregation in Milan as an act of public penance.

In the context of that conflict Ambrose developed the idea that "where matters of faith are concerned it is the custom for bishops to judge Christian emperors, not for emperors to judge bishops." For, he said, "the Empire is within the church, not above the church."[2]

In the same tenor, Augustine in his *City of God* asserted that while the state has a place in God's plan, serving to promote the church's welfare, the Christians' ultimate loyalty must be to the city of God. Ironically, although Augustine himself never absolutely identified God's city with the institutional church, many later church leaders, claiming to follow Augustine, did precisely that. They demanded that all church members, including kings, accept the final authority of the church over all areas of life.

Such dominance of church over state was never Augustine's intention. But those who followed him found it easy to use the *City of God*

to champion their cause for the church's preeminence. Pope Gelasius in particular continued to develop the claims of the church, thus setting the stage for the great conflict of the Middle Ages between church and state.

Under Frankish Rulers

The beginnings of that conflict were relatively peaceful. Clovis (c. 500) became an orthodox Christian, loyal to the papacy, and brought his tribe into the church. The king and his successors tended to treat the church as their own property: they made royal approval a requirement for anyone seeking ordination as a priest and determined which priests were eligible to be elected bishop by the clergy of a diocese. The popes, however, were too busy in Italy to do battle over these matters; and perhaps the Frankish kings sensed and the popes agreed that without control of the church they could not rule their realm. So from 500 to 700 this society was essentially sacral in character.

However, that situation began to change when the Carolingian Mayors of the Palace, the true ruling family behind the Merovingian figureheads (Clovis's successors), decided they wanted both power and crown. In 752, Pepin the Short decided to seize the sceptre. To prevent possible rebellion by the landed nobility and to gain church sanction of his action, he took a momentous step. He appealed to the pope,

Charlemagne crowned emperor by Leo III, A.D. 800

asking him to decide who should be king. That politically sagacious church head responded by saying that "it was better for the man who had power [Pepin] to be called king." By this action "he commanded by apostolic authority that Pepin should be king."[3]

This act set a new stage in church-state relations. By appealing to the pope, Pepin seemed to be conceding the papacy's right to determine who held secular power. As if to confirm this, Boniface, the pope's representative, anointed Pepin as king.

Still a long, mutually beneficial, cooperative relationship did develop between popes and Frankish rulers. For instance, in the early 750s, Pepin brought his army into Italy to protect the papacy. After driving out invading Lombards, he gave the conquered lands of central Italy "to St. Peter and the Roman Church" in perpetuity (Donation of Pepin). By this act he began the papal states, established popes as temporal rulers, and excluded the Eastern Roman Empire from any voice in central Italian affairs.

Charlemagne (768–814), Pepin's son, continued the same policy. He added to the Papal States (Donation of Charlemagne). And when Pope Leo III crowned him Western Roman Emperor in A.D. 800, the position of both was strengthened. A *bona fide* Roman emperor now supported papal claims to central Italy. The Eastern Roman rulers' claims had become ineffective and a factual basis had been laid for the later claims that popes created the emperors.

Yet, even though Charlemagne had accepted the imperial crown from the pope, he did not consider himself in any way subordinate to him. By virtue of his anointing as king and emperor, Charlemagne believed he had been placed in authority over church and state. He considered himself the equal of David and Solomon, the one empowered to be "the representative of God in the leadership of the church, not only in external but also in internal affairs."[4] As such he stood above bishops and felt free to reject the pope's advice. He called thirty-three councils to deal with problems of discipline in the church. He had scholars prepare sermons which clerics were forced to memorize and recite to the people. He nominated candidates for bishops, who were then rubber-stamped by diocesan clergy and laity. He reformed lax monasteries, imposing the Benedictine Rule once again. He imposed uniform dress on Western clergy. He reformed the church's music and liturgy. Fortunately, these reforms were conducted with full papal support and, for the most part, were beneficial to both the church and the empire.

Charlemagne's theological decisions created more tension. As the head of the church he had no qualms whatever about his ability to alter important creeds and to make theological decisions which seemed to run counter to the broader wisdom of the church. For example, at the Council held in Aachen (809), Charlemagne insisted the Western church add to the venerable Nicene Creed the Latin words *filioque* (and the Son); so we now confess "I believe in the Holy Spirit, the Lord and giver of life; who proceedeth from the Father and the Son." The change was made in spite of the pope's warning that such an alteration in an age-old creed would be repugnant to the Eastern church and alienate them further. Charlemagne was clearly the master of the Western church.

And for the most part he was a good master, genuinely concerned with the church's welfare. In at least two areas, however, Charlemagne used the church to enhance his own political ends. First, he compelled monasteries, cathedrals, and parishes to educate qualified lay students—so that he would have capable civil servants for his administration. Second, he made use of Christian missions in expanding his kingdom. He brought missionaries along on his battles with the pagan German tribes. The conquered had a choice: death or baptism. Thousands chose death. But other thousands "converted," probably reasoning, "What does it profit a man to have his own way and lose his life?"

Charlemagne's practice was quite consistent. He found it necessary to abandon Boniface's peaceful missionary methods in favor of forced conversions because missionary activity was an integral part of his wars of conquest. He reasoned that those who refused to convert were, by that very act, proven rebels—and rebels deserve to die. Such reasoning is typical of the logical but disastrous results of combining church and state, interlocking questions of faith with those of political obedience.

The Investiture Conflict

Not long after Charlemagne's death, his empire began to disintegrate. His grandsons divided the empire into three parts and then, scrabbling together in involved civil wars, drained away its strength. At just this inopportune time (from the empire's viewpoint), Magyars from the east and Vikings from the north invaded, spreading ruin and desolation.

The effects of these invasions and civil wars on the church were devastating. By the year 900 there were no strong kings or powerful bishops left. In that context of anarchy, local, petty lords began to grab church lands and monastic properties—sometimes by outright force; more often indirectly, by appointing relatives as priests, abbots, or bishops. Sometimes such offices were even sold to the highest bidder (simony).

Such a clergy, chosen not for spiritual gifts but for political or family ties, became progressively less spiritual. It gave little leadership in faith and its interests and values became quite worldly. Some church leaders married and tried to pass on to their children church positions and lands. A church so led was rapidly decaying.

But then, in 910, a reform movement began within the church. The center and fountainhead of this movement was a new monastery

86

founded at Cluny, in central France. From there a flow of reform went out, purifying monasteries, bringing monastic life back under the strict Benedictine Rule, reviving the life of the church at large.

The key to such reform was independence of church from state. The monasteries had to become free of local landed nobility, the bishops of local lords, and the papacy of local political factions in Rome. Ironically to achieve such independence, the church had to depend on the kings, leaders of the state.

A classic example of how this worked is the case of Henry III, emperor of the Holy Roman Empire. After freeing the church in Germany of local lords, he marched to Rome (1046), deposed the three rival popes, and enthroned his own candidate—who promptly died, probably poisoned by some Roman faction. That happened a second time. But Henry's third appointee, Leo IX, managed to avoid poisoners and ruled the church for five years.

Leo immediately appointed several reform leaders as cardinals and decreed that all future popes be elected by the College of Cardinals. He forbade simony, clerical marriages, and concubinage. All these acts were meant not only to spiritually cleanse the church but also to make it strong and independent of state powers.

Even though the reform party owed much to Henry III, they saw that to carry through reform they could permit no king to retain the power to appoint popes and bishops. Ties with the state corrupted. Only a free church would stay pure. This became known as the "lay investiture" issue—whether laymen had the right to appoint church officers.

On this issue the clash of church and state came to focus. By 1073 the empire had a new king, Henry IV, and the church had a new pope, Gregory VII. Both king and pope needed the power to make church appointments—Henry to rule effectively and Gregory to carry on reforms. So the stage was set for confrontation.

Pope Gregory began the struggle. He issued a decree called *Dictatus Papae* (one of the most impor-

Hildebrand—Gregory VII

tant church documents ever published). It read, "The Roman Pontiff alone is rightly to be called universal. He alone can depose or reinstate bishops. The Pope is the only one whose feet are to be kissed by all princes. He may depose Emperors. He himself can be judged by no one. The Roman Church has never erred, nor ever, by the witness of Scripture, shall err to all eternity."[5] Gregory logically summarized the earlier papal claims by asserting that the pope is the highest authority on earth.

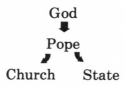

God
↓
Pope
Church   State

Henry IV was outraged by these claims. In his opinion kingly authority came directly from God, not via a pope. The king then, unless he deviated from the orthodox faith, was judged by God alone.

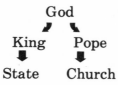

God
King   Pope
↓   ↓
State   Church

The practical issue of these clashing claims was lay investiture. Henry defied Gregory and made his own candidate the bishop of Milan. Gregory retaliated by excommunicating Henry and deposing him. The conflict may have remained unresolved for some time if Henry's situation had been more stable. But German nobles, who were opposed to Henry's attempts to consolidate power, immediately and joyfully chose this opportunity to revolt, putting Henry in a precarious position. He was further weakened when the common bishops who had earlier supported him turned against him. After such a substantial loss of power, Henry was forced to surrender. In January of 1077 the humbled king came to meet Pope Gregory at Canossa (in the Alps). There he waited three days in the snow as a penitent sinner. Finally, since Christ's vicar must forgive the penitent, Gregory lifted the excommunication; but he did not restore Henry to the German throne. The German nobles proceeded to elect Rudolph of Swabia as their new king—and civil war broke out.

If Gregory had supported either Henry or Rudolf, the war might have ended quickly. But he miscalculated badly. It was a year before he finally endorsed Rudolph. By then public opinion had changed. Many felt Gregory had treated Henry shabbily. So Henry rallied support and, after defeating Rudolph, placed an "antipope," Clement III, on the papal throne in Rome. Gregory fled to southern Italy and died there a few months later (1085). His last words were, "I have loved justice and hated iniquity—and so I die in exile."

****

No one won the investiture conflict. In spite of Gregory VII's claims, kings continued to have a vital role in church elections. But Henry IV's claims of the right to invest clergy in office were also not accepted.

After the death of both combatants, a compromise developed. The Synod of Worms, 1122, decided that clergy in a diocese should elect their own bishops. However, the king should be present and receive homage from the newly elected bishop. Practically, this gave kings veto power since they could refuse to accept homage from unacceptable candidates. It also reflected the realities of the situation since bishops did possess great political power.

So ended almost a thousand years of highly varied church-state relations in the Western empire area. But this compromise did not dissipate the tension. In the West neither king nor pope were finally able to unify the society under themselves.

The entire Middle Ages experience suggests strongly to us that no permanent, clean-cut resolution to this problem is possible in this present era.

We, contemporary Westerners, live in a time when a complete separation is often presented as the ideal resolution. But we know that such a separation is never truly complete or really ideal. The church may not remain aloof from "secular affairs" and the state cannot ignore "religious activities." These are not isolated spheres of human activity, hermetically sealed from each other.

So the tension remains and seemingly will remain until Christ, the Lord of both church and state, comes again.

Emperor Henry IV at the Gate of Canossa

CHAPTER 9
ISLAM, THE EASTERN CHURCH, AND THE CRUSADES

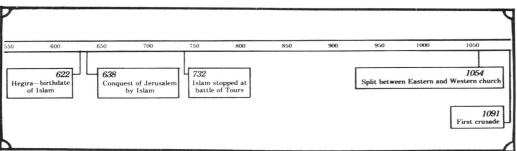

| 550 | 600 | 650 | 700 | 750 | 800 | 850 | 900 | 950 | 1000 | 1050 |

622 — Hegira—birthdate of Islam

638 — Conquest of Jerusalem by Islam

732 — Islam stopped at battle of Tours

1054 — Split between Eastern and Western church

1091 — First crusade

Imagine yourself an observer, a student of religion, from another planet. For almost five centuries (A.D. 500–950) you've been living in an orbiting space station, watching the movement of religious beliefs across the surface of planet Earth.

During this long period North and South America, most of Africa, Australia, and other outlying territories have remained a mottled grey of Animism and idolatry. But universal, "higher" religions have been spreading over the rest of the world.

The bright, saffron yellow of Buddhism has covered central Asia and China and crept over Southeast Asia, the East Indies, Korea, and Japan. But by 950, in its birthland of India and in China, it has begun to fade, losing its bright intensity. The rich green of Christianity has spread from its base around the Mediterranean Sea, to Ireland in the west, Scotland and Germany in the north, parts of China in the east, and Sudan in the south.

Then suddenly during the seventh century a new color, the flaming red of Islam, begins to burn. From Arabia, like fire through underbrush, it flashes out over Palestine, Syria, and Armenia to the east; over Egypt, North Africa, and Spain to the west. All these are engulfed. Even parts of Southern Italy and Sicily are temporarily red. The Mediterranean "heartland" of the Christian faith on the east, south, and west has fallen to this new religion. Large numbers of Christians in these territories have converted and the church, if it remains at all, is a small, ineffective remnant. By 950 Islam is almost as widely spread as Christianity and has captured the most powerful nations in this part of the world. The Christian faith is fighting defensively to recover Spain in the west and to hold the bulwark of Constantinople in the east.

If you, this planetary student of religion, are yourself a Christian, this shift of colors probably disturbs you deeply. For if church history records the agelong, world-wide battle between the Lord of Light and Prince of Darkness for the hearts, minds, and lives of peoples, and if, as the Bible testifies, Christ has already defeated Satan and will surely lead his church to victory, then how do we explain such losses of great territories? The Lord preserved his church through the harshest persecutions. Why would he permit it to be engulfed and virtually eradicated in some lands by this new faith?

This is the unavoidable question raised by the spread of Islam, the losing struggles of the Eastern church, and the failure of the Crusades.

The Rise and Spread of Islam

In the year 613 a man called Mohammed began publicly preaching a new faith in the city of Mecca, Arabia. This Mohammed, an Arabian who claimed to be a descendant of Ishmael, Abraham's son,

had been a businessman and caravan leader. Religiously alienated from pagan and polytheistic Arabian society, he had frequently retreated to a cave outside Mecca to meditate. There, at the age of forty, he had a dramatic religious experience which transformed him into a prophet.

Mohammed proclaimed an austere monotheism, calling on his fellow citizens to abandon their many gods and materialistic interests and submit to the will of Allah (*Islam* means "submission"; a *Muslim* means "one who has submitted"). Like the *Hanifs* who had earlier preached a similar message in Arabia, this new prophet was singularly unsuccessful. Most thought him weird. Businesspeople saw him as a threat to the pilgrim trade (Mecca was filled with sacred shrines). So in 622 Mohammed and his seventy followers were forced to flee Mecca and seek refuge in the city of Medina. This journey (the *Hegira*) is considered the birthdate of Islam. The Islamic calendar begins with the Christian year 622.

In strife-torn Medina, Mohammed became the peacemaker. His new religion united the warring factors. And from this base, the prophet was able to win over most of the Arab people. "He [became] not only a venerated prophet and the father of a new religion but also the uncrowned king of Arabia and the founder of a rapidly expanding empire."[1]

The method Mohammed encouraged for spreading Islam was the holy war (*Jihad*). Followers raided caravans, using some of the booty

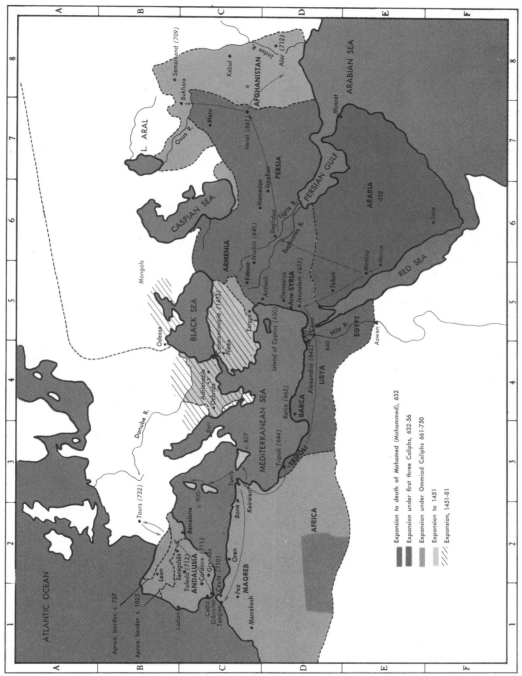

Muslim Expansion to 1481

ATLANTIC OCEAN

Aprox. border. c. 737
Aprox. border c. 1025

Tours (732)

Lisbon
Leon
Saragossa
Toledo
Cordova (711)
Granada
ANDALUSIA
Cadiz
Gibraltar
Tanger
Ceuta (710)
Fez
Marrakesh
MAGREB

Barcelona
c. 900
Oran

AFRICA

Kairwan
Bona
Tunis
c. 827
Bari
Tripoli (644)
TRIPOLI
Barca (643)
BARCA
LIBYA
MEDITERRANEAN SEA

Danube R.
Ochrida
Adrianople
Constantinople (1453)
Aleppo
Tarsus
Island of Cyprus (650)
Alexandria (642)

Mongols
Odessa
BLACK SEA

ARMENIA
Edessa
Antioch
Damascus
Acre 'SYRIA
Jerusalem (637)
Cairo
Nile R.
EGYPT
640
Aswan

CASPIAN SEA
L. ARAL
Oxus R.
Bukhara
Merv
Herat (661)
PERSIA
Ispahan
Hamadan
Nisibis (641)
Baghdad
Tigris R.
Euphrates R.

Samarkand (709)
Kabul
Indus R.
AFGHANISTAN
Alor (712)

Muscat
ARABIAN SEA

PERSIAN GULF
ARABIA
632
Medina
Mecca
Tébuk
Sana
RED SEA

Expansion to death of Mohamed (Mohammed), 632
Expansion under first three Caliphs, 632-56
Expansion under Ommiad Caliphs 661-750
Expansion to 1451
Expansion, 1451-81

Charles Martel halts the Muslim invasion at Tours.

to support Islam's cause. Later it was the sword that brought even Mecca to accept Mohammed as leader. That strong sword won successive victories for the new faith in the Near East and Africa. Yet this sword of political conquest was not used to force conversion. People in conquered territories were allowed, if they wished, to practice their own religions. Still the religion spread rapidly, following close on the political conquests.

In 636, four years after the prophet's death, Syria fell. In 638 Jerusalem was conquered, an event that shocked the Christian world. In 642 Alexandria, the great Christian center in Egypt, fell. By 650 Mesopotamia and much of North Africa was under Muslim control. By 697 Carthage had been conquered. And by 715 the Muslim tide flowed over the Straits of Gibraltar into Spain. In 732 Charles Martel, A Christian Frank, stemmed the tide in Tours, France. And in the East the Christian emperor, Leo III, stopped the Muslims at Constantinople. But in 1453 the Eastern empire finally yielded and the Muslim tide advanced into Eastern Europe.

That, in brief, is the record of the greatest loss of territory Christianity has ever experienced.

Why the Muslim Successes?

It is difficult for us, as Christians, to understand and explain why the Muslims were so successful in winning people to their faith. Since Christianity was officially tolerated, why did so many believers convert to Islam?

It's easier for us to explain the political successes.

The Muslim armies were welcomed as liberators by some Christians. When the Council of Chalcedon (451) defined the relationship of divine and human natures in Christ, many Christians in Egypt and Syria disagreed. They rejected the Formula of Chalcedon and argued that Jesus Christ had one nature after the incarnation (Monophysites).

These dissenters left the Eastern Catholic church and became alienated from the main body of believers in that part of the empire. When orthodox emperors persecuted them to force uniformity, they became both strongly anti-Catholic and anti-imperial. Hoping for better conditions under the Arabs, these Christians in Egypt and Syria welcomed the Muslim armies.

Furthermore, there had been a military power vacuum in much of the Near East and North Africa. Persia and the Eastern Roman Empire had fought for years until both were exhausted. The Eastern emperor had lost his hold on the Carthage area. The Roman elite there were disenchanted by Constantinople's excessive tax levies, and the native Berbers had little loyalty to the Carthage elite. So when the unified Arabian armies appeared they found little resistance and many willing allies.

The religious successes are harder to explain.

There was, it does seem, a strong attraction for many to the rigorous monotheism of Islam and its clear proclamation: "There is no God but Allah [God], and Mohammed is his prophet." This new faith also, in contrast to both the pagans and the contemporary Christian churches, radically rejected any use of images in worship. It permitted no idols, no pictures, no graven forms of human or beast.

There was a further attraction in Islam's claims to ties with Judaism and Christianity. The earlier prophets—Adam, Noah, Abraham, Moses, Jesus—and the shrines dear to Jews and Christians were still honored by Muslims.

This was a religion that prescribed regular prayers, five times each day, in specified postures. It required also, where possible, a service of prayer and preaching each Friday noon. At first believers were told to bow in prayer toward Jerusalem. But when the Jews rejected Islam, Mohammed made Mecca the holy city. Every Muslim, again if possible, was to make a pilgrimage to Mecca.

Islam was a religion without clergy or formal structure. Any believer who owned a prayer carpet had a place of worship and was, therefore, equal to any other believer. It was also a faith that greatly emphasized divine judgment; it promised a glorious heaven "with comely maidens, delicious drinks, and excellent foods" to those who submitted to Allah, but consigned unbelievers to a gruesome hell where they would be roasted in scorching fire, watered at a boiling fountain, and fed cactus thorns.[2]

Still, from a Christian viewpoint, the attractions of this new religion don't explain the mass conversions of both pagan and Christian peoples to Islam. The Muslim rulers were remarkably tolerant. Even Christians in the civil service were permitted to practice their own religion. They were not forced to convert.

True, there were distinct disadvantages in being non-Muslim. Taxes were heavier. Christians were forbidden to evangelize the invaders; so church growth was limited to births among members. By 700 it also became illegal to build new church buildings, to hold public processions on Christian holidays, or to ring church bells. So all outward promotion of Christianity was strictly forbidden.

Very likely these restrictions were enough to convince most nominal Christians that they could expect a better future under Islam.

But unless almost all the people in these conquered territories were just nominal Christians, mere economic and legal disabilities do not explain the mass defection to Islam. Early Christians had faced far worse and yet remained loyal to their Lord.

Mohammed

Some have suggested that the defective view of Christ held by Monophysite (one nature) Christians may have caused the conversions. Perhaps their resistance was weak because they did not faithfully serve the Christ of Scripture. But if that were true, why didn't all Monophysites convert to Islam? The once prosperous Monophysite churches, though reduced to a struggling remnant, still exist today.

There seems to be no easy or ready answer to this question. Perhaps we do not stand far enough along in the course of history to be able to understand the purpose of God and the exercise of his faithfulness to his people even in these seemingly disastrous events.

The Eastern Church

Thanks to Emperor Leo III's heroic defense of Constantinople, the Eastern Catholic church survived and continued to prosper in the area of present-day Turkey.

Unlike the papal church of the West, this church was emperor-dominated. The emperor was spoken of as "divine," "the equal of the Apostles," "holy," even "a god on earth." So he was clearly a "Christ figure," head both of state and church, ruler and pastor of the people. He presided over church councils, appointed and dismissed bishops, and helped shape dogma.

Whether for this reason or not, the Eastern church had a clear propensity for heated doctrinal debate. In the East consensus on matters of teaching seemed to come only when those who disagreed, like the Monophysites, split from the church.

Two major controversies shook the Eastern church.

The first debate concerned the question of whether Jesus Christ had one divine will or two wills, one divine and one human. After long and strenuous argumentation, the Ecumenical Council held in Constantinople (680–81) resolved the issue. The Eastern emperor and Western papacy united to insist that two wills was the orthodox position; they dismissed the Monothelites (who believed Christ had one will) as "instruments of the devil."

The second debate (the Iconoclastic Controversy) concerned the place of images in Christian worship. It began in 725 when Leo III, presumably because of taunts by Muslims and Jews that Christians were idolaters, tried to eliminate images in churches. Leo and the other iconoclasts (image destroyers) were strongly opposed by many monks and the vast majority of ordinary Christians. These iconophiles (image lovers) found images useful for edification. Riots and general discontent forced the emperors and iconoclastic bishops to back off. At the Second Council of Nicea (787), Empress Irene, supported by the Western pope, tried to restore religious peace by endorsing the use of images in worship. The council argued that since the Old Testament (ark of covenant and cherubims) and church fathers used images, since in the incarnation God had taken on a human, material form, and since icons were "venerated," not "worshiped" in the church, they were permissible. Despite Charlemagne's objection, this remained the official position of both Roman Catholic and Eastern Orthodox churches.

Still the Eastern church did not expend all its energies in theological wrangling. While losing huge southern areas to Islam, it successfully evangelized the barbarian Slavic peoples to the north. From 800–1000 missionaries like Cyril and Methodius proclaimed the gospel to the Bulgarians, Russians, and other Slavs. To help win them to the faith, these evangelists invented a Slavic alphabet, translated the Bible, and developed liturgies in the native language. In this the East took a far different tack from the West, where Latin was maintained as the standard tongue of worship.

Through all these centuries the Eastern and Western branches of the Catholic church, despite variations and some tensions, had maintained a basic unity in doctrine and worship. Intercommunion was practiced and officials honored. But the multiplying of differences led to a major rift, the Schism of 1054, and to a final break in about 1350. The status of the papacy was a major point of disagreement. Another was the Western prohibition of clerical marriage. The Eastern church in 692 approved marriage of lower clergy—deacons and presbyters—though not of bishops. Still another was differences of doctrine. Charlemagne's addition of the "filioque" clause to the Nicene Creed was a continual irritant to the East.

But it was encounters in mission territories that made differences most apparent. Here the separate paths the two churches had taken were placed boldly side by side. Eastern clergy were married while Western were not; Western liturgies were in Latin while Eastern were in native tongues. Even the creeds the churches used were different.

In the year 1054, Pope Leo IX's representatives excommunicated the Patriarch of Constantinople, and Patriarch Cerularius returned the favor. Yet despite this major division and recurrent animosities, there were continued efforts to heal the breach and restore some measure of cooperation.

The Crusades

By the eleventh century Islam under the Seljuk Turks, was again expanding, threatening the Eastern empire, and making Christian pilgrimages to the shrines in Jerusalem very difficult. So the Eastern emperors, hoping for some mercenary soldiers to help fight the Turks, appealed to the West. What they got was unexpected and unwelcome—the Crusades.

Why did people come crusading? Reasons were probably as varied as the crusaders, but we can identify a few of them.

Some desired to recapture the Holy Land and Jerusalem from infidel hands. The papacy hoped to maintain the Eastern empire as a last bastion against the Muslims. Many shared this sense of Christian responsibility as well as a desire to promote unity with the Eastern church.

Others wished to visit these holy places and view the relics, thereby winning divine favor. The pope promised crusaders full forgiveness for past sins and for sins com-

Godfrey of Bouillon, a French nobleman, leads a crusade into Jerusalem.

mitted while on the crusade.

Still others sought reward and excitement. They included the second and third sons of nobility who saw a chance to win fiefs in the East, the restless souls seeking adventure, and the ambitious souls seeking new trade routes. All these added to a great mass movement to the East.

Only the First Crusade could be labeled successful. Incited in 1096 by a sermon of Pope Urban II in Clermont, France, it began with a first wave of 15,000 persons, mostly peasants. Led by enthusiastic preachers like Peter the Hermit ("he had an odor as strong and impressive as his personality and message")[3] and Walter the Penniless, the first wave was utterly destroyed by the Turks in Asia Minor. The second wave was better organized and led. It conquered Antioch in 1098, slaughtering nearly all of the Turks who lived there. Famine and plague followed. "They killed their own horses for meat and drank one another's urine to quench their thirst."[4] Still they survived and conquered Jerusalem in 1099. The blood of slaughtered Jews and Muslims ran in the streets knee-deep, one observer said.

Having conquered the Holy Land, the crusaders set up so-called Crusader States, which declared themselves independent of the empire (to the annoyance of the Eastern emperor) and which established Roman Catholic churches (to the annoyance of the Eastern church). So the First Crusade sharpened tensions between East and West instead of effecting reunion.

When the Crusader States toppled like dominoes before Turkish attacks in the mid-twelfth century, St. Bernard of Clairvaux proclaimed a Second Crusade. While militarily stronger than the first and led by kings of France, England, and the Holy Roman Empire, this second crusade proved a total failure. When in 1187 the crusading armies were decimated at the Battle of Hattim, many in Europe began to wonder if God favored these Eastern adventurers.

Following Crusades showed less dedication and spirit. The Fourth, in a total perversion of the original ideal, conquered Christian Constantinople (1204), making it a Western colony for fifty years. That attack seriously weakened the Eastern empire and increased the alienation between the two parts of the church.

Religiously the crusades were disastrous. They fostered the idea that violence and bloodshed were acceptable means of spreading Christian faith. Infidels were treated worse than animals. Anti-Semitism was promoted. Papal hunger for power and the Western lords' hunger for land were joined in Christ's name, to the credit of neither papacy nor nobility. Islam, Eastern Christianity, and Western Christianity came in close contact. The result was enhanced distaste of each group for the others.

****

Seen from the perspective of our time, these years were a time of Christian recession. There were, in total, more losses than gains, more defeats than victories.

Numberless people within the conquered territories defected to Islam. The Eastern church ended up far weaker in numbers and position. And the requested help from Western Christian brothers and sisters served only to weaken the East even more and alienate it further.

Still, within Muslim countries, small groups of Christians, Monophysite and Nestorian churches, did survive and do exist to the present day. The Eastern church, even after Constantinople fell, continued and expanded north and east. Today in numbers, worldwide, it has over 250 million members. And the Western church, despite the failure of the Crusades, continued to grow toward the north and east also.

The failings and flaws of Christians and churches during this period cannot and should not be ignored. They are numerous and obvious. Yet in spite of such faithlessness, the church survived under the care of its faithful Lord. The gospel was still preserved and still proclaimed to new peoples.

In the long sweep of history, this time of recession should be seen as part of that wider advance. The battle of the church continues and the victory is still assured in the name of its Lord.

CHAPTER 10
NEW REFORM MOVEMENTS

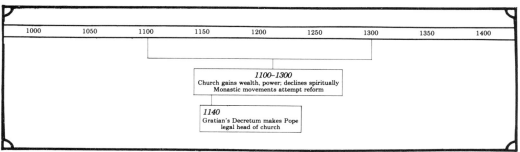

| 1000 | 1050 | 1100 | 1150 | 1200 | 1250 | 1300 | 1350 | 1400 |

1100–1300
Church gains wealth, power; declines spiritually
Monastic movements attempt reform

1140
Gratian's Decretum makes Pope
legal head of church

When we Protestants say "reform" we usually think of "the Protestant Reformation"—as if there has only been one reform movement in the church's long experience. But church history quickly teaches us something different.

The church of Jesus Christ has been reformed again and again. And each reform movement, zealous to purify corrupt institutions, idealistically seeking to serve the Lord and build his church, soon loses those original ideals, becomes self-seeking and corrupt. Again and again there have been those—like the children of Cluny—striving for the independence and power to cleanse the church of abuses, willing to sacrifice themselves to bring the church back to its true mission

of service. Yet within a few centuries independence and power have become ends in themselves, means to lord it over the rulers and people of the nations.

That image of the church as always reforming and always needing to be reformed can be very discouraging. Where then is the holy city, the bride of Christ, the immovable temple built on the rock of faith?

But viewed differently this continuing reform can be an encouraging sign. For like a tree planted by the river of life, the church has the inner vitality to renew itself, the Spirit-given strength to cut away dead branches and to grow new limbs—to serve its Lord's purposes and to bear proper fruit.

The Bureaucratic Church

The history of the church in the twelfth and thirteenth centuries is a prime example of how well-meant but misguided efforts at organization and too much concentrated power can corrupt the church.

The story began in 1138. Innocent II, after eight years of struggle, finally gained full control of the papacy. Trying to solidify lines of authority and insure the ability of himself and future popes to deal with local problems, Pope Innocent found Gratian's Decretum, issued in 1140, very helpful. This was a new, ecclesiastical, legal code based on Roman law. It clearly established the pope as legal head of the church and became the tool for developing "papal omnipotence." It was "the creed of the century."[1]

This Decretum made the pope supreme judge and legislator of the church. It gave him the right to hear all appeals and settle even the most insignificant local squabbles. Appeals promptly began pouring into Rome—on marriage, on ordination, on canonization, and on a host of other church affairs. To handle this vast influx of church business the pope needed a bureaucracy. He built one, the Curia, able to handle thousands of cases each year. But bureaucracies are expensive: the pope needed to raise new funds. And that made him appear greedy and money-hungry to church people. Some bureaucrats were corrupt and gave favorable rulings in exchange for bribes. That intensified the bad, unspiritual image.

As the pope grew more and more powerful, he became, and was perceived to be, the chief legal officer rather than the spiritual pastor of the church. Growing papal power progressively undermined the role and consequently the morale of regional bishops: as they lost influence, they lost interest in diocesan affairs. The growing practice of papal appointments to local offices was also corrupting. Such appointees were responsive and loyal to Rome, not to local church needs. Besides many were absentee officers, holding local office and being paid from there, but working in Rome.

The greatest of the "lawyer popes" who dominated the church during this period was unquestionably Innocent III (1198–1216), although he was neither very innocent nor very wise. Under him the papacy gained incredible power, but at tremendous cost to the church. His autocratic use of papal authority was destructive to any real pastoral function.

For instance, the bishops of France had annulled King Philip Augustus's marriage to Ingeborg of Denmark since the marriage had never been consummated. Arguing that the pope can intervene in secular affairs "where sin is involved," Innocent placed France under interdict, drastically curtailing religious services throughout the country. Philip was forced to take Ingeborg back as wife.

Again when King John of England made the person of his choice bishop of Canterbury, Innocent III set this candidate aside in favor of his own. When John rejected the pope's choice, Innocent placed all England under interdict. When John reacted by driving out ecclesiastics favoring the pope, Innocent excommunicated the king and declared his throne forfeit. Finally John capitulated and received England back as a fief from the pope, a concession that so irked English nobility that for this and other reasons they forced the famous Magna Charta on John.

Not that Innocent himself was corrupt. He did weed out the worst abuses in the Curia, especially bribery. But in his consuming concern to strengthen papal power, he neglected spiritual considerations. So his actions both hurt the spiritual welfare of the church and widened the gap between clergy and laity.

The result was a deep and broad reaction throughout Europe which surfaced in two forms: heretical sects which left the church and reform movements within the church.

Heretical Sects

A movement appeared in southern France during the twelfth century and spread rapidly among the common people there. By the end of the century the majority of people in southern France—even a number of landed nobility—supported it. The people of this movement were called Cathari or Albigensians.

Much like early Gnosticism (to which roots can be traced), the

Pope Innocent III urging the war against the Albigenses

Cathari believed that the material world is evil, the devil's creation. In an age of materialism and luxury worship, even within the church, that seemed a plausible tenet. To escape from evil matter and the devil's rule, Cathari taught, people must seek to free their good souls from evil's bondage by meditation and ascetic living. This idea of salvation led to some rather bizarre practices. The "perfect" abstained from all sexual intercourse since such acts could entrap new souls in matter. They became vegetarian, refusing to eat any food such as eggs or milk related to reproduction. And they refused to hold property since that also belonged to Satan's kingdom.

Still not all Cathari were "perfect." The majority were called the "believers." These sect followers could hold property and even, to avoid trouble, conform to the Catholic church. However, to be saved, "believers" had to support the "perfect," and, before death, repent and receive the "consolation" which would assure their entry into heaven.

So threatened was Catholicism by this movement of protest against wealth, power, and legalism in the church, that in 1208 Pope Innocent III proclaimed a crusade against it. That crusade, followed by Dominican preaching among the remnant and an Inquisition search for heretics, almost totally destroyed the Cathari. Yet the very fact that such a movement could arise was a warning that the church might not safely neglect the spiritual needs of the people.

Another movement, called the

Peter Waldo

Waldensians, is usually considered heretical by Roman Catholics, though not by Protestants. Peter Waldo, of northern Italy, and his followers took seriously Christ's command (to the rich young man) to sell all, give to the poor, and follow him. Wishing to keep his movement within the church, Peter asked papal approval to preach among the people. This request was denied by the Lateran Council (1179) and when Peter and his followers preached anyway, they were excommunicated in 1184. Once separated, the Waldensians became much more radical in their criticisms of the pope and the Catholic church.

The Waldensians were generally simple people, those who wished to serve Christ humbly and faithfully and felt abandoned by an unconcerned church. Believing that only personal faith was needed for salvation, this movement attacked the church's whole sacramental structure. It rejected as extra-biblical the cult of the saints, prayers for the dead, and purgatory. It affirmed the Bible, especially the New Testament, as the sole source of authority and translated the Bible into the people's language.

The Waldensian church was harshly persecuted by the Inquisition. Dominican preachers also tried to convince adherents of their errors. But these efforts failed. This separated church continued and several centuries later joined forces with the Protestant Reformation. Still today one can worship in Waldensian churches in Italy.

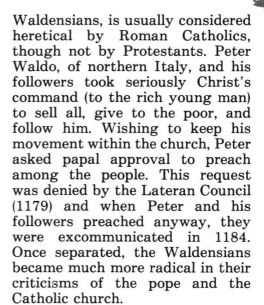

*Reform Movements Within
the Church*

Not all the reform forces were thrust out. There were those which, perhaps because they followed the pattern of Cluny and operated from within monastic orders, were able to work effectively within the Catholic church.

The first of these was called the Cistercians, named after the cisterns near the monastery at Citeaux. Begun in 1098 by a monk named Robert, this movement rigidly enforced the Rule of St. Benedict, holding high in contrast to a wealthy and powerful church the ideals of Christian poverty and humility. As the church sank deeper into a morass of wealth and legalism, the Cistercian order rose higher in the general believer's opinion. By 1188 there were 288 monasteries associated with this order.

The greatest figure in this reform movement was St. Bernard, abbot of Clairvaux (1090–1153). A man of deep piety and utter simplicity, he preached and practiced a humility which challenged the church's splendor and wealth. In contrast to the prevalent sacramentalism and religious legalism, he taught that salvation comes only through meditation, a practice by which one forgets self and turns to God. He clearly criticized the papal political activities and pleaded with the popes to restore to their office a spiritual and pastoral function.

Addressing the church at large from the strategic position of the monasteries, Bernard and other Cistercians were able to criticize papal abuses and yet remain loyal to the papacy, to expose the church's worldiness and yet steer it toward a greater spirituality. These efforts had a profound impact on the church at large, instilling a new, reforming spirit into many.

Bernard of Clairvaux's emphasis on divine grace as the motivating power to salvation was of special importance for the later Protestant reformers. Both Luther and Calvin looked back on this man as a great medieval saint, one who faithfully honored Jesus Christ in a hopelessly corrupt age.

Bernard, like most monks of his time, worked from dedicated seclusion to call the church back to its Lord. In the thirteenth century, however, two new orders, the Dominicans and the Franciscans, rejected the need for seclusion and developed a dramatically new kind of monasticism. The Dominicans and Franciscans referred to themselves as friars—monks who adhere to rules of poverty, chastity, and obedience, but are forbidden monastic isolation. Members of these new orders were called instead to live and work in society, to "save themselves by losing themselves in saving others."[2] Their task was to fill the unmet need among the people, to serve those the church was neglecting.

Both of these orders were approved by the papacy—which may have learned from the Waldensian experience that it was better to keep the reform spirit within the church than to drive it out. Both were well organized. Both began as mendicant orders—friars were expected to beg for their food. Both found an important place for women in teaching and social service. Both were totally loyal to the papacy. Both became the important missionary arms of the church. Yet there were differences between these two orders, springing partially from the experiences and insights of their founders.

Dominic was a Spaniard, born in 1170. Since most of Spain was still Muslim, he viewed unorthodox teachings as the greatest threat to the church, and as a result directed his efforts as a zealous, devout preacher toward converting the heretics in Europe, especially the Cathari and Waldensians. Already in 1206 he founded a school in southern France to instruct women who had fallen into the error of Catharism.

At first a lonely preacher with few followers, Dominic's successes attracted many adherents. So in 1215 the archbishop of Toulouse gave him a house and church, and in 1216 the order received papal approval. Dominic saw that to convert heretics, teachers of orthodoxy must be as zealous and self-denying as the "perfect" of the Cathari and the preachers of the Waldensians. So Dominican preachers had to meet extremely high moral standards. Besides, since debate with heretics involved one also in intellectual questions, these preachers had to be well educated. Dominicans combined purity of life with depth of knowledge. This explains why they soon came to hold key chairs in the new universities

rising throughout western Europe.

Unfortunately when preaching to the heretics proved relatively unsuccessful, Dominicans turned to other means. They collaborated with the papacy in the Inquisition and helped to execute thousands of stubborn heretics who refused to submit to the papal demands.

Francis of Assisi, founder of the Franciscans, was born in 1182 of a middle-class family in Italy. In his early life of revelry and self-indulgence, there was nothing to foreshadow what he became after conversion—one of the greatest saints in Christian history. It was after he nearly died of disease that Francis's life changed. He began to follow literally the command of his new-found master, Jesus Christ, "untroubled by any difficulties of exegesis" which would have made discipleship easier.[3] Sure that the best way to serve Christ was to pattern his life after his Lord's, Francis dressed in rags, worked among lepers, and ate only what others gave him.

His family thought he was crazy. His father, to prevent Francis from giving the family fortune to the poor and making himself the laughing stock of the town, confined him to the house cellar. Fortunately the local bishop intervened. He urged Francis to give up his inheritance to alleviate his father's justified annoyance.

Francis took the bishop's advice and became free as the birds, who, he believed, lived the perfect life. The birds, he noted, build no barns, yet sing continuously. So Francis became "the troubadour of the peo-

Francis of Assisi surrounded by scenes from his life

ple singing to them...the songs of Divine love."[4]

Having soon acquired an extensive following of men and women, Francis in 1210 went to Rome and received Pope Innocent III's somewhat reluctant approval of the new movement and its simple Rule. The order grew rapidly. Soon the Franciscans, or Lesser Brethren as they were called, could be found throughout Europe sharing the life of the poor and preaching the good news of God's love. Francis also founded a "Second Order" of spiritual sisters, nuns who wished to follow Christ in the way of St. Francis.

As the order grew, however, extravagances appeared and against Francis's will a new, more complex Rule was imposed. Sensing that the original simplicity of the movement was being destroyed by its success, Francis in 1220 resigned as order head and became again a private brother. Four years later he died, aware that his original ideals for the movement would not long survive.

In summary, the Franciscans may be evaluated as a highly successful lay movement that reached the neglected masses. In an age when ordinary people found little place for their talents in the church, Francis opened the door to a life of service for every serious-minded Christian. Without any caste distinctions, whether married or single, fulltime or parttime, all those who wished to live a life of poverty, obedience, and service were pressed into social and church work. "In an age when a dominant sacerdotalism had established an impassible gulf between clergy and laity, [Francis] attempted a revolution whose ideal...was the priesthood of all believers."[5]

It was also an order which shared St. Francis's love of nature. Bees and flowers made Francis praise God. For him creation testified to God's love, not to evil. Historians have credited a like love of nature among his followers for aiding the rise of science in the West by encouraging people to look more closely at nature. The best evidence to support this is the Franciscan scholar, Roger Bacon (d. 1291), who advocated observation and experiment as the proper method to understanding nature.

The Franciscans also sent many missionaries to the Muslims. Some lost their lives in this work, including six who were beheaded by Muslims in Morocco in 1220. In 1275 Raymond of Lull established a missionary college to prepare Franciscan friars, teaching them Arabic and Chaldean to equip them to present the gospel in the languages of the "infidels."

Finally the Franciscans, like the Dominicans, became teachers in the new universities. Recognizing that a successful reform movement requires more than mystical experience and that dealing with unbelief and other religions requires careful study, Francis's followers rejected his fear of higher learning. By the end of the thirteenth century most of the great scholars of Europe belonged either to the Franciscan or Dominican orders.

****

There seems to be a "law" in Christian history. Whenever the gospel is threatened by frozen rigidity or dead corruption, a new vitality emerges like a flame, melting the rigidity or burning away the dead branches. That flame rekindles a living light of Christian faith.

God does not leave his church in darkness. He revives it again and again. When the Cluny reforms had lost their cleansing power in the twelfth and thirteenth centuries, other movements arose as God's instruments of church reform. When in the fifteenth century, these movements in turn had lost their vitality, new reformers appeared to press on the church the gospel's claims.

Church history is the story of a church ever needing reform but also ever reforming. In every age God has provided his witness. Never has the church become so dark that new light has been unable to break forth.

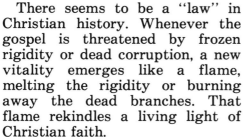

CHAPTER 11
THE FLOWERING OF THEOLOGY

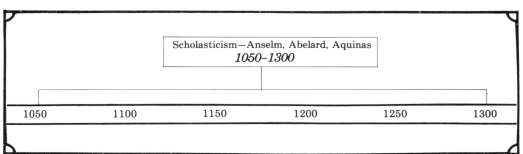

Scholasticism—Anselm, Abelard, Aquinas
1050–1300

| 1050 | 1100 | 1150 | 1200 | 1250 | 1300 |

O Lord, how long?
How long, Lord, will you turn your face from us?
   When will you look upon us and hear us?
When will you enlighten our eyes and show us your face?
   When will you give yourself to us again?
   Look upon us, Lord, and hear us,
   enlighten us and show yourself to us.
Give yourself to us again that it may be well with us,
   for without you it is ill with us.
     Have mercy on us,
   as we strive and labour to come to you,
   for without you we can do nothing well.
   I confess, Lord, with thanksgiving,
   that you have made me in your image,
so that I can remember you, think of you, and love you.
But that image is so worn and blotted out by faults,
   so darkened by the smoke of sin,
   that it cannot do that for which it was made,
   unless you renew and refashion it.

Lord, I am not trying to make my way to your height,
for my understanding is in no way equal to that,
but I do desire to understand a little of your truth
   which my heart already believes and loves.
I do not seek to understand so that I may believe,
   but I believe so that I may understand:
      and what is more,
I believe that unless I do believe I shall not understand.

This is not, as one might suppose, a mystic's poetic outburst or the rephrasing of some ancient religious poem. It's part of Anselm's *Proslogion*, a profoundly intellectual attempt to think theologically about belief and an example of the blending of reason and faith typical of one of the most remarkable phenomena in the medieval church—Scholasticism. The third from last line in this quote might almost be called the motto of the movement: "I believe so that I may understand."

By the end of the early Middle Ages (1050), Europe had become an intellectual desert. The Viking invasions, like a scorching wind, had burned away centers of education and higher culture. The arid disinterest in learning had dried up others. Only a few monastic and cathedral schools survived like oases in an intellectual wilderness.

Then unexpectedly, like a spring flood, came an outburst of interest in learning. Schools sprang up in many towns and universities grew in major cities. The first three centuries of the new millenium were like a wonderful spring, full of new intellectual life, a flowering of study and education.

Scholasticism

At the heart of this revival were the theological scholars. Like the Apologists of the earlier church, these Scholastics were concerned with questions of faith and reason—but for a different purpose. The Apologists had struggled to defend and define their faith against philosophically derived, heretical misunderstandings of it. The Scholastics, on the other hand, were not as interested in defending as in discovering. They dedicated themselves to a consideration of non-Christian systems of thought, trying to find ways in which these ancient beliefs would help Christians better understand what they believed. The questions they raised were these: Can human wisdom make understandable the mysteries of Christian faith? Can the wisdom of pagan philosophers (Plato and Aristotle) help us order and make coherent the tenets of our faith?

The modern image of Scholastics is one of ivory-tower scholars debating unrealistic matters such as whether Adam had a navel or how many angels can dance on the head of a pin. But the name Scholasticism was given them only because most of these learned people were associated with the *schools* of the period—initially monastic and cathedral schools, later the new universities. Their interests were not centered in ivory towers, far from the world's realities. Instead they were trying to help ordinary, thinking people understand better the supernatural truths of the Christian faith. They hoped to answer some of the rational criticisms leveled at the truths of revelation.[1]

Generally the Scholastics were conservative. They accepted the Bible as the authoritative source of revealed truth, "binding, sacrosanct, and obligatory."[2] They also accepted the traditional content of faith expressed in the Nicene and Chalcedon Creeds by the great church fathers. So while valuing highly the great philosophers of antiquity, they admitted that these thinkers diverged from Christian truth at several points. The Scholastics, then, were not radical liberals, seeking to establish a new, rational form of the Christian faith. Rather they used both ancient philosophies and traditional doctrines in new, refreshing, vital ways to make Christianity meaningful to a new age.

To the Scholastics truth revealed and truth derived by natural reason could not be antithetical since God is author of both. So most maintained the "unity of truth" while asserting also the superiority of revealed truth to reason. No one during this period,

not even the opponents of Scholasticism, like Bernard of Clairvaux or Hugo of St. Victor, took a Tertullian-type position, saying, "I believe because it is absurd." It was an age that respected reason as a gift from God.

Remaining within the Roman Catholic church and, like Abelard, submitting to its ruling even when their teachings were condemned as error, Scholastics worked to serve the church of Christ. Encouraging this scholarly effort by the best minds of the day, the church came to be called the "mother of learning" and theology became the "queen of the sciences."

Anselm

Anselm (1033–1109) was a man of the church, abbot of the monastery of Bec in Normandy, France, and later archbishop of Canterbury, England. Supporting Pope Gregory VII's efforts to reform the church and preserve its independence, Anselm clashed with both William the Conqueror and Henry I over lay investiture. He also demonstrated a genuine pastoral care for the people in his diocese. He was a man of prayer whose meditations inspire believers yet today and whose theological work is the fruit of a living faith.

Although perhaps best known for his ontological argument to prove God's existence, Anselm's most important theological contribution was his explanation of the

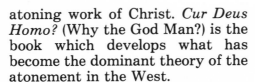

atoning work of Christ. *Cur Deus Homo?* (Why the God Man?) is the book which develops what has become the dominant theory of the atonement in the West.

Anselm's reasoning in this work progresses as follows: God created humankind to honor him. However, humans sinned, thereby dishonoring God and challenging his will for creation. Under the circumstances God couldn't simply forgive this sin—to do so would upset the moral order of the universe and contradict God's own nature. In overlooking this act of defiance, God would himself have become immoral. This is impossible. So to restore creation and sustain his own integrity God must demand *satisfaction*. Since humankind sinned, a human must give this satisfaction. Yet what human being can offer God anything over and above what is already owed him? No ordinary person can satisfy God and undo the fall's evil. At the same time God cannot leave us in our sins, for that would frustrate his plan for creation: God created humanity to enjoy and honor him. God's solution to this dilemma was to become incarnate in Jesus Christ, a person who both shared our humanity and was infinite, therefore able to offer satisfaction to God. By his perfect life and sacrificial death, Jesus Christ did satisfy God's honor and make salvation possible for his fellow humans.

By this satisfaction theory of the atonement, Anselm attempted through reason to demonstrate that the atonement is rational. Many have rejected this view as excessively legalistic or as forcing God into the limitations of human reason. But Anselm's theory does give structured form to a New Testament theme which is deeply imbedded in Western Christendom.

Abelard

Abelard (1079–1142) was a Frenchman who lived two generations after Anselm. Abrasive and often arrogant, Abelard was a brilliant teacher who—both because of his personality and because of his often heretical ideas—attracted many students but also many controversies.

When already a middle-aged, established teacher, Abelard fell in love with Heloise, one of his private students, half his age. She willingly, even joyfully, submitted to him and bore him a son. Her doting uncle, Fulbert, angrily demanded marriage. But when word of the secret ceremony spread, endangering Abelard's teaching career, both he and Heloise denied a marriage had taken place. Now enraged, Fulbert hired thugs who castrated Abelard. After this tragedy Heloise became a nun and Abelard a monk.

Some find a connection between this celebrated romance and Abelard's theory of ethics. He taught that good and evil depend on the motivation or intention of the doer rather than on the concrete character of the acts themselves. That is, if someone acts out of love (as Abelard felt he had done in his affair with Heloise), then even seemingly evil actions need not necessarily be condemned. At first glance this view seems to have merit. After all, Christianity has consistently held that motive is important: good works done for bad reasons are not good at all. But Abelard is too extreme. He makes the same mistake as followers of the modern situation ethics make: he sharply separates intention and action, failing to recognize that ideally good intentions always produce good actions.

Abelard also had his own theory of the atonement. He rejected Anselm's satisfaction theory in favor of what is now called the moral influence theory. Anselm's interpretation, said Abelard, insults God. For if God is love, then forgiveness is an act of grace, free of any demand for satisfaction. Out of his immense love God has voluntarily, not necessarily, taken on himself the suffering caused by human sin. This gracious, free act of God in Christ, said Abelard, awakens human gratitude and love and results in a Christ-centered life. How is that gratitude and love awakened? By the Spirit of Christ, said Abelard, indwelling and moving a person to love and thankfulness. It is at this point that Abelard's theory reveals its

Peter Abelard (1079–1142) lectures on theology.

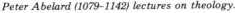

117

mystical side, proving that in spite of what some of his critics said, Abelard did believe Christ was more than a great moral example.

Still, in his atonement view, in his seeming denial of the Trinity in favor of a sort of tritheism, and in other doctrines, Abelard's ideas often appeared heretical. Furthermore, even though such was not his intention, his theological methodology expressed in his book *Sic et Non* (Yes and No) seemed to undermine faith's certitude. He set contradictory passages from the fathers in juxtaposition with no attempt at harmonizing them. This suggested strongly that for him traditional teachings were filled with insurmountable contradictions.

Because of his abrasive personality and difficult, questionable writings, Abelard was hounded by those who feared him and felt he threatened the orthodox faith. Bernard of Clairvaux, his most notable opponent, succeeded in 1140 in having him condemned on several counts. Abelard submitted to the church and was reconciled to Bernard, but died a broken man in an isolated monastery two years later.

Still his theological method dominated the later Scholastics. Peter Lombard (1095–1160) used the "yes and no" approach to develop a system of Christian doctrine called *The Four Books of Sentences*. This became the primary textbook for theological students up to the Protestant Reformation. It combined citations from the fathers and the creeds in a way that demonstrated an essen-

tial unity of the traditional theological teachings.

Misgivings about Scholasticism

Not all church leaders of the eleventh century shared Scholasticism's enthusiasm about the theological usefulness of philosophy and reason. Bernard of Clairvaux, for example, believed that since God's ways don't necessarily coincide with human reason, we can't simply ally reason and revelation. Furthermore, he rejected the idea that reason gives greater certainty to faith, teaching instead that certainty comes through mystical union with Christ and through humbly following the Holy Spirit's leading. Philosophy and reason can add nothing to such assured faith.[3]

Hugo of St. Victor (d. 1141) agreed with Bernard that mystical knowledge is the sole road to religious understanding. Faith, he said, is essentially an act of will. Faith knowledge is distinct from reason knowledge. The former does not rest on or gain certainty from the latter. In fact the understanding that springs from faith may well confound reason; for it comes through the church's sacraments and is strengthened by pious meditation of the soul free from all creaturely things—including reason and philosophy.[4]

These men reflect a debate found within the church in every age. Where some theologians find reason a marvelous tool to deepen the believer's understanding of faith, others fear it will rob faith of its mysterious depths of meaning. In this period of church history, however, the Scholastics were the favored party.

The High Water Mark of Scholasticism: Thomas Aquinas

The twelfth and thirteenth centuries experienced a new flood of learning and a new flowering of theology. The two new religious orders, Dominicans and Franciscans, contributed to this by their interest in education and their outstanding scholars. But the major impetus came from the discovery of a new, old philosophy. Aristotle was rediscovered. Accompanied by writings of Muslim and Jewish interpreters (such as Averroes and Moses Maimonodes), Aristotelian thought came to Europe in Latin translation. New issues were raised, new solutions offered, as thinkers in Europe faced this new challenge.

The greatest Scholastic of this period was Thomas Aquinas (1225–74). Born of a noble Italian family and a member of the Dominican order, Thomas taught at the University of Paris, the contemporary intellectual center of Europe. Surely one of the greatest theologians in Christian history, his thought has been compared to a gothic cathedral, encompassing all aspects of reality, earthly and heavenly, in a form both beautiful and symetrical. His greatest achievement, the *Summa Theolog-*

ica, is an encyclopedic work that uses selected ideas and methods of Aristotle to explain the major themes of the Christian faith. This theology became the established one of the Roman Catholic church and remains so, at least officially, to the present.

Aquinas, like the other Scholastics, taught that Scripture, as interpreted by the church councils and the fathers, is the final theological authority and that reason and faith are not contradictory since both come from God. But unlike Anselm, he held that many Christian truths cannot be rationally demonstrated, even to believers. Aquinas believed that most revealed truths, while not contrary to reason, can't be fully grasped even by redeemed reason.

Aquinas's view of humanity's fall remains the official Roman Catholic teaching. Adam, he taught, possessed a *donum superadditum* (a super-added gift) that enabled him to worship God and live a godly life. In falling Adam lost that gift and as a result, he and his descendants have turned for worship to lower, earthly things (Rom. 1). Without this lost gift, human beings can still live lives of natural virtue, but cannot experience God. By the grace won through Christ's satisfaction, the elect receive again the *donum superadditum* and thus are potentially able to live in faith, hope, and love (the supernatural virtues).

Salvation thus is God's work in humanity. But having received this new possibility by grace, believers are then able to perform works that

Thomas Aquinas surrounded by those who influenced and benefited from his Summa Theologica

gain merit with God, earnings that add to those of Christ and the saints. If such earned merits outweigh evil actions, a Christian may even avoid purgatory and at death go directly to heaven.

In Aquinas's scheme of salvation, penance has a key role. If believers' sins are greater than their merits, they must do penance. This includes confession (preferably to a priest) and ideally contrition (true sorrow) and leads to forgiveness. But even the forgiven sinner must pay certain "temporal penalties." If these are unpaid, the believer after death must go to purgatory to be purged of impurity and prepared for heaven.

But there is another way out besides personally earned merit. The church has the authority to transfer to the sinner merits earned by Christ and the saints, thus offsetting the "temporal penalties." At first such transfers usually came through acts of outstanding service to the church such as participating in crusades or visiting shrines. Later these transfers of merit (indulgences) were granted by money payments.

Aquinas reaffirmed Lombard's teaching that the church has seven sacraments (baptism, confirmation, the mass, penance, extreme unction, ordination, and marriage) and that God's grace comes to humanity only through these sacraments which belong to the church. He also gave a philosophical grounding for the doctrine of the mass already officially approved by the Fourth Lateran Council in 1215. The Roman Catholic teaching, transubstantiation, maintains that communion bread and wine become literally Christ's body and blood, and at every mass Jesus Christ is offered up again as a sacrifice for sin. Using Aristotle's categories, Aquinas argued that while the *accidens* (external form) of the bread and wine remain the same, so that the communion bread and wine looks and tastes like ordinary bread and wine, the *substantia* (underlying substance) changes into the real body and blood in Christ.

Although many of the doctrines he developed were attacked three centuries later by the Protestant reformers, Aquinas himself is not unworthy of our admiration. At a time when many argued for two truths, philosophical and theological, which could be completely at odds (one could as a philosopher deny the immortality of the soul and as a theologian affirm it), Aquinas rejected such a notion of double truth and drew the boundaries of faith and reason. He prevented an uncritical acceptance of ancient philosophy which might well have led to denial or compromise of cardinal Christian doctrines. He also affirmed the necessity of grace both for redemption and Christian living. Meritorious works to him were only possible because God gave the ability to believers to perform them and because God graciously chose to view them as merit. Aquinas would have been appalled by the abuses that developed based on his ideas—although it should be recognized that his scheme of salvation opened the door to these very abuses.

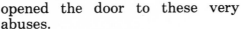

The problem of relating faith and reason, Christian truths and human philosophies, has no easy solution. To reject reason leaves one with an unsatisfactorily contentless faith, built on feeling and undefined affirmations. But to affirm that faith and reason are mutually supportive, forces one into the difficult task of evaluating philosophies from a Christian perspective and determining the role and limits of reason in relation to faith.

We Calvinists usually affirm, with the Scholastics, the unity of truth and the legitimate place of reason and human wisdom in the realm of Christian doctrine. But we also need to beware lest we uncritically allow foreign elements to enter into the content of our faith.

CHAPTER 12
THE CHURCH
MOVES TOWARD REFORMATION

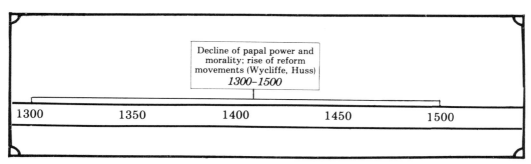

		Decline of papal power and morality; rise of reform movements (Wycliffe, Huss) *1300–1500*		
1300	1350	1400	1450	1500

The years 1300 to 1500 have been variously described by church historians as the "centuries of decay," the "years of decline," and the "restlessness before the storm." These descriptions share a common element: they perceive a decay before the new growth, a decline before the upward surge, a depression before the winds of fresh air and showers of life-giving rain. In other words, they all view the centuries we'll be studying in this chapter as a prelude to that momentous event, the Protestant Reformation.

The danger of this rather typical Protestant understanding is that we prejudge events and movements in the church's life during this period. To justify the division that produced our own independent church existence, we may unconsciously do a negative apology. We may shade the Catholic church of those years darker so that the Protestant cause appears brighter, stressing the bad to make clearer the Reformation's good.

Yet even without prejudice these centuries present a depressing picture of church life. The papacy lost power. Intellectual unity waned. The quality of the everyday believer's life declined. And the many attempts to correct abuses and improve the church's spiritual life generally failed. Some people remained faithful to their Lord, strong and alive members of his body, but many more were faithless, weak, and seemingly dying. The church, Christ's body, did not appear during these centuries to be the healthy, growing, serving vehicle it should have been.

Papal Decline and Nationalism

In the year 1250 the papacy seemed to be still gaining strength. Using the same intrigues and tricks as the secular rulers, perfecting and expanding its tax structures, the church hierarchy was a power in Europe. But at the same time, new nation states were emerging. The kings of these developing states were consolidating their power over the nobility and establishing a central control over national affairs.

Under those circumstances, the fourteenth-century collision between a power-seeking papacy and secular rulers of the nation states was inevitable. Perhaps the most dramatic confrontation occurred when Pope Boniface VIII (1294–1303) challenged the efforts of Philip IV (1285–1314) to centralize the government of France. That clash came in two areas: taxes and trials.

Philip, to finance war with England, imposed a tax on the church (which controlled some 25 percent of France's wealth). Boniface responded to clergy complaints by forbidding the payment of any taxes on church properties. Philip replied by prohibiting the export of all money from France, effectively cutting off much of the pope's revenue. Boniface was forced to allow the churches to make "voluntary payments equivalent to the tax.

A few years later Philip accused a bishop, who represented the pope, of high treason, arrested him, and prepared to try him. Boniface, contending that clerics should be tried only in church courts, ordered the bishop's release. He supported that claim with a famous bill, *Unam Sanctam.* In it he argued that both temporal and spiritual swords are ultimately in the pope's hands, and therefore secular rulers rule only with papal approval. Philip answered by pressuring a council of French bishops to condemn Boniface as a heretic (because he held unusual ideas of the soul's existence after death) and a usurper of the papal throne (because he was suspected of maltreating the preceding pope, forcing his resignation). In addition, Philip sent an army into Italy. His soldiers roughed up Boniface, an act which so shocked the pope that he died a short time later.

With these dual defeats, papal influence in secular affairs declined markedly. Never again would an "imperial pope" force his will on reluctant rulers. This loss of papal power was not just the inevitable result of the new nationalism. It also reflected a general loss of respect toward a church that unscrupulously grasped for temporal power.

Papal Decline and Conciliarism

The period after Boniface's defeat (1309–76) to the end of the

Great Schism is one of the darkest in the church's history. It is called the "Babylonian captivity of the Papacy" or the "French exile of the Papacy."[1] Dominated by French kings, the popes lived in Avignon, France. The Curia and College of Cardinals were both French dominated and only Frenchmen were elected popes. Yet ironically, blind to realities of power, the papacy continued to expand its money-gathering activities, enlarge its bureaucracy, maintain a magnificent court, and try to intrude on European political affairs.

When in 1376 the papacy tried to move back to Rome, the situation deteriorated even further. The cardinals, under pressure from the Roman populace, elected an Italian pope. Four months later the French cardinals declared the election invalid and chose a French pope. So came the Great Schism. The opposing popes excommunicated each other and each other's followers. The entire Western church divided into two parties, and the papacy lost tremendous amounts of prestige.

To resolve this intolerable division, some church leaders—including two outstanding theologians, Marsiglio of Padua and William of Occam—developed new theories about church government and papal authority. These were called conciliarism.

Marsiglio of Padua (c. 1290–1342) argued that the church should not be identified with the papacy or the clerical hierarchy. The church is the entire body of Christians. Giving the analogy of the "sovereignty of the people" in a state, he further argued that every Christian has the right, as a citizen of the body of Christ, to have a say in the church's decision-making. Such involvement is possible if the church is governed by a representative general council. Under such a system the pope becomes the administrator who carries out this council's will. Marsiglio was promoting a parliamentary sort of church government strikingly similar to the national pattern of government that emerged in England.

William of Occam (1285–1347), an English Franciscan, maintained similar conciliar ideas. Occam, who had been personally in conflict with the Avignon papacy, claimed the pope was too involved in politics and in extracting money, too little concerned with saving souls.[2] The papacy, he said, should be limited to spiritual functions. Furthermore, Occam argued, it is not the papacy but church councils who over the years have defined orthodox doctrine. So even in spiritual matters the church council takes precedence over popes. The popes hold power not from Peter, but from the faithful members of the church. Therefore popes should submit to the will of the church represented in and by councils. Also, Occam contended, the pope is not the only person who may call a general council. "Even a woman has the power to convoke a council without the permission of the Pope."[3]

Conciliarism provided the theory needed to end the Great Schism. But the actual resolution of the in-

125

tolerable situation required two councils. In 1409 the College of Cardinals called a council in Pisa. This church gathering deposed both popes and elected a third. But when neither pope accepted the deposition, the church was left with three popes.

Five years later, the Holy Roman Emperor Sigismund summoned another general council to meet in Constance (1414–18). Thoroughly dominated by conciliar ideas, this council deposed all three popes and selected a new one, Martin V, requiring of him a verbal agreement with the principles of conciliarism. The decree *Haec Sancta* asserted that the council represented the "catholic church militant" and held power "directly from Christ." All persons, it claimed, "even a pope," are bound to obey the council of the church "in matters relating to faith" as well as in matters relating to "the general reformation of the church."[4] The council also required, in its decree *Frequens,* that the pope, with the approval of the most recent council, set specific dates for future council meetings.

Council participants believed a new era had dawned in the church and that a reform had begun of the worst papal abuses of authority. But that was not the case. Martin V and his successors, while calling regular councils for a time, effectively undermined them and reconsolidated papal power. By 1459 Pope Pius II was able to condemn conciliarism as "an execrable outrage unheard of in earlier times."

From 1459 to 1517 the so-called "Renaissance Papacy" reasserted its control over the church. It was unsurpassed in luxury, immorality, avarice, and ruthlessness. Deaf to the rising "cry for reform" developing in the church, it claimed that reform would be forced to move outside the papal church to be effective. To us, in retrospect, it's astounding that a church leadership, challenged to reform the church in "head and members," coldly rejected that call and instead tried in every way and at all costs to retain its own prerogatives, indulging itself in unspiritual activities.

The Breakdown of High Scholasticism

The years 1300 to 1500 also brought disruption of the church's former intellectual unity. There were growing efforts to "disengage faith from reason," philosophy from theology.[5] Two figures stand out.

Duns Scotus (1270–1308) taught that God is Absolute Will. Since God acts according to that will, his acts need not conform to our ideas of what is rational. We know God not through intellect but through a union of our human will with God's— that is, through faith. It follows, argued Scotus, that theology is not a science (as Scholasticism supposed) but a group of beliefs based solely on faith. Reason and philosophy can contribute nothing to the assurance of faith.

William of Occam agreed with Scotus that reason can never be the foundation for faith or give faith

John Huss

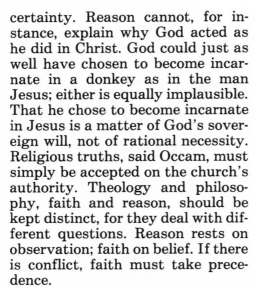

certainty. Reason cannot, for instance, explain why God acted as he did in Christ. God could just as well have chosen to become incarnate in a donkey as in the man Jesus; either is equally implausible. That he chose to become incarnate in Jesus is a matter of God's sovereign will, not of rational necessity. Religious truths, said Occam, must simply be accepted on the church's authority. Theology and philosophy, faith and reason, should be kept distinct, for they deal with different questions. Reason rests on observation; faith on belief. If there is conflict, faith must take precedence.

Both these men separated what the earlier Scholastics had tried to bring together, faith and reason. In so doing they had profound impact on the late Middle Ages and prepared the way for the Reformation. Martin Luther, in fact, called William of Occam "his master," the one who taught him to think properly on the relationship between faith and reason.

The Decline of Popular Piety

During this same period Europe was a shambles, torn by wars, plagues, and peasant revolts. The result was a "morbid preoccupation with death" and a dominant "melancholy imagination."[6] Fleeing from a painful existence, people sought refuge and solace in religious activities: unprecedented numbers of people went on pilgrimages, visited sacred shrines, viewed holy relics, listened to preaching, and read devotional literature. There seemed to be a flowering of popular piety.

But if quantity of religious activity increased, quality decreased. Most of the religion was inspired by fear and expressed in shallow, superstitious forms. Some people went on witch hunts, killing thousands of odd innocents. Others visited shrines dedicated to the Virgin or to some saint, hoping to experience cures or shorten sufferings in purgatory. Many traveled long distances to view a piece of the burning bush, milk from the breast of Mary, the tablecloth used at the last supper, a piece of the crown of thorns, or a splinter from the cross of Christ. We're told (an exaggeration doubtlessly) that over eighty thousand people each day visited the cathedral at Aachen to view the seamless robe of Christ. People also flocked to see "bleeding hosts," that is, the body of Christ consecrated for the mass which supposedly dripped blood. Such pious actions, these people believed, would assure them salvation and perhaps present blessings.

This frenzied religious activity generated a need for more clergy. Officially approved people were needed to consecrate the host and say masses for the dead. But of the large number who became clerics, many lacked any education at all and fewer than 1 percent held any sort of academic degree. Crash courses were given that, while insufficient to teach priests what they were really doing, still enabled them to perform masses.

The result was a flood of bad clergy. Cologne, for example, with a population of only forty thousand, had six thousand clerics. Since few of these were well qualified, serious abuses resulted. Priests often sold their religious "goods" for a price. The majority of them had concubines—for which privilege they paid the bishops a fee. Such fees became a major source of the bishop's income in Constance. On an average, in this rather small diocese, fifteen hundred illegitimate children were born to priests each year.[7] Even some popes had concubines. Innocent VIII had several children and held gala wedding celebrations for them in the papal palace.

Many monasteries became more like men's clubs than places of religious devotion, and many convents were little more than comfortable boarding houses for unmarried daughters of the wealthy.[8] Even the orders committed to poverty, like Franciscans and Dominicans, became wealthy and corrupt in some parts of Europe.

In brief, the piety of most in this period was one of external practices, not of heart or moral behavior. There was a bull market in religious services and, for a price, the church gladly sold these services.

Efforts at Reform

It would be a mistake to finish painting this dismal picture without including some rays of hope.

There were in this period of church history also the faithful ones who struggled to reform the church in "head and members." We've mentioned conciliarism. We should briefly describe some other reform efforts. Each of these had a distinct effect on the Protestant Reformation that finally erupted in the sixteenth century.

The first of these efforts was German Mysticism, a reform movement that reacted against the typical external religious acts that people performed to "save their skins." The German Mystics taught that people should seek God only because this is what God desires, not for their own spiritual well-being or to avoid hell (a form of egotism). Religious practices are useless unless one is in true communion with God. Furthermore they taught that salvation is wholly God's work; only by grace can people be saved.

The Mystics, and especially their most famous leader, Johann Tauler (d. 1361), played a key role in Martin Luther's later understanding of the gospel. They also influenced thousands in the fifteenth century who read and dearly loved *The German Theology,* a devotional work produced by the movement.

Another movement of this period that breathed a similar reforming spirit was the Brethren of the Common Life. This group, which began in the Netherlands in the late fourteenth century, tried to develop in all believers, laity or clergy, a simple inward piety expressed in acts of kindness to the poor and social outcasts. They set up houses throughout Europe from which the

129

Brethren practiced pious philanthropy. Thomas a Kempis's *Imitation of Christ,* the most widely read book in Europe during the late medieval period, was a work that sprang from this movement and reflected its belief that proper Christian living involves obedient following of Christ's pattern.

The Brethren also set up schools throughout Europe which, avoiding abstract theological speculations, taught students to live practical Christian lives of service. Both Erasmus (the great Christian humanist) and Martin Luther were educated in Brethren schools. If the church had followed the Brethren's example of following Christ, Luther observed, the church in Europe would not have needed the Reformation.

This period also produced two theologians who are often called "forerunners of the Reformation": the Englishman, Wycliffe, and the Czech, Huss. These men challenged not just papal authority (like Marsiglio and Occam) but the very sacramental structure and theology of the Roman Catholic church. Consequently both were condemned and burned (Wycliffe posthumously).

John Wycliffe (1320–84) taught that all tradition, including church council decisions and doctrines, must be tested by the Bible. "Holy Scripture," he said, "is the highest authority for every Christian."[9] He applied that principle by working to have the Bible translated into native English. Wycliffe agreed with Augustine that the church is the body of the predestined and must not be identified with the papal church. Formal membership is no proof of salvation. He also advocated a return to the poverty of the early church. Ecclesiastical lords, he said, if unrighteous, should have their property confiscated—advice secular rulers were glad to follow. In later life he even suggested the pope and cardinals do not belong to the true church but are Antichrists.

Wycliffe also challenged the sacramental practices and especially the doctrine of transubstantiation. Scripture, he said, teaches that "the body of Christ is concealed in [the elements]" but the bread and wine do not change.[10] Raising the Host for the people's adoration is a practice that leads to idolatry.

John Wycliffe

John Wycliffe sends forth his followers, the Lollards.

Basically Wycliffe was a practical intellectual. He trained a number of "poor preachers," called Lollards, to evangelize the English people. Challenging many aspects of the Catholic sacramental system, these preachers were severely persecuted and driven underground. Yet some survived to welcome joyfully Luther's ideas, so similar to those of their founder.

In spite of the church's condemnation, Wycliffe died a natural death—probably solely because of the protection of the English kings who used him to demonstrate their own independence of Rome. But even after his death Wycliffe and his "heresy" were not forgotten— years later the Council of Constance ordered his body exhumed and publicly burned.

John Huss (1374–1415) continued Wycliffe's work. Clearly influenced by the English theologian's ideas which had traveled to his homeland in central Europe, Huss, professor and later rector of the University of Prague, became the leader of the reform movement in Bohemia. He echoed Wycliffe's teachings on the Bible and the church. Advocating reform of church abuses, Huss gained a widespread popular following. In fact, his popularity was even greater than Wycliffe's had been—probably because his reform efforts were identified with rising Bohemian nationalism.

In 1415 Huss appeared before the Council of Constance. There, in spite of his safe conduct from the emperor and the conciliar ideas of

John Huss is burned at the stake.

the council members, he was condemned. And when he refused to recant his teaching, the council had Huss burned at the stake. But they couldn't "burn" the movement. By 1416 all the churches in the Prague were in the hands of the "Hussite" reform party. The papacy, recognizing its inability to destroy this movement, finally compromised, granting members of the movement communion in both kinds (bread and wine). A majority of the Hussites accepted the papal concessions; the rest refused this compromise and became an independent church. These Bohemian Brethren, like the Lollards in England, survived to greet the Protestant Reformation. In fact, descendants of these Brethren, Moravian churches, can still be found in Canada and the United States today.

One final movement, Christian Humanism, helped awaken many to the need for church reform and greatly influenced the Protestant Reformation. Christian Humanism was a northern European phenomenon with roots in the Italian Renaissance. Its greatest leader was the Dutchman Desiderius Erasmus (c. 1466–1536), known as the "Prince of the Humanists." Although the Humanists did not directly challenge the theology of the Roman Catholic church, they did point out numerous flaws in the church, often in a forceful way, bringing out a "cry for reform." The movement has, as a result, been called the "John the Baptist" of the Reformation.

How did the Humanists hope to effect reform? First, as noted above, by pointing out the flaws in the church. Second, by going "back to the sources," that is, to the Bible and the church fathers, to reclaim what had been lost by the church over the years (it was Erasmus's edition of the Greek New Testament, in fact, which played a key role in the Protestant Reformation). Third, by seeking a better education for both clergy and laity in these sources of Christianity, Erasmus hoped to teach children and clergy the "philosophy of Christ."

****

Unfortunately, all these efforts at reform were resisted by the leaders of the church. None were able to turn the church to the right path.

Still the papacy's resistance to these witnesses to the truth and its stubborn refusal to cooperate with the reform movements was unable to still the voices. The best it could do was to postpone reform. During the years 1300 to 1500 the papacy "sowed the wind." In the following years it "reaped the whirlwind." If the leaders of the church had only taken a different attitude, the deep division of the body of Christ that we call the Protestant Reformation might never have occurred.

CHAPTER 13
LUTHER INAUGURATES THE PROTESTANT REFORMATION

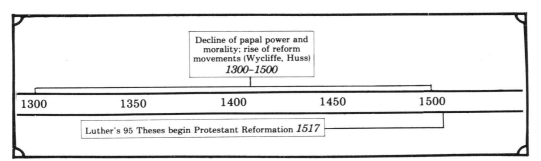

Decline of papal power and morality; rise of reform movements (Wycliffe, Huss)
1300–1500

1300	1350	1400	1450	1500

Luther's 95 Theses begin Protestant Reformation *1517*

Rarely in human history has one man so thoroughly shaken his world as Martin Luther did. He touched the hearts and minds of vast numbers of people in Europe and became the "spokesman for all [the] pent-up feelings of frustration, moral indignation, and downright anger at the Roman hierarchy, from the pope to the exploiting clergy and ignorant monks."[1] Grasping better than anyone else the situation and its causes, he was able to move people to rebel against it.

Unquestionably Luther is one of the greatest genuises in Christian history. He embodied something of several reform movements that preceded him: the Christian Humanist's desire to correct church abuses, the German Mystic's emphasis on divine grace as the only path to salvation, and William of Occam's understanding of God. Yet more than a summation of these, Luther was "a religious genuis of profound faith and theological insight, [who] made a deeper plunge into the meaning of the gospel than perhaps any other man since St. Paul."[2]

Still conditions must be right even for genuises and when Luther appeared, Europe was ready for reform. The preparatory movements had made people in Europe painfully aware of the desperate conditions in the church. The newly invented printing press made it possible for reform ideas to spread quickly and widely. All was ready. So God provided the man for the time and the result was a radical change in the church's structure and course.

Luther's Quest for Religious Certainty

Luther's path to a new understanding of the gospel was no coolly rational and exegetical walk through the Bible; it was the anguished pilgrimage of a turbulent, troubled spirit, wracked by the religious anxiety and fear of death so common in his day. The breakthrough to truth was slow and painful. As Luther said, "I did not learn my theology all at once, but I had to search deeply for it." And it came as a result of his "living, nay dying, and feeling damned."[3]

Luther was born in 1483 in the German state of Saxony. His father, Hans, was a miner who had worked himself up to middle-class status as part owner of six copper mines. Luther's early life was typically severe, although Martin, an extraordinarily sensitive child, tended to exaggerate its negative aspects. He claims, "My mother caned me for stealing a nut, until the blood came," but adds, "She meant it well." He also tells us, "My father once whipped me so that I ran away and felt ugly toward him until he was at pains to win me back." Some have speculated that the severe authority of his own father helped form Luther's early view of God as a vengeful, unforgiving Father.

Luther recalls his early education as a boring time when seemingly heartless teachers "drummed" facts into the students' heads, and if that failed "drummed" them into the students' behinds instead. "One day," he said, "I was caned in a single morning fifteen times for nothing at all. I was required to decline and conjugate and hadn't learned my lesson." Such schooling probably contributed to Luther's deep sense of anxiety and personal uncertainty.

Recognized as a highly gifted student, Luther was sent by his parents to the University of Erfurt in 1501. He received an A.B. degree in 1502 and an M.A. degree in 1505. His proud father urged Martin to enter law school and contract a good marriage—both of which would have confirmed the family's newly won middle-class status. His course of life seemed clear.

But underneath the seeming success, Luther was wracked by fear of devils seeking his destruction. Even though angels, saints, and the Holy Virgin might help against these devils, Luther still trembled that he might die and face a vengeful God who would punish him for his innumerable sins. He was *always* aware of his sins; they utterly oppressed him. Then one day in 1505, shortly before he was to enter law school, Luther was nearly struck by lightning. Terrified he cried to the patroness of miners, "St. Anne, help me! Help and I will become a monk."

Fifteen days later, on May 20, 1505, Luther gave a beer party to friends and announced his decision. Over the furious protests of an outraged father, he entered the

Augustinian monastery in Erfurt.

His first years as a monk gave him some peace and assurance. But soon he was designated to become a priest, and with his first mass the religious distress and uncertainty returned. Aware that (according to the doctrine of transubstantiation) he was handling the real body and blood of Jesus Christ, he was overcome with "fear and trembling" and could not finish the service alone. He felt wholly unworthy to hold divinity in his hands. "How could a pygmy stand before divine majesty? How could a transgressor confront divine Holiness?"[4] His father, come to see his son's first mass, added to Luther's insecurity by suggesting that the voice from heaven out of the thunder cloud which had called him to monastic life might have been "an apparition of the devil." Martin was no longer sure.

Although entrusted with several leadership positions in the monastery, Luther still struggled mightily with the question of facing a holy, righteous God. He performed vigils, prayers, and readings. He starved himself until his "belly-button touched his backbone." He strove to "outmonk the monks." He confessed even the most insignificant things in such detail that finally one exasperated confessor rebuked him, "Man, God is not angry with you. You are angry with God. Don't you know that God commands you to hope?" But Luther could not hope. Gradually he came to realize that sin is not a list of specific offenses, but a condition. Every person's nature is corrupt; it must be changed if that person is to stand before God.

Perhaps to take his mind off his religious state and certainly because of his great promise, Luther was sent to study further. In 1512 he received a doctorate in theology from the University of Wittenberg and was appointed to the chair of biblical studies, a position he held until his death. This assignment, to teach students the Bible, proved to be the means by which he himself came to a true understanding of the gospel.

Luther's breakthrough came in 1515 or 1516. He was editing *The German Theology* of the German Mystics and lecturing on Psalms and then on Romans. The combination of these helped him to read familiar texts in a very new way. Luther later wrote:

> I greatly longed to understand Paul's Epistle to the Romans and nothing stood in the way but that one expression, "the justice of God," because I took it to mean that justice whereby God is just and deals justly in punishing the unjust. My situation was that, although an impeccable monk, I stood before God as a sinner troubled in conscience, and I had no confidence that my merit would assuage him. Therefore I did not love a just and angry God, but rather hated and murmured against him. Yet I clung to the dear Paul and had a great yearning to know what he meant.

> Night and day I pondered until I saw the connection be-

tween the justice of God and the statement that "the just shall live by his faith." Then I grasped that the justice of God is that righteousness by which through grace and sheer mercy God justifies us through faith. Thereupon I felt myself to be reborn and to have gone through open doors into paradise. The whole of Scripture took on a new meaning, and whereas before the "justice of God" had filled me with hate, now it became to me inexpressibly sweet in greater love. This passage of Paul became to me a gate to heaven.

It had dawned on Luther that we do not make ourselves holy enough to withstand God's justice by pious practices. Rather, through faith, God views us *as if* we were holy, thanks to Christ's sacrifice. God gives us his righteousness (justice) through Christ and so makes us able to stand before him.

With this newfound understanding of the gospel, Luther began to judge the church's teachings and practices. Of course the full implications of all this only came to Luther over a period of time and as a result of many conflicts.

Luther's Reform Activities

Pope Leo X was building the magnificent and very expensive Cathedral of St. Peter in Rome. To help finance it, he appointed Albert, the bishop of Magdeburg, as the new archbishop of Mains—for a fee of about a million dollars. As part of the deal and to assist the new archbishop in raising the money, the pope authorized Albert to sell papal indulgences in northern Germany. Half of the proceeds were to go for the building of St. Peter's, the other half to the archbishop. John Tetzel, a Dominican monk and supersalesman, was hired to market this new offer of religious securities. "Ironically, one of the grandest monuments in Christendom, St. Peter's Cathedral in Rome, became the occasion for and the lasting reminder of the division of the church."[5]

Tetzel assured indulgence purchasers full remission of past sins. He also encouraged them to buy indulgences for dead loved ones, with the sales slogan, "Just when the coin in the coffer drops, a soul out of purgatory hops."

Luther, who was now serving also as a pastor, was deeply disturbed by these sales. He no longer believed the church could draw on a "treasury of merit" to forgive sin, but rather that each person must repent and receive a change of mind and heart. So in response to Tetzel, Luther formulated in 1517 Ninety-five Theses on indulgences. He sent these to Archbishop Albert and also (according to Melanchthon) posted them on the door of the Castle Church in Wittenberg.

To Luther's surprise these theses, intended for academic debate, were quickly printed and translated into several languages, unleashing a storm in Europe. We can understand better how this happened if we catch the tenor of these theses by reading a few of them.

32. "Those who believe that, through letters of pardon, they are made sure of their own salvation, will be eternally damned along with their teachers."

37. "Every *true* Christian, whether living or dead, has a share in all the benefits of the Church, *given him by God*, even without letters of pardon."

86. "Why doesn't the Pope,

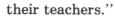

Martin Luther nails his 95 theses to the door of Wittenberg Church.

whose riches this day are more ample than those of the wealthiest of the wealthy, build the basilica of St. Peter with his own money, rather than with that of poor believers?"

What Luther had done in these theses was to categorically deny the notion of pardon for sin for a fee, thus challenging the system on which the church depended for income. Tetzel threatened to have this upstart burned within three weeks. Albert and Pope Leo, also upset by the decline in indulgences sales, tried to silence this obscure monk. But Luther kept writing and speaking and Frederick the Wise, Prince of Saxony, resisted all attempts by emperor and papacy to force Luther to appear for trial in Rome.

Quickly Luther went further. At the Disputation of Leipzig in 1519, discussing the condemnation of John Huss, he maintained that popes and councils err and contradict each other. Then in 1520 he wrote three major treatises that assured an irrevocable break with the Roman Catholic church:

Address to the Nobility of the German Nations called on the secular German princes to reform the church, since the clergy refused to do so.

Babylonian Captivity of the Church attacked the sacramental system, reducing the sacraments to three—baptism, the Lord's supper, and confession (or penance). The three "captivities of the church," said Luther, are withholding the cup from laity in the supper, the doctrine of transubstantiation, and the teaching that the mass is a sacrifice.

On Christian Liberty presented Luther's teaching on the Christian life. Faith, he said, frees the believer *from* slavery to a law code and *for* loving obedience. Good works are not performed out of anxiety or fear of judgment. "The good man does good works" but "good works do not make a man good."

In June, 1520, Pope Leo X took decisive action. He gave Luther sixty days to recant a list of forty-one heresies and burnt his books publicly. Luther responded by burning books of papal canon law and several scholastic writings. In January, 1521, Luther was excommunicated. That April he appeared before the Holy Roman Emperor, Charles V (1519–55), at the Diet of Worms. When he refused to recant, Luther was put under the ban of the empire and a price was placed on his head. For the rest of his life he remained under this threat of execution.

Fearing betrayal after the Diet of Worms, Prince Frederick sent horsemen who kidnapped Luther and hid him in the castle of Wartburg. During the next ten months of "enforced leisure," Luther translated the New Testament into German. This became "his and his nation's most complete literary achievement."[6] Only Shakespeare could compare to Luther in his mastery of language and ability to

Luther defends himself before the Diet of Worms.

express reality in a way that touched the hearts of all people.

But while Luther was confined in Wartburg Castle, the rapidly spreading Reformation began to get out of hand, particularly in Wittenberg. Some priests, followers of Luther, ignored people's feelings and celebrated the Lord's supper in plain clothes. Others began to destroy images and all aids to worship. Luther's teaching on Christian liberty was understood as license. The "heavenly prophets" of Zwickau came to Wittenberg claiming direct revelations from God and denying the need to be subject to either ecclesiastical authority or Scripture. Some of these prophets even advocated community of goods and sharing of wives.

Melancthon (left) and Luther (wearing hat) with two associates making the first German translation of the Bible in 1532.

Philip Melanchthon (1497–1560), Luther's right-hand man in Wittenberg, could not stem this tide of lawlessness. So in early 1522 Luther returned and in eight sermons clarified his position in opposition to this disorderly tumult. He argued that there is a place for images, since it is through the senses God has chosen to come to us. He taught that to reform in love we must consider the sensitivities of weaker brothers and sisters. And the "heavenly prophets," he said, "have swallowed the Holy Spirit, feathers and all." The Spirit, Luther said, works through the Word, not through independent revelations. Since the church of Christ is expressed within ecclesiastical structures, true reform does not mean abolishing the external church, as the prophets were teaching. Luther would not permit radicalism and spiritualism to swallow up the Reformation.

Fifteen twenty-five was a crucial year that largely determined the course of the Lutheran Reformation. That was the year in which the exploited German peasants, misunderstanding Luther's teaching on Christian liberty in social and political ways, rose in revolt against the nobility. Luther had to take a stand on this radical step taken in the name of his teachings. He did. In a savage pamphlet, "Against the Murderous and Thieving Rabble of Peasants," he asked the princes to put down the revolt—which they did enthusiastically. One tragic result was a mutual loss of trust between Luther and the peasant class; they no longer believed him and he, rather than allowing common people to govern Christ's church, turned its control over to secular rulers. Lutheran churches became, as time passed, Caesaropapist.

Luther preaches to Prince Frederick and others in Wartburg Castle.

This was also the year Luther married the ex-nun, Katherine von Bora. Katie, as he called her, had responded to Luther's teaching and escaped, with Luther's help, by hiding with eight others in the smelly wagon that delivered fish to the convent. Luther tried unsuccessfully to find her a husband and then, on her suggestion, married her himself. By this public act he confirmed the right of clergy to marry. Later he said he married Katie to "please his father, rile the Pope, and make angels laugh and devils weep."[7]

It was a good marriage. It changed Luther's initial view of marriage as "chains" to "the greatest sphere for good works, because it rests on love."[8] Katie presented Luther with six children and sustained him in his frequent times of stress so that he said, "I would not change Katie for France or for Venice" or for the "riches of Croesus."[9] She was an excellent business manager who ran the Luther household with outstanding efficiency and provided a model for a clerical home. She was, in short, God's marvelous gift to Luther in a critical period in his life.

The year 1525 included another important event. The Christian humanist, Erasmus, had supported Luther in early years. But when he saw that Luther's reform would divide the church and alter its theology, Erasmus attacked him. In *Freedom of the Will*, he developed a moralistic approach which, while rejecting Catholic abuses, combined God's grace and human works in a sort of "steps of Jacob's ladder" to God.

Luther responded in 1525 with what became a key work of the Protestant Reformation, *The Bondage of the Will*. This book, which affirmed humanity's total enslavement to Satan and complete inability to be saved except by divine grace, symbolized the break of the Reformation with the ideas and efforts of Christian Humanism. It also propounded what Luther himself called *the most basic doctrine of the Reformation*—predestination, or the absolute sovereignty of God in salvation. All the other mainline Reformers shared this emphasis. At the heart of the Reformation was a rejection of any role of works in salvation and an affirmation of God's sovereign act in turning people to himself.

The Evangelical Church

In the years 1517 to 1530 Luther was deeply involved in developing the new Evangelical church. His *German Order of Worship*, which appeared in 1526, helped determine that body's liturgy and church order. The essential position he took was to maintain old Roman practices as long as they did not contradict the faith. Zwingli and Calvin later took a different approach.

Luther retained the basic structure of the mass for his worship services, but made central a sermon given in the people's language, not Latin. Also the Lord's supper followed the sermon and people received both bread and wine.

His church order granted the congregation authority over doctrine, calling of pastors, finances, and discipline—at least in theory. In practice, princes and city councils came to control such church affairs. In Saxony, for instance, parish priests came under the administrative (not spiritual) control of district superintendents directly responsible to the prince.

In 1530, at the request of Emperor Charles V, the Lutheran position was clearly expressed in the Augsburg Confession. This creed, authored by Melanchthon and approved by Luther, presented Lutheranism as no new teaching but rather the doctrine of the early church councils. With beautiful classical clarity, it stated Luther's position on justification.

> We cannot obtain forgiveness of sin and righteousness before God by our own merits, works, or satisfactions.... [Rather] we receive forgiveness of sin, and become righteous before God by grace, for Christ's sake, through faith. ...For God will regard and reckon this faith as righteousness.

Rejecting the teaching that the church structures are redundant because believers receive direct revelations from the Holy Spirit, this creed teaches that the gospel comes through the church and its offices. But it also asserts that without faith "we are too weak to do good works." Good deeds are a fruit of faith, not a means to gain God's acceptance.

Perhaps it's a blessing that because of the ban which kept Luther away from Augsburg, Melanchthon composed this classical creed. Luther said he could not have walked "so soft and gently" as this document. Still he agreed with it.

Several of the strongest princes of Germany signed the Augsburg Confession, affirming it as the theological position of their states. What an incredible change! In 1521 Luther stood alone at the Diet of Worms. By 1530, despite the emperor's continued opposition, several princes were willing to support him.

****

More has been written about Luther than about any person except Jesus Christ.[10] This fact reflects a bit of the greatness of this man. Still today people study him to understand the genius that inaugurated the Protestant Reformation and altered the face of Europe. Even Roman Catholics are more and more recognizing his unique abililty and remarkably sensible grasp of the gospel's meaning.

We must not overlook his flaws. Luther was not always gracious. He was often harsh and unforgiving—his polemical writings show this. He was often uncouth, using street language in the context of the highest dialogue.

Yet this man, with his genius and his flaws, was used by God to touch the hearts of people who had despaired of finding peace with God. He was a faithful servant through whom Christ led his church into a period of fundamental reform.

CHAPTER 14
THE REFORMATION SPREADS: ZWINGLI AND THE RADICALS

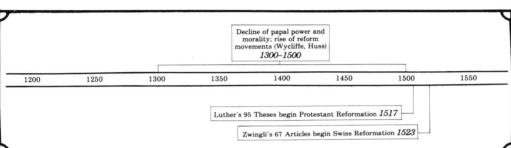

Decline of papal power and morality; rise of reform movements (Wycliffe, Huss) *1300–1500*

| 1200 | 1250 | 1300 | 1350 | 1400 | 1450 | 1500 | 1550 |

Luther's 95 Theses begin Protestant Reformation *1517*

Zwingli's 67 Articles begin Swiss Reformation *1523*

Humpty Dumpty sat on a wall,
Humpty Dumpty had a great fall.
All the king's horses and all the king's men
Couldn't put Humpty Dumpty together again.

If, as some experts contend, most nursery rhymes reflected contemporary social and political events, this well-known children's ditty might well have been occasioned by a happening like the Protestant Reformation. Once the egg of Roman Catholic unity was broken—once that sanctified religious authority was successfully challenged by Martin Luther—then "all the king's men" could neither put it together again nor prevent the broken parts from fragmenting further. The story of the Reformation's spread reflects a growing disunity and a disheartening inability to resolve differences of doctrine and practice.

Once the church as an external organization had been shattered, it threatened to disintegrate into isolated, individualistic segments. Once the shell was broken, could anyone put it together again? Was, as some Roman Catholics have argued, the loss of unity caused by Protestantism too high a price to pay to achieve reform? Or was, as most Protestants have argued, doctrinal purity and a reformed church life well worth the cost paid in disunity?

This basic value question rises in

the minds of historical observers as they see the spread of the Reformation result in not one, single Protestant church but in a number of diverse, divided, and often mutually antagonistic churches on the European continent.

Zwingli Establishes the Reformed Church in Switzerland

Contrary to general opinion, it was not John Calvin who established the Reformed churches in Switzerland. Calvin, who assumed the leadership of this branch of Protestantism in the thirties, was a relative latecomer. Ulrich Zwingli was the initial reformer.

In 1516, before Luther had nailed the celebrated Ninety-five Theses on the cathedral door, the young priest Zwingli (1484–1531) began publicly criticizing certain abuses in the Roman Catholic church. In his post as pastor of the church at Einsiedeln, location of the famous Shrine of the Black Image of the Virgin Mary, Zwingli observed the thousands who flocked to this shrine to earn pardon for past sins. Convinced that such pilgrimages were wrong, Zwingli insisted, "Christ alone saves and he saves everywhere."

There are interesting similarities and differences between Zwingli and Luther. Both were born of peasant stock. Both were precocious students whose parents provided them with a good education. Both were scholars of the Bible and sharp critics of the church's

abuses. But Zwingli, deeply influenced by the Christian Humanists to love the New Testament, also learned from them to dislike Scholasticism, monasticism, and a mechanical, materialistic idea of the sacraments. Zwingli didn't experience the hell of religious anxiety that tormented Luther. His movement toward reform was more coolly rational—though still deeply spiritual. Zwingli also lacked Luther's early ascetic tendencies: in 1518 he admitted to an affair with a promiscuous, and at that point pregnant, young woman and only gained the pastorate at Zurich because his chief competitor was found to be father of six illegitimate children.

In 1519 Zwingli began his ministry in the prestigious church at Zurich by announcing his intention to preach through the New Testament without using "human interpreters." He would, he said, allow the clear meaning of the text to emerge and lead where it would. That radical departure from current practice led eventually to a break with Rome.

Zwingli was an "electrifying" preacher; his sermons, it is said, lifted people up between heaven and earth and his style was so clear even the uneducated could understand. That magnetic preaching, plus a warm personality, established a solid following that supported Zwingli's reform activity.

The actual break came over a minor matter. On Ash Wednesday, a fast day, some parishioners, influenced by Zwingli's sermons, ate sausage (rather than fish). Zwingli's defense of that action occasioned a public debate before the city council in Zurich in 1523. In preparation for this debate Zwingli drew up a document expressing not just his position on the practice regarding fast days, but other "reformed" ideas as well—his Sixty-seven Articles. In these articles he asserted that:

—the Bible is the only source of authority for the church; all tradition, all councils, all papal pronouncements must be judged by the Bible.

—Jesus Christ is the only head of the church and its only eternal priest; the papacy does not have absolute authority over the church.

—the mass is not a sacrifice; it is rather a remembrance of Christ's already accomplished sacrifice on Calvary.

—pilgrimages and other supposedly meritorious works are detrimental to salvation since they give only a false security.

—civil rulers have the duty to promulgate and enforce laws that bring society into conformity with the divine will.

In this last point Zwingli, unlike Luther, appeared to aim at a "Holy Commonwealth," a reform of the whole of life in Zurich, not just the church.

Zwingli argued, in the debate before the city council, that these ideas were not new. The defenders of the papacy were the innovators while Zwingli himself was urging a return from the false practices of the Middle Ages to the purity of ancient times.

Apparently convinced, the city council approved Zwingli's articles and urged him "to continue to preach the holy gospel as hereto-

Ulrich Zwingli

fore." It warned other pastors in the city "not to preach anything they could not establish by the holy gospel and other divine scriptures." However it took several more years before the magistrates mustered the courage to abolish the mass and introduce the Zwinglian form of the Lord's supper (with the congregation seated at tables, receiving both bread and wine). Also in 1525 the liturgy was simplified, images removed, artwork in churches covered with whitewash, choirs eliminated, organs chopped up, and psalms sung without accompaniment. Reform had come to Zurich, more extreme in its rejection of liturgical practices than the reform in Germany.

Already in 1522 Zwingli had secretly married a widow in Zurich, defying the bishop of Constance. In 1524 he celebrated that marriage publicly, supported by the city council. Other German-speaking cities in Switzerland soon followed Zurich's lead. By 1530 Zwingli was the recognized leader of a large, rapidly expanding Protestant movement and, as it turned out, a competitor of Martin Luther.

The Marburg Colloquy

Because of the continued Roman Catholic opposition, many Protestants felt that the Zwinglian and Lutheran movements should form a united front. In 1529 Luther, Zwingli, and their adherents met to try to resolve their differences.

Although this colloquy at Marburg was able to agree on a list of fourteen points, the fifteenth of these articles of faith, dealing with the Lord's supper, brought out unreconcilable disagreements. Luther believed that Christ's statement at the last supper, "This is my body," must be taken literally. Zwingli took these words as a figure of speech, meaning, "This represents my body." Luther insisted that in the sacrament the benefits of Christ's work are actually and objectively received by believers. Zwingli believed the sacrament was a sign of divine grace already possessed by the believer. Furthermore, Zwingli questioned how Christ could be physically present in the sacrament since he had physically ascended to

heaven. The most he would reluctantly concede to Luther was that Christ was in some sense "spiritually" present. This was not enough for Luther who insisted that the whole Christ, divine and human, is present at the Lord's supper. Luther remarked sadly to the Zwinglians, "You have a different spirit than we."

But there were other differences as well. Luther loved a liturgy that used the senses; Zwingli disliked all such "externals." To Luther the Christian life demanded a spontaneity of faith apart from the law; to Zwingli the law of Christ was all-important for Christian living. Luther, while willing to accept the aid of princes to reform the church, disapproved of using violence and war to force reform on all citizens; Zwingli wanted church and state to work cooperatively to fashion a total Christian community among all the people.

When confessional agreement proved impossible, some of the princes at the Marburg Colloquy tried to form at least a political alliance. But the Germans would not agree to this. So the two Protestant groups remained divided, confessionally and politically. This was surely one of the sadder days in Protestant history.

Shortly thereafter, civil war between Catholic and Protestants erupted in Switzerland. At the second battle of Kappel, in 1531, Zwingli was killed in the fighting. Upon hearing the news, Luther commented, "Those who live by the sword will also die by the sword."

Luther, Zwingli, and other figures of the Reformation attend a conference at Marburg to discuss doctrinal differences and promote unity in a Protestant Germany.

The Anabaptist Movement

Following Zwingli's successful break with Rome, others appeared who were satisfied neither with the Roman Catholic church nor with Zwingli's reformed church. In 1525 a group of people left the church in Zurich because they felt Zwingli's reform efforts were too slow and too moderate. Led by Conrad Grebel (1448–1526), this group defied the city council and its approved program and began to worship and practice "believer's baptism" in private homes. Nicknamed Anabaptists (rebaptizers) because of this practice, this "truly New Testament church" was severely persecuted. In 1526 the Zurich authorities ordered many Anabaptists drowned in a hideous parody of their beliefs regarding baptism.

Instead of destroying the movement, persecution simply dispersed it into other parts of Switzerland and Europe. Spreading like wildfire, it also took on new, radical forms. In Moravia, Jacob Hutter (d. 1536) formed the Anabaptists into a communistic sect (the Hutterites). In the Netherlands, Menno Simons (1496–1561) formed a saner group, but one which still held many teachings that departed from the historic faith (the Mennonites). In Germany the unstable Melchoir Hofmann (1495–1543), proclaiming the imminent return of Christ, formed a fanatical group that tended toward revolutionary action.

Because the movement was so diverse and widespread, it is difficult to describe accurately their views. However, the following generalizations seem to apply to most Anabaptists.

At the heart of Anabaptist teaching was the belief that the Bible must be the sole standard of faith and practice. Every ordinary believer, they insisted, has a right to interpret Scripture for him- or herself. In practice they tended toward "a canon within the canon," elevating the Sermon on the Mount above the rest of the New Testament.

Rejecting the state churches of the Lutherans, Zwinglians, and Roman Catholics with their inherent compulsion, the Anabaptists taught the "gathered church"—a voluntary association of only those serious about their discipleship. Logically they also argued for separation of church and state and toleration of religious minorities.

In this voluntary, gathered church, they further argued, a high New Testament standard of behavior could and should be maintained. Through rigorous discipline and by "banning" those who do not live according to Christ's commands, they believed they could separate "tares" from "wheat" and attain a truly pure church. While most Anabaptists *did* put other Protestants to shame by their exemplary lifestyle, their positions also opened the way for strong tendencies toward legalism, judgmentalism, and schism.

Carrying their voluntarism to the extreme, Anabaptists concluded that only adult baptism was permissible; after all, infants could

152

make no responsible decision for Christ. Since on New Testament grounds they considered infant baptism no baptism at all, they also objected to the name their enemies gave them: rebaptizers.

Perhaps partly because of the ill treatment they received, Anabaptists had a very negative view of the state. Although they believed the state was instituted by God, its purpose, they said, was to keep believers in check, not to build a righteous society. Since civil governments are "outside the realm of grace," "under the power of the evil one," and use force, execution, and war to achieve their ends, they should be left to unbelievers. Christians—required to turn the other cheek, to be meek, lowly, and long-suffering—should not become involved in the state's efforts to keep order in a sinful world.

Accordingly Anabaptists were pacifists. They refused to bear arms for the state or take part in any other violent activities. Accusations of cowardice and treason merely confirmed their belief that the true disciple of Christ must expect suffering and abuse. As Conrad Grebel said, "True Christian believers are sheep among wolves . . . and must be baptized in affliction, tribulation, persecution, suffering, and death. Whatever their opponents might do, they would remain sheep."

It should be noted that a substantial number of Anabaptists taught doctrines that were not orthodox. Some asserted that Jesus' flesh was "celestial," that he was born *through*, not *of*, the Virgin Mary; they seemed, like the radical Alexandrians of the fifth century, to have "swallowed up Christ's humanity in his divinity." Others, uncomfortable with the doctrine of justification by faith alone, spoke of a "natural grace" that enables people to turn to Christ, or of faith as a good work which brings reward. Some tended to emphasize human actions rather than God's grace in a way that seemed to put them closer to Catholicism than to Protestantism.

It should also be noted that occasionally fanatical strains in the movement could erupt into violence. The famous Münster experiment is an example of such an eruption. Believing the world was about to end, Jan of Leyden led an uprising that took over the city of Münster in 1534. Proclaiming the New Jerusalem, an Anabaptist kingdom, he invited all true believers to come; and "they came, Frisians and other scoundrels," by the thousands. In preparation for Christ's glorious return to this city, Jan established a "holy government" —but this kingdom of heaven on earth soon turned into a living hell. Jan declared that all private property must be surrendered. Those who refused were executed or, if they were lucky, driven out of the city. Polygamy was made mandatory with Jan setting a marvelous example by taking sixteen wives. Finally, after the behavior of this group had become even more bizarre, a coalition of Protestant and Catholic armies attacked and reconquered Münster.

These fanatical extremes of some

Zwingli left his family at Zurich to act as chaplain for the evangelical Swiss forces in the country's civil war of 1531.

of the Anabaptists were partly caused by the severe persecutions they encountered. However, their revolutionary violence only led to more persecutions: their opponents "felt themselves more justified than ever in identifying Anabaptism with revolution."[1] The more balanced Anabaptists had great difficulty living down that reputation.

But even if these fanatical extremes had not existed, the issues that divided Anabaptists from the other reformers were substantial. The Anabaptists represented a unique and profoundly different approach to Christianity in a wide spectrum of areas. In some respects they were a people ahead of their time. The wisdom of many of their ideas came to be recognized in later years by the descendants of those who violently opposed them in their own time.

The Free Spirits

The Free Spirits were the far extreme of the Protestant movement: religious individualism run rampant. Their final authority was the individual conscience—the inward word which church, tradition, and even the Bible (for some) had no right to judge.

Let us take one person as representative of this movement. Kaspar Schwenkfeld (1484–1561) left Lutheranism, judging it "too doctrinal" and ineffective in improving morality. Turning away from clergy and the church, he took as his authority the "inner word" or "inner spirit." Each Christian could, he believed, through contemplation, meditation, and reliance on the "inner word" commune directly with God. Sacraments and the Bible, he conceded, might help weaker believers, but truly spiritual Christians gain wisdom directly from God through the "inner spirit."

While Schwenkfeld avoided all religious bodies, maintaining they worshiped "the letter" rather than the Spirit, he did meet informally with a small group of fellow Free Spirits. At such gatherings there were no preaching or sacraments; like the Quakers of a century later, they waited on the Lord.

The Free Spirits were a sort of *reductio ad absurdum* of the Protestant spirit. They carried to its logical extreme Luther's statement at the Diet of Worms in 1521: "Unless I am convicted by Scripture and plain reason...I cannot and will not recant anything, for to go against conscience is neither right nor safe." But unlike Luther they refused to let their consciences be directed by the Word and the fellowship of believers. Their consciences were, in a sense, their god.

****

Like a river breaking through its dikes, the Reformation begun by Luther quickly flooded over northern Europe and spread out in a variety of differing movements. To some that diversification was an unmitigated tragedy. But while no Christians can rejoice when the unity of the church, the unity for which Christ prayed, is severely marred, yet it seems clear that Luther and Zwingli were unable to apply their understanding of God's grace to the church's life without challenging the unifying authority of Roman Catholicism. And it also seems clear that the new understanding of Christ's gracious salvation was more important than a unity based on an improper understanding and manifestation of the Christian faith.

Were Luther and Zwingli indirectly responsible for the radicals? Yes. Without their challenge to authority the radicals would have been unthinkable. Yet extreme as they were, these radicals brought to light the ideas of pluralism, religious freedom, and a church of serious-minded believers that together have become very important in later church history.

In the realities of human existence, it seems, a price must be paid even to bring truth to light. The price paid in the Reformation period was disunity and much human suffering.

CHAPTER 15
CALVIN AND CALVINISM

1350	1400	1450	1500	1550

Luther's 95 Theses begin Protestant Reformation *1517*

Zwingli's 67 Articles begin Swiss Reformation *1523*

Calvin's Institutes advance Reformation cause *1536*

After Luther, the greatest Reformation figure was a quiet, sensitive, intellectual Frenchman: John Calvin. Quite unlike robust, volatile Luther (toward whom he felt a deep kinship), Calvin described himself as "a poor, timid scholar."

Yet through his genius, this sensitive scholar became one of the most influential and controversial people in church history. To some he was the great systematizer of Protestant theology, the man who orchestrated the tunes written by fertile Luther.[1] To others he was the harsh "dictator" of Geneva, "ambitious, presumptuous, arrogant, cruel, malicious, vindictive, and above all, ignorant."[2] But the report of a fairly neutral observer, the Venetian ambassador in Geneva, describes him thus:

Your Serenity will hardly believe the influence and the great power which the principal minister of Geneva, by name Calvin, a Frenchman and a native of Picardy, possesses in this Kingdom; he is a man of extraordinary authority, who by his mode of life, his doctrines and his writings rises superior to all the rest.[3]

Perhaps the best way to describe John Calvin is as the great, second-generation reformer who took the best of the earlier reforming efforts and formed these ideas into what became the most influential and most explosive of the Reformation movements. He developed the new, total way of life that was to shake the foundations of Europe—Calvinism.

John Calvin, called "the greatest gift of France to the Reformation," was born in Noyon, France, in 1509. His family was quite well-to-do, his father being a bureaucrat employed both by the city and by the bishop of Noyon. The family's frequent contacts with area nobility probably occasioned Calvin's rather aristocratic tastes and manners—in later life he preferred "Monsieur Calvin" to the more egalitarian "Brother Calvin."

When he was twelve years old, Calvin was appointed to a sinecure (a do-nothing position) as chaplain of the altar at the Noyon Cathedral. This and two later added sinecures assured him a good education at church expense. But it also involved him in the pervasive corruption of the church. It has even been suggested that fear of losing this income may be one reason Calvin was slow in joining the Reformation movement.

At fourteen he left home to attend the University of Paris. At the College de la Marche, part of that university, Calvin developed the lucid Latin style that characterized his writing. Later he transferred to the very conservative and scholastic College de Montaigu. Erasmus had earlier found this college oppressive; Calvin found it an opening to the exciting world of the church fathers, especially Augustine. It was at this college that Calvin formed his first friendships with Christian Humanists—including King Francis I's physician, William Cop, and his three sons. These Humanist friends introduced Calvin to Luther's writings but with little impact; at this point in his life Calvin was still obstinately loyal to the papacy.[4]

In 1528 Calvin received his Master of Arts degree. Then, at his father's urging, he abandoned his intended religious vocation and went to study law at the University of Orleans. There the atmosphere was very different from College de Montaigu's rigid Catholic orthodoxy; Orleans was a center of Christian Humanism. Calvin's involvement with the movement became almost total and his commitment to the papacy began to waver.

In 1531 his father died. Free then to determine his own future, Calvin returned to Paris to continue his humanistic studies. That year he published his first book, a commentary on Seneca's *De Clementia.* Calvin showed in this work an astounding knowledge of both pagan antiquities and early church leaders, as well as a mastery of the humanistic techniques of literary and historical criticism.

Although for a number of years already he had been considering the relative merits of Catholic orthodoxy, Christian Humanism, and Protestantism, Calvin seems not to have experienced a long or troubled struggle. His conversion to Protestantism was relatively calm, yet sudden and decisive. He says:

> At first, since I was too obstinately devoted to the superstitions of Popery...God by a sudden conversion subdued and brought my mind to a teachable

frame. Having thus received some taste and knowledge of true godliness, I was immediately inflamed with so intense a desire to make progress therein, that although I did not altogether leave off other studies, I yet pursued them with less ardour.[5]

It was shortly after this conversion that Calvin became involved in his friend Nicolas Cop's inaugural address as rector of the University of Paris. If Calvin did not actually write the speech, he at least influenced its tone and content—which were pronouncedly Protestant. Both Cop and Calvin were forced to flee Paris. Calvin traveled south and for a time, under the protection of influential friends, was able to carry on reforming activities. But the situation in France worsened. In 1534 some leading Protestants posted placards intemperately attacking "the horrible abuse of the papal mass." King Francis I reacted with the determination once for all to rid France of "the poison of the Protestants." Hundreds were imprisoned, including Calvin for two brief periods. Many were executed, including Calvin's brother. It was clearly time to seek a safer environment.

Calvin went first to Basel, Switzerland. There he spent two years quietly studying and writing. By 1536 he completed the first edition of *The Institutes of the Christian Religion*, "the most influential single book of the Protestant Reformation."[6] It was not the originality but the clarity of argument, excellent style, and orderly arrangement that made this book a lucid statement of the Protestant position and a useful manual for instructing people new to this faith. "As a systematic presentation of Christian theology, it became the handbook of militant Protestantism and exercised an enormous influence upon Western thought, among friends and foes alike.[7]

In 1536 Calvin left Basel intending to continue his quiet study and writing in Strassburg. But something occurred en route that redirected his life. Calvin himself describes the fateful encounter:

...At length William Farel detained me at Geneva, not so much by counsel and exhortation, as by a dreadful imprecation, which I felt to be as if God had from heaven laid his mighty hand upon me to accept me. As the most direct road to Strassburg, to which I then intended to retire, was shut up by the wars, I had resolved to pass quickly by Geneva, without staying longer than a single night in that city. A little before this, popery had been driven from it...but matters were not yet brought to a settled state, and the city was divided into unholy and dangerous factions. Then an individual...discovered me and made me known to others. Upon this, Farel, who burned with an extraordinary zeal to advance the gospel, immediately strained every nerve to detain me. And after having learned that my heart was set upon devoting myself to private studies, for which I wished to keep myself free from other

Farel threatens Calvin with God's judgment if Calvin does not remain and carry on the reforming of Geneva.

pursuits, and finding that he gained nothing from entreaties, he proceeded to utter an imprecation that God would curse my retirement, and the tranquility of the studies which I sought, if I should withdraw and refuse to give assistance when the necessity was so urgent. By this imprecation I was so stricken with terror that I desisted from the journey which I had undertaken; but sensible of my natural bashfulness and timidity, I would not bring myself under obligation to discharge any particular office.[8]

The reform of Geneva had come through a city council that—in its struggle for independence from the bishop who had ruled the city— adopted Protestantism, drove out bishop and Catholic clergy, confiscated church property, and took over administration of charity. Calvin and Farel now wanted to establish a Reformed church in Geneva, a church relatively free of council control. In 1537 Calvin developed the *Ordinances* which tried to establish church control over the moral life of Geneva. That made the city council distinctly uneasy. "[The Magistrates] did not want to trade what they regarded as Catholic clerical tyranny for a new Protestant yoke."[9] To reestablish their

160

control of the Reformation in Geneva the council ordered Calvin and Farel to cease preaching. Both disobeyed that order and refused to administer the sacrament. So in 1538 the city council expelled them from Geneva.

Calvin went first to Basel and then, on the urging (and threat of divine wrath) of Martin Bucer (1491–1551), traveled on to Strassburg and became pastor of the French Reformed refugee congregation there. He also taught exegesis at the Reformed Academy.

This period was important for Calvin's development. Bucer helped form Calvin's thinking on predestination, the Lord's supper, church organization, the liturgy, and the place of the academy in the reform movement. These influences became evident later in Geneva. It was also during this time that Calvin married Idelette de Bure, the widow of an Anabaptist. Although for much of their short marriage (1541–49) Idelette was an invalid, she was still a great comfort to Calvin. The baby she bore him in 1542 died shortly after birth and Idelette never fully recovered. When she died in 1549 Calvin was heartbroken. "I have been bereaved of the best companion of my life," he said, "who not only would have been the willing sharer of my indigence, but even of my death."[10] Calvin never remarried.

Meanwhile in Geneva the situation had deteriorated. Some feared (others hoped) for a return to Catholicism or a drift into wild, radical Protestantism. Finally, in 1541, the city council—unable to restore religious social order—asked Calvin to return. Happy in Strassburg, Calvin most decidedly did not wish to return to Geneva. He said, "I would prefer a hundred other deaths to that cross, on which I should have to die a thousand times a day." But finally Farel persuaded him to return, and Calvin remained in Geneva until his death in 1564.

From 1541 to 1555 Calvin was often opposed and thwarted in Geneva, failing many times to convince the city council that the changes he suggested would be beneficial to church and city. But from 1555 until his death eleven years later, Calvin was able to get most of his programs enacted into law. Still it is important to note that Geneva was never a theocracy ruled by Calvin. John Calvin never had ". . . even a fraction of the legal power of the deposed Catholic bishop. Political power remained in the hands of the elected council. . . . Calvin and the other pastors were only employees of the municipal government."[11] What they accomplished was done through moral suasion, preaching, and consultation. To think of Calvin as dictator of a theocracy is a ludicrous myth concocted by those hostile to him and his reform movement.

The Structure of Reform in Geneva

Calvin's Ecclesiastical Ordinances of 1537 were the regulations that structured the Genevan Re-

161

Calvin confers with the Geneva Council.

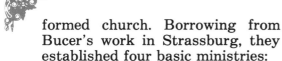

formed church. Borrowing from Bucer's work in Strassburg, they established four basic ministries:

—The pastors preached and administered the sacraments.

—The doctors studied the Word and taught.

—The elders carried out discipline.

—The deacons supervised charitable work.

These ministries were organized in four institutions:

—The *company of pastors* included all the clergy in Geneva. Subject to city council approval, this group determined who should be pastor in the Genevan churches and other similar pastoral matters.

—The *consistory* was a far more important organization. It included all the Genevan pastors and twelve elders. The Ordinances stipulated that two elders should be members of the Small Council (the executive group usually called the city council), four should be members of the Council of Sixty, and six members of the Council of Two Hundred. All elder members were chosen by the Small Council. This organization disciplined, by punishment or excommunication, those in error either in doctrine or life. But contrary to Calvin's wishes, the consistory's decisions were (at least in the early years) subject to review by the city council.

—The *school* was the institution in which the doctors educated children for the ministry or for civil government. The doc-

tors were chosen by the pastors and the city council. Finally, in 1559, the Geneva Academy was established, providing university level instruction.

—The *deacons* had no comparable institution, but appeared to have organized charitable work through the *Hospital-General.*

Calvin also developed a liturgy and a catechism for the Genevan church. The liturgy was outlined in his Form of the Ecclesiastical Prayers and Hymns. Like Zwingli, Calvin had no use for organs and choirs; he preferred congregational singing of psalms without instrumental accompaniment. Yet, though still very simple, Calvin's liturgy was more formal and elaborate than Zwingli's and became the standard in the Genevan church. Calvin's *Geneva Catechism* also played a key role in church life, contributing to the religious training of generations of Protestant believers. All children in Geneva were nurtured on this clear little catechism and through it grew as Christians.

Practices of Reformed Geneva

Many historians have asserted that the people of Geneva were subjected to a "moral reign of terror." Undoubtedly by our standards "Christian discipline [at times] degenerated into pettiness, foolishness, and even cruelty...."[12] Yet this is not the full or true picture.

The consistory met weekly to deal with domestic quarrels, lying, fornication, rebellion against parents, drunkenness, superstition, ignorance of doctrine, gambling, laziness, and like offenses. To give examples, a woman of seventy-two was disciplined for becoming engaged to a man of twenty-five; a barber was censured for tonsuring a priest; a man was reprimanded for making a noise during a sermon; another man was forced to make public confession for naming his dog "Calvin." At times it appeared that "the authorities went

John Calvin

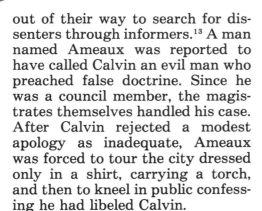

out of their way to search for dissenters through informers.[13] A man named Ameaux was reported to have called Calvin an evil man who preached false doctrine. Since he was a council member, the magistrates themselves handled his case. After Calvin rejected a modest apology as inadequate, Ameaux was forced to tour the city dressed only in a shirt, carrying a torch, and then to kneel in public confessing he had libeled Calvin.

Although it is easy to pick out such ludicrous examples of moral discipline, in general the consistory's actions were relatively mild and its concern was not to condemn but to lead sinners to repentance. Because of such insistence on a high standard of moral life for its citizens, Geneva was probably a better than average place to live.

More important, in Geneva there was a genuine concern to create a just society, to restructure societal relations in a way that would at least begin to establish God's kingdom on earth. Calvin taught that church and state must work together for justice. That meant that the church should not only pray for political leaders and the justice they established but also, through clear gospel counsel, encourage them to defend the defenseless and check the rich and powerful. In carrying this out Calvin, the company of pastors, and the deacons became deeply involved in what to many people would seem "nonspiritual matters"; they were concerned with regulation of wages, development of sewer systems, setting fair interest rates, establish-

ing cloth factories, socializing medicine, and so on. Although it has been often asserted that Calvin and Calvinists were instrumental in the rise of capitalism, in Geneva they formed a "social welfare state" in which social justice had clear priority over selfish economic interests, and where exploitation of poor by rich was more successfully resisted than in any other European city of that day.

For Calvin, the church—through its pastors—became a prophetic voice, a conscience of the state. "The minister . . . has the duty of speaking out against all injustices, all neglect of duty, all ungodliness in high places."[14]

The Heritage of Calvin: Calvinism

Building upon the doctrines of God and predestination, Calvin developed an activistic form of Protestantism quite unlike that of Luther. Both Luther and Calvin believed that a sovereign God would certainly accomplish his purposes in the world. But Luther tended to limit his interest in this work of God to personal salvation, while Calvin believed God also intended to establish a holy commonwealth on earth. In Geneva, Calvin attempted to found such a commonwealth which would honor God in every area of life. When like attempts occurred wherever Calvinism spread, this reform movement rapidly developed a reputation for being revolutionary.

Many have suggested that the

Calvinist belief in predestination (that all is predetermined and nothing humans do can alter anything) must of necessity kill any Christian activism. But historically this has not been true. Calvinists, more than any other group, have held to predestination and used predestination as a motivating force to achieve change. They have reasoned: if God is sovereign, he will necessarily achieve his purpose in history; it follows that we can work knowing that since God is for us, no one can stop us—we're in the vanguard of an irrepressible movement. It is interesting that the Marxists, who hold an atheistic form of historical determinism, have also proven revolutionary and activistic. They believe they cannot fail because "history" is on their side.

Calvin believed, with Augustine and Luther, that the institutional church will always have "tares" mixed with "wheat." But he was unwilling to conclude that therefore the church should accept gross violations of basic norms within its members. Calvin also believed, with the Anabaptists, that the church should be a community of committed believers whose lives reflect their faith. But more modest than the Anabaptists, Calvin did not claim to know who were or were not "true Christians." Rather those who make public profession of faith, live uprightly, and participate in the sacraments should, he said, be presumed to be Christians. Still, since the true church is made up of committed believers, discipline becomes an important function. And under such circumstances there can be a tendency, as in Geneva and later among the Puritans, to define precisely what is meant by an upright life, a too narrow definition that has led some Calvinists to take "a certain pride in their pale faces," faces that did not show the ravages of drunkenness and other fleshly excesses.[15]

Finally there is little in Calvin of the introspective religiousness of Luther, the Anabaptists, and many Roman Catholics. Christians who know they are elected "stand in the external and immutable good will of God toward [them] and that cannot be altered by any of the storms of the world."[16] Election, Calvin believed, gave assurance of salvation so that believers were freed from concern for self and liberated to serve God and their fellow human beings. As Bainton notes, such an attitude "bred a race of heroes."[17] Free from inner anxiety, Calvinists were able to turn the world upside-down for their Lord.

****

Calvin was the quiet scholar who founded the most activistic form of Protestantism. He was the tranquil theologian (by nature) who became embroiled against his own wishes in the religious and social turmoil of Geneva and worked a revolution in that city.

All this came about because Calvin was a man of faith who obediently followed his Lord's leading even when it went against his own deepest desires. As he wrote to Farel on October 24, 1540:

If I had any choice I would rather do anything than give in

to you in this matter [of returning to Geneva], but since I remember that I no longer belong to myself, I offer my heart to God as a sacrifice.[18]

Such a faithful servant of God can and was used by the church's Lord to reform and transform his church.

Farel, Calvin, Beza, and Knox occupy central positions on the International Monument of Reformation *in Geneva.*

CHAPTER 16
THE ENGLISH REFORMATION

1350	1400	1450	1500	1550	1600

Luther's 95 Theses begin Protestant Reformation *1517*

Zwingli's 67 Articles begin Swiss Reformation *1523*

Calvin's Institutes advance Reformation cause *1536*

1558–1603
The "Middle Way"
Reformation—
Elizabeth I

A map of the Protestant Reformation's spread presents a striking picture of a three-layered division of Europe. In the central north, like a giant tulip, is Lutheranism—ranging from southern Germany upward into the Scandinavian countries. Across the whole southern half, like a great half moon, lie the solidly Roman Catholic lands. Between these two is the third main faith grouping: in an interrupted belt from Transylvania and Hungary on the east, through Switzerland, and along the Rhine valley into Holland on the west, stretches the predominantly Reformed area. Scattered among the Lutheran and Reformed were the Anabaptists.*

Many have speculated and theorized about why the Reformation movements spread as they did and why they took hold in some areas and not in others. It's an intriguing question. Perhaps, as some church historians contend, it has to do with the entrenched Latin culture of the south and the strong Germanic culture of the middle north. If so, the Reformed faith seems to have taken root most strongly in the borderline between these two.[1]

If the map is broadened to include the British Isles, another interesting feature emerges. The Reformed belt appears to leap across the North Sea into Scotland. But there the pattern breaks. Unlike

*Note: This picture of Europe needs qualification, of course. Most of the Rhine valley remained solidly Catholic as did southern Germany and Austria into Bavaria. Southwestern Germany, between these, was strongly influenced by Protestantism.

southern Europe, the southern half of the islands (England in particular) did *not* remain Roman Catholic. England experienced a reformation.

However, the English Reformation was not like the Reformation on the continent. In fact, some historians question whether what occurred to the church in England was truly a Reformation at all. As the eighteenth-century cynic, Voltaire, remarked, "England separated from the Pope because King Henry fell in love."

Yet that judgment seems too shallow. A real change did occur in the Christian church in England. What began under Henry as "Catholicism without the pope" turned into a church distinct from both Roman Catholicism and the continental reform movements. England followed a "Reformation of the Middle Way."

Henry VIII (1491–1547) and the Separation of the English Church from Rome

In the early 1520s King Henry VIII was still regarded by the pope as a "defender of the faith," a true son of the church. But currents of reform thought were already beginning to flow through England. The Lollards, John Wycliff's followers—although poorly organized and largely a working-class movement—remained a significant "undercurrent of dissent," critical of Rome. The Lutherans also were growing in influence: in Cambridge, university dons like William Tyndale (the

Bible translator), Robert Barnes (the antipapal writer), and John Foxe (the great martyrologist) met regularly at the White Horse Tavern (dubbed "little Germany") to discuss Luther's teachings. A third group, the Christian Humanists, strongly demanded moral reform in the church. It was probably the Humanists who convinced many English men and women that such reform was not only necessary but also that it should be moderate and gradual, not sudden and cataclysmic (as on the continent).

These three movements grew rapidly—partly because of the widespread "anticlerical feeling" in England. Even those English citizens who were unconcerned about reform were still thoroughly tired of the greedy dissolute clergy who harassed them with the confessional and ecclesiastical courts. They also remembered the destructive civil wars of the past century. For those reasons many preferred order under a strong king to chaos without him; and they preferred "royal tyranny to ecclesiastical."[2]

The occasion for such a choice (between king and pope) was "the twinkle in Anne Boleyn's eyes." Actually it went beyond Henry's lust for this pretty woman. The king wanted a male heir to the throne, a legitimate son (he already had an illegitimate one). Catherine, the queen, had borne him only one living child, Mary. At forty-one she was unlikely to give him the desired son. But Anne probably could.

Then Henry found an excuse. He had, with a special dispensation

Henry VIII

from Pope Julius II, married his brother Arthur's widow. But Leviticus 20:21 says clearly, "If a man takes his brother's wife it is impurity...they shall be childless." Perhaps the pope had not been able to set aside the explicit curse. By 1527 Henry had convinced himself that his marriage to Catherine was illegitimate. He asked Pope Clement VII for an annulment. That put Pope Clement in a fix. Catherine's nephew, Emperor Charles V, was his near neighbor and would be highly displeased by such an annulment. Clement refused to grant Henry's request.

In 1533 Anne Boleyn became pregnant, and Henry became urgent. If the baby, hoped to be a boy, was to be a legitimate heir, Henry must marry Anne before the birth. So Henry acted. He fired the chancellor, Cardinal Wolsey, who had failed to procure the annulment, charging him with treason. He appointed the more sympathetic Thomas Cranmer as Archbishop of Canterbury. (Pope Clement approved that.) Then Henry called in session the great "Reformation Parliament" (1529–36) and gave it the task of legally separating the church of England from Rome and handing to Henry all ecclesiastical authority.[3]

In 1533 this Parliament passed an *Act in Restraint of Appeals* which determined that "matters of divine law" should be settled in England without "the inter-meddling of any exterior person" (that is, the pope). Archbishop Cranmer promptly annulled Henry's marriage to Catherine and legitimized the rela-

tion with Anne Boleyn. The same year an *Acts of Succession* stipulated that the children of Henry and Anne would be the legitimate heirs to the throne. Henry had won. And Anne shortly bore Henry not the hoped for son, but a daughter, Elizabeth.

So Henry still had no male heir, but he did have the Church of England. He was, in effect, its new pope. A few refused to accept this, including two Christian Humanists, Sir Thomas More (the "man for all seasons") and Bishop John Fisher. Both were executed. Only in the late 1530s when Henry, supposedly because of corruption but actually for financial gain, began to dissolve the monasteries and confiscate their properties, did substantial opposition develop. But Henry dealt quickly and brutally with these uprisings in northern England (called "the pilgrimage of grace"). He had gained and retained firm control of the church.

The "Reform" Under Henry VIII

In spite of Henry's questionable motives, some reform did occur during his reign—thanks to Archbishop Cranmer. A book of prayers in the English language was introduced and Tyndale's English Bible was placed on church lecterns. And in a document called the Ten Articles, some doctrinal concessions were also made, thanks to Henry's desire to win the support of Lutheran princes in Germany: these Ten Articles mention only three sacraments and teach a rather ambiguous doctrine of justification designed to please both Catholics and Lutherans. Also, while they do not condemn honoring images, venerating saints, and promoting relics, the articles do admit that such practices frequently contribute to superstition. The Ten Articles were "the first of the ingeniously ambiguous documents which were so often used to maintain a degree of unity in the various stages of the English Reformation."[4]

Later, no longer seeking accommodation with German Lutherans, Henry took a more distinctly Catholic stance. The Six Articles of 1539 teach transubstantiation, communion in one kind (only bread for laypeople), seven sacraments, and clerical celibacy. So strong was Henry on this last point that poor Cranmer, secretly married, had to keep his wife hidden in the house or, when he traveled, to transport her in a chest. Bainton suggests Mrs. Cranmer should be regarded as one of the minor martyrs of the Reformation, bumping along stage roads in a comfortless and stuffy chest and often, no doubt, thrown about by careless luggage handlers.[5] Henry was clearly Catholic, though not Roman. Those who refused to accept the Six Articles were persecuted, and some burned at the stake.

By 1547 Henry had gone through five wives—divorcing some, beheading others. He got one male heir, Edward, from Jane Seymour who died in childbirth. Only the last wife survived him. His marriages confirm his extreme egotism

William Tyndale translating the Scriptures

and his ability to tailor his conscience to fit his political and personal wishes. What reform occurred during his reign was in spite of, rather than because of, Henry. Yet through this unadmirable man, God did bring a Reformation to his church in England.

The English Reformation Under King Edward VI (1547–53)

Edward was only nine when Henry VIII died. Officially the boy became king, but England was actually ruled by regents during his short reign—first Somerset, then Northumberland. Both regents feared a Catholic reaction that

173

would bring back the papacy and take away government revenues; so they encouraged the "protestant-ization" of the Church of England. Cranmer, with his Lutheran (later Zwinglian) leanings, cooperated eagerly.

Among various reforms, the Second Prayer Book stands out. It provided an English worship service which expressed a clearly Protestant understanding of the Lord's supper: in place of the altar (for the sacrifice of the mass) came the communion table, across which the priest faced the congregation. Yet this prayer book was a classic example of studied ambiguity, vague enough to satisfy both Lutherans and Zwinglians. It also maintained the use of medieval clerical vestments and church appointments. It left intact the basic medieval structure of the church.

As sickly Edward approached death in late 1552, the regent Northumberland, trying to maintain his power, convinced Edward to bypass Catholic Mary and declare his cousin, Lady Jane, heir to the throne. In reaction to this power-grabbing attempt, the English people supported Mary's claims. Some may have done so in spite of her Roman Catholicism, but others perhaps preferred a return to Catholicism to the protestantizing tendencies of Edward's reign.

Bloody Mary (1553–58)

Mary badly misjudged the English mood. She supposed her enthusiastic reception meant her subjects wished to submit totally to papal authority. But that was far from true. If the majority disliked explicit Protestantism, they also had a marked distaste for extreme Catholicism. In addition, Mary's marriage to the arch-Catholic Prince, Philip II (later king of Spain), aroused fears of Spanish domination and a Spanish-type inquisition against heresy.

Such fears were well-founded. Mary's Act of Repeal of 1554 reimposed papal authority and tried where possible to restore England to the situation in 1529. That act was followed by a counter revolu-

The future Queen Elizabeth is confined to the Tower during the days of Bloody Mary.

tionary reign of terror. Many Protestants fled to Europe as "Marian exiles." Nearly three hundred less fortunate persons were burned at the stake or killed in other painful ways. John Foxe's famous *Book of Martyrs* memorialized them.

One pathetic victim of this persecution was the deposed Archbishop of Canterbury, Thomas Cranmer. Condemned to death for past reform activities, he tried to escape sentence by recanting his Protestant beliefs. Seven times he recanted—to no avail. Mary was adamant. Finally Cranmer recanted his recantations, choosing to die a Protestant. When they led him to the stake, he first placed the hand that had signed the earlier recantations in the flames so that it might be burned before the rest of the body.

Like Cranmer (but more successfully) most clergy accommodated themselves as easily to Mary as they had to Edward. Only a few surrendered pastorates rather than conform. This adaptability seems to indicate an almost total lack of conviction among English clergy. How, one wonders, could they change their loyalty so completely and then change again and yet again, adapting also to Elizabeth's form of Protestantism?

At any rate, disliking extremism, the English detested Mary's brutality. The execution of three hundred Protestants was, if nothing else, in very poor taste. A growing revulsion toward Catholicism developed and a sympathy for the Protestant party deepened. When Mary died in 1558, England did not weep. It hoped instead for a more moderate and balanced religious future.

The Elizabethan Settlement

Elizabeth (1558–1603) brought the desired balanced and moderate religious settlement. During her reign England became a truly Protestant nation, yet in a *middle way* between Roman Catholicism and continental Protestantism. Elizabeth had a deep distaste for all dogmatism and religious fanaticism. Her sympathies were essentially Protestant, yet she loved the splendor of the medieval Catholic worship service and she wanted to personally assume the headship of the English church. Out of these ingredients, these tastes and distastes, came the *middle way* of the English Reformation.

Elizabeth reintroduced the Second Prayer Book of Edward VI. She also, in 1563, adopted the Thirty-nine Articles, a moderate but thoroughly Protestant formulation of Anglican belief. These she made normative for the church; any dissenting clergy were abruptly removed from office. After the years of religious upheaval, conformity was, Elizabeth felt, crucial for church and nation.

Elizabeth's Protestantism aroused intense opposition from Roman Catholics, both in England and abroad. In 1570 the pope excommunicated her and urged her subjects to rebel. He sent many zealous Jesuits into England to convert people to Catholicism and foment discontent. He endorsed at least one of the many plots to assassinate the queen. More openly Philip II, Bloody Mary's husband, tried to destroy Elizabeth by military power; only the destruction of his great armada by a storm blocked that major threat.

In response to this dangerous opposition, Elizabeth tightened restrictions on English Catholics. While permitting them private worship in their homes, she dealt stringently with all treasonous activity. Parliament supported her with anti-papal laws that made it a crime to accuse the queen of heresy or schism and with an anti-Jesuit act in 1585. Still it's remarkable how mildly Elizabeth dealt with the Roman Catholics; only two hundred and twenty-one were executed during her forty-five-year reign compared to three hundred in Queen Mary's brief reign. Furthermore most of those who died were not religious martyrs in the narrowest sense; they were executed for treasonous activities against the crown.

It is ironic that while Elizabeth was Protestant enough to earn Catholic hostility, she wasn't Protestant enough to satisfy the Puritan party. The Puritans, deeply influenced by continental Calvinism, felt Elizabeth had not gone far enough in reforming the English church. They wished to "purify" the church from within, removing the vestiges of medieval Catholicism like ministerial vestments, prescribed prayers, and the episcopal structure with its bishops, archbishops, dioceses, priests, and the like. They wanted to simplify the worship and clerical garb and make the English church a Presbyterian body comparable to the Calvinist church on the continent.

But Elizabeth would have none of this. She believed that for the peace of the church and the nation she must resist the dogmatism and extremism of the Puritans just as she was resisting that of the Catholics. And she did this very successfully. Only after her death did they come to pose a real threat to the Anglican *middle way*.

What was this *middle way*? It has been called "a mood rather than a system."[6] It affirmed a Protestant stance but without precision on doctrinal and liturgical matters. It sought unity through lack of clarity. Its goal was "to compromise as many as possible in a single church by making minimal and ambiguous demands."[7]

To some this seems too bland to be called a Reformation at all. But Elizabeth, wiser than her Puritan and Catholic opponents, knew what could be done in late sixteenth-century England. Torn by religious conflicts during the previous three reigns, the nation was tired of extremes—it wanted a settlement.

Extremism of either variety, Bainton suggests, might have brought England the sort of religious wars that wracked Europe during this time. It may be seriously questioned whether the "studied ambiguities" of Elizabeth's settlement were a less satisfactory solution of religious strife than the "blinding clarity of the fires of Smithfield" where those with unambiguous religious positions burned to death those with equally unambiguous, opposing positions.[8]

The Scottish Reformation

Later than, and in a sense apart from, the English Reformation was the reform of the church in Scotland. John Knox (1513–72), often called the "father of Presbyterianism," was serving as a pastor in England already during the reign of Edward VI. Like many Puritans he was critical of what he considered the incomplete Reformation of that time. The Calvinistic reform in Geneva was for him the "perfect school of Christ."

Forced to flee England when Bloody Mary came to power, he later returned under Elizabeth but was then banned from the country when he wrote a fiery tract attacking government by women as "re-pugnant to nature and contumely of God."

In 1559 Knox returned to his native Scotland. This was also the year in which the Scottish Protestants, with English military aid, gained control of the country. The strong anti-French feelings of that time were paired with anti-Catholicism—so by 1560 laws were passed outlawing the Roman Catholic church in Scotland. Knox enthusiastically supported these laws. He also helped give the Scottish Reformation a distinctly Calvinistic

John Knox preaching

cast, making sure that the basic documents, the Scottish Confession of Faith, *The Book of Common Order,* and *The First Book of Discipline,* were all patterned on Genevan models.

The political feelings of the time combined with Knox's strong leadership to make of Scotland, eventually, a solidly Protestant land. "No established church of the Reformation outside of Switzerland was more deeply rooted in the life of the people."[9]

****

The English Reformation is an enigma, especially when we compare it to the reform in Scotland. It seems to lack the greatness and boldness of the Lutheran and Calvinist movements. It produced no single, outstanding theological figure, no one to compare with a John Knox or Philip Melanchthon, let alone a Luther or Calvin. It held no hard, fixed position, except perhaps the position that one should avoid fixed positions. It seemed to be motivated more by political than religious aims (although it can't be denied that political motives played a major role in other lands, such as Scotland). Its leader, Archbishop Cranmer, accepted martyrdom only when there were no other options. Its priests seemed not to care whether they were Protestant or Catholic; they appeared to follow public policy rather than religious conviction. Can this truly be called a Reformation?

Yet the documents produced by this Reformation, The Second Prayer Book and the Thirty-nine Articles, while lacking the Genevan stamp of the Scottish documents, are clearly Protestant. The gospel is present in and proclaimed through these documents. Perhaps it is the genius of the English Reformation that it defied all categories. In an age of religious strife it found a way to be Christian without choosing one particular brand. To some that ambiguity seems unfortunate. To others it seems a brilliant way to keep peace in a restless age.

CHAPTER 17
CATHOLIC REFORM AND COUNTERREFORM

1350	1400	1450	1500	1550

Luther's 95 Theses begin Protestant Reformation *1517*

Council of Trent convenes and launches Counter-Reformation *1545*

To a loyal Roman Catholic the decade of the 1530s must have been most disquieting. What began in 1517 as the scholarly dissent of a single German monk had within a few years turned into a major defection from the papal church. In Germany, in Switzerland, in most of northern Europe—with echoes through much of the south—there had risen a swell of protest against Roman Catholic teaching and practice, a growing cry of condemnation against the pope and his faithful followers.

These Protestants were saying and writing terrible accusations against the papal church. For instance, infamous Martin Luther had written:

The ungodly papists prefer the authority of the church far above God's Word; a blasphemy abominable and not to be endured; wherewith, void of all shame and pity, they spit in God's face. Truly, God's patience is exceedingly great, in that they be not destroyed; but so it always has been.[1]

And another leader of these Protestants, John Calvin, had seriously questioned, "Does there exist in Rome any church or bishopric at all?" He had concluded that for all practical purposes there was none.[2] There were even popular cartoons circulating which portrayed the passion of Jesus and the acts of the pope, contrasting these two as Christ and Antichrist.

How was a good, loyal Roman Catholic to react to such vehement attacks or deal with such extreme

Passional Christi vnd

Christ is given a crown of thorns . . .
(*John* 19)

Antichrist.

The Pope claims to have received an
emperor's crown from Emperor
Constantine

Passional Christi vnd

Christ washes his disciples' feet . . .
(*John* 13)

Antichristi.

The Pope demands that his feet be
kissed

Pages from the widely read Passional of Christ and Antichrist of 1521

Christ drives the money-changers
out of the temple . . . (*John* 2)

The Pope sells special favours

Christ ascends to heaven . . .
(*John* 12)

The Pope will descend into hell

accusations? To be called Antichrist is something no follower of the Lord Jesus can dismiss with a careless shrug. Surprisingly the first reaction of many who remained loyal to the Catholic church was to try to reform that church and, by doing so, to bridge the gaping rift between Catholics and Protestants.

The Catholic Reformation, 1525–45

The leading influence in promoting such reform was Christian Humanism. We have already seen what a key role that movement played in the lives of many who became Protestant reformers. But Erasmus and his followers remained, first of all, a strong voice within the Roman Catholic church. This voice called for a return to gospel simplicity and a revival of the traditions that ruled the early church. That sustained cry had a profound impact on the Catholic church and succeeded in producing some significant improvements in its life.

Christian Humanism stood for tolerance. It had no patience with excessive dogmatism. Thus it was a force that kept open lines of communication between the old mother church and the new dissenters. True, few messages flowed along those lines, but the channels did exist. Christian Humanism loved the Catholic church and would not leave it, despite its flaws. It recognized that within Christendom there should be a Christian unity and it testified of that need to the Protestant reformers.

Among the outstanding Humanists who worked for reform within the Catholic church were people like Erasmus, Gasparo Contarini, and Jacob Sadoleto. But the best representative of that movement and its spirit was perhaps George Witzel (1501–73).

Witzel originally followed Luther. But becoming, as he said, thoroughly disenchanted with "the Pope on the Elbe," he returned to the Roman Catholic church and became a priest. Still his disappointment with Protestantism did not prevent him from seeking to reconcile that movement with Rome. As a step in such a direction, Witzel tried to lead a reform of Catholicism along lines he outlined in a proposed program called, *A Means for Ecclesiastical Harmony* (1539).

Before anything else, he said, the Catholic church must return to the simplicity and flexibility of the ancient church. It must abandon all those later, fine scholastic distinctions and theological subtleties, for these lead only to misunderstandings and schisms. With Erasmus, Witzel believed that "the more we pile up definitions, the more we lay the foundations for dissensions."[3] If the church would abandon these later layers, it would open a path to concessions that might lead to reunion with the Protestants. What both Witzel and Erasmus didn't realize was that even if the Catholic church had returned to some (supposed) original flexibility, the impenetrable obstacle of Protestant inflexible dogmatism would have remained.

A second path to reconciliation, Witzel believed, would be translating the Bible into the languages of the people and preaching sermons based on biblical texts. Witzel acknowledged that the tradition of the church had great value. But with the other Christian Humanists he believed that the Bible should be the heart of the Christian's faith. This greater emphasis on Scripture, he hoped, would bring Catholics and Protestants closer together.

One Catholic practice Witzel strongly attacked was the private mass. This, he believed, was a corrupt addition to the liturgical practice of the early church which had viewed the mass as a "communal petition and thanking of God." Private masses denied this. Furthermore they promoted abuses—masses for money, masses for the dead—and encouraged a magical understanding of the Lord's supper. A return to the communal sacrament of the early church would bring Protestant and Catholic closer together.

Witzel also advocated education for ordinary church members, who he believed could and should be taught the deeper spiritual meaning of the church's rituals and ceremonies. Such education would eliminate the prevalent magical view of religion, encourage laity to function actively in worship, and aid in developing "a family of the children of God." Again this would tend to bring Protestant and Catholic closer together.

Finally, Witzel emphasized the common roots of both mother church and dissenters in the ancient church. Such a recognition of their common source would, he believed, work toward reunion.

This Humanistic quest for unity, so well typified in Witzel's program, failed. Although Catholic and Protestant leaders conversed and even arrived at some surprising compromises, they finally rejected this approach. Both felt the Humanist way was an evasion rather than a resolution of important issues. Regarding the central question of divine grace and how it operated, there was basic division that couldn't be overcome or ignored. Ambiguous statements on doctrine and moderate concessions by the Catholics on celibacy, mass, and church structures could not heal a wound that reached to the heart.

Another major attempt to reunify the church was strongly urged not only by the Christian Humanists but also by many political leaders in Europe—Emperor Charles V, for example. Remembering the conciliar movement of the last century and faced by a papacy seemingly unwilling to reform itself, these people raised the call for a general church council. Perhaps such a council could thoroughly reform the church and restore the unity of Christ's earthly body.

But the papacy feared such a council. It might undermine the power so painfully won back after the disaster of Constance in 1415. Until it was absolutely certain it could completely dominate such a council, the papacy stalled, promising to call a council at some unspecified future date. Wars, Muslim attacks from the East, and debates over the appropriate location all helped the papacy's delaying tactics.

But many in Europe became impatient. The opinion grew that "the Pope shrinks from a council in order to save himself from reform."[4] In response to such pressures, the pope finally convoked a general council in 1545. But by then he had made sure that this council would be totally dominated by Italian and Spanish bishops unquestioningly loyal to papal authority, that Protestant participants would be tolerated only if they accepted that authority, and that nothing would be imposed on the papacy that he could not accept.

Counter-Reformation, 1545–1600: The Council of Trent

The Council of Trent was called into being by the pope in 1545. It met in three sessions: 1545–49, 1551–52, 1559–63. Its long-term effects on Catholicism "far surpassed any council before or since"[5]—although some might argue that the Second Vatican Council in the early 1960s had an even greater impact.

The Council of Trent rejected any conciliatory approach to Protestantism, sealed the breach between the two wings of the Christian church in Europe, and emphatically defended those aspects of Catholicism attacked by Protestant reformers and criticized by Catholic reformers. It turned the Catholic church away from dialogue and toward a crusade to define clearly the Catholic position against Protestantism and to try to win back lost areas of Europe.

The best way to show what the Council of Trent was about is to delineate the stand it took on a number of key Protestant teachings:

Sole Authority of Scripture. Trent asserted that Scripture and tradition have equal authority and both may be interpreted only by mother church. Further, the Latin Vulgate edition of the Bible (disliked by both Protestants and reform Catholics) is the "only authentic edition" and "no one should presume or dare to reject it under any pretext whatever."

Justification by faith. Trent taught that faith is but "the beginning of man's salvation," which must also include hope and charity. Salvation is *not* wholly the work of God, but requires human cooperation with God. There is *not* certainty about salvation, for "no one can know with the certitude of faith . . . that he has obtained God's grace." Saving grace must come through sacraments *administered by the Roman Catholic Church,* "for all true justification either begins through the sacraments, or once begun, increases through them, or when lost, is regained through them."

Number of sacraments. Trent reaffirmed seven sacraments, declaring that anyone who denied any of these sacraments should be "anathema."

The Council of Trent

Besides such open doctrinal opposition to the reformers, Trent also defended many of the widely criticized abuses of Catholic practice. It insisted the church has the right and power to grant indulgences. It reaffirmed the practices of venerating saints and relics, for through these means Christians may "obtain favors with God" and "many benefits are granted to men by God." It even maintained the Latin liturgy.

The Council of Trent placed the future of the Roman Catholic church in papal hands. And the papal power was firmly entrenched with Italians. This is obvious from the statistics for the official acts of the last session of the Council: they "were signed by 255 prelates, of whom 189 were Italian."[6]

Trent did accomplish a few small reforms, the most significant of which was mandating seminaries for training priests. But even this was a reactionary move, intended to remove future priests from the universities, the mainstream of European intellectual life. Seminaries guaranteed "educational inbreeding" and shielded the clergy from "critical study based on historical arguments."[7] In short, seminaries became centers for indoctrination.

The Council of Trent sealed the breach between Roman Catholicism and Protestantism, a breach that would remain until Vatican II in the early 1960s. It ended the moderate, conciliatory reform movements within the Catholic church.

The Counter-Reformation: The Jesuit Order

Ignatius of Loyola (1491–1556) was the founder of the Jesuit Order which served to actualize the aggressive, dogmatic Catholicism of Trent. Loyola was born into an ardently Catholic, noble family in Spain and raised "in an atmosphere redolent of the centuries-long Christian crusade against [Muslims], with all its accompaniment of devout knighthood and gallant adventures in honor of the saints."[8] When, at thirty, his leg was shattered by a cannonball and he was left a lifelong cripple, this knightly soldier chose to become a spiritual knight for his Lord and his church and to lead a spiritual campaign against those devil's servants who threatened his church.

Preparation included a period of personal religious struggling in a monastery, the outcome of which was very different from Luther's struggle. Then at the age of thirty-three Loyola went to grammar school and at thirty-eight entered the College de Montaign at the University of Paris. (His study there overlapped Calvin's, and they may have met.) In 1535 Ignatius had received both his master of arts and bachelor of divinity degrees and was ready to crusade as a knight for his Lord Jesus Christ.

Loyola began to form a new order, gathering followers (notably) Francis Xavier) and perfecting a Christian soldier's handbook, the *Spiritual Exercises*. This was a manual intended to lead candidates for membership in the new order along a path of intense self-examination. Step one, *the way of purgation*, forced the candidate to recognize his own sinfulness. Step two, *the way of illumination*, taught Christ's redeeming work and the believer's warfare with Satan. Step three, *the way of unity*, led the candidate to a complete surrender of will and mind to God, to Christ, and to Christ's church. The exercises produced an army of unquestioning servants, ready to serve the church in its battles against unbelief.

In 1540, after Ignatius had agreed that all members take a special vow to obey the pope and accept any mission he might assign, the Society of Jesus was proclaimed an official order within the Roman Catholic church. It became the pope's arm to promote the aggressive Catholicism of Trent.

The Jesuits set up elementary and secondary schools throughout Europe, intended primarily for children of politically and socially influential people. Indoctrinating students in Catholicism and teaching facility in speaking and arguing, these schools produced many of the later leaders of the Counter-Reformation. They helped stop the

Ignatius Loyola

Reformation tide in southern Germany, Poland, Austria, and Hungary and brought thousands of Protestants back within the Catholic fold. They moved the Catholic stance from defensive to offensive and made being a Roman Catholic once more respectable.

The Jesuits also became confessors of many influential political figures in the princely courts of Europe. Their popularity in this role was partly due to their famous ability to justify questionable moral actions, especially if these promoted Catholic welfare. Such opportunistic tactics led Protestants to refer to them as "Machiavellians," that is, people who believe the end justifies the means.[9]

Besides being effective preachers (presenting a practical and understandable form of Catholicism) and effective catechists (borrowing the Protestant tool of catechism instruction), the Jesuits were also highly successful foreign missionaries. At a time when most Protestants thought the great commission had already been fulfilled in New Testament times, Jesuit missionaries were working in the far corners of the earth. Francis Xavier (1506–52) began work in far lands like India, Japan, and China. Matthew Ricci (1552–1610) worked mainly in China, opening that kingdom to Catholic presence. Typically Jesuit in their methods, both of these great missionaries attempted, first of all, to reach those in leadership positions in these Oriental lands. They also made what many consider excessive concessions to local cultures and religions, seeking to build a Catholic presence on such non-Christian foundations.

But Jesuit activities markedly strengthened the Roman Catholic church not just in numbers but also in confidence. The new, aggressive Catholicism of Trent gained much of its explosive impact from these "spiritual knights" of the Jesuit order.

****

We are likely to wonder why the mild, conciliatory, reform-minded Catholicism of the early sixteenth century failed, giving way to a dogmatic, unbending, crusading, anti-Protestant form. From our perspective, the first seems so much more attractive. If it had succeeded, would not the church of Christ now be far closer to a desired unity as the one body of believers, the one building founded on the one cornerstone of Jesus Christ?

In human terms, we can understand possible reasons for the failure of the Catholic reformers. Vague and rather undefined in contrast to vigorous Protestantism, that movement probably stirred up little enthusiasm. Catholics looked for a well-defined and self-confident form of their faith that they could promote as zealously as any ardent Protestant.

Also in human terms we can understand something of the success of aggressive Counter-Reformation Catholicism. By 1550 some of the initial enthusiasm of the Protestant Reformation had waned since it had become evident that Protestantism was no panacea for the illness that plagued Europe. The morality, for instance, in Lutheran territories was no higher than in neighboring Catholic lands, despite Luther's hopes that good doctrine would bring improved behavior. Furthermore, the religious disunity and mutual antagonism of the various branches of Protestantism disillusioned many, turning them to the resurgent Catholic church as a better hope for some Christian unity.

What God's purpose was in this developing bifurcation of the Christian church in Europe is something we may perhaps be able better to grasp in future years, when the new shape of modern Catholicism and the new relationship it has to our own branch of Christ's church becomes clearer.

CHAPTER 18
THE POST-REFORMATION PERIOD
(1560–1775)

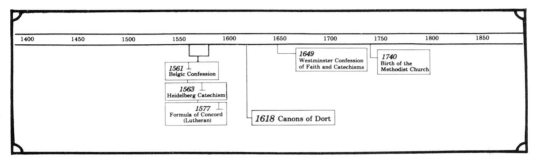

By the year 1560, Protestant churches had taken firm root in much of Europe and the British Isles and had developed into varied but vigorous bodies. They had become progressively distinct from Catholic churches so that to modern observers *Catholic* and *Protestant* seem to have emerged as two subspecies of the genus *Christian church.* Yet to themselves such was not the case. Both churches claimed to be the full genus; Catholic and Protestant were mutually antagonistic, standing in radical and bloody opposition.

The post-Reformation period tells the story of that antagonism and its results. Again, to modern observers, most striking is the intense political entanglement of the religious bodies. Beliefs were primary political issues and faith was like a powder, burning furiously and threatening to explode the West into seared fragments. "One of the major fruits of the Reformation was a century and a half of social and political upheaval that was immensely destructive of peace, prosperity, and human life."[1]

But there were other fruits. The Reformation brought to many a renewed spiritual vitality and a better grasp of divine grace and the reality of God's salvation. It also produced the great creeds and confessions of the reforming faith: in the face of internal and external threats such defined doctrines were necessary to preserve the faith of the reformers. Yet many were turned off by these documents.

191

People who have come to be called Pietists viewed the creeds and confessions and the systematic theologies that followed them as faith frozen into lifeless Scholasticism. So a new Christian piety might also be seen as a late development in this post-Reformation period.

Germany

Martin Luther's teachings on Christian liberty have often been viewed as "the hot spark in a trail of gunpowder" that set off the Peasants' Revolt.[2] Actually it was not so much what Luther said which proved volatile, but the way in which the peasants interpreted it. The result was a bloodbath in which thousands of peasants lost their lives while gaining few concessions from the nobility.

Even after that sad uprising, peace did not come to Germany. Some of the princes who became Protestant did so not because of Luther's justification by faith doctrine, but because turning Protestant excused seizing church lands for themselves and strengthened their position over against their emperor, Charles V. When Charles reacted strongly against such religiously disguised rebellion, civil war resulted. Marauding Catholic and Protestant armies tore Germany apart—all in the name of "true religion."

In 1555 the Peace of Augsburg brought an end to that civil war which neither side could win. On the principles that the leaders had the right to choose each territory's religions and that Calvinists should have no place in the empire, this treaty established Lutheran and Catholic territories side by side. Most Germans thought the Peace of Augsburg was the solution. Few would have guessed that in less than sixty years they would become embroiled in what would prove to be the most awful of all religious conflicts, the Thirty Years War (1618–48).

During this period of unrest in Germany, the Lutheran church itself was torn by bitter controversies. These concerned such basic teachings as justification by faith (some revived the idea that good works were necessary to be saved; others reacted by saying good works interfered with salvation), freedom of the will (some said fallen people can prepare themselves for God's grace and choose freely for Christ), and the understanding of the Lord's supper (some, called crypto-Calvinists, said the mode of Christ's presence in the sacrament was only spiritual). Key teachings of Luther were being disputed.

The resolution and the definitive statement of Lutheran teaching on these important issues and the rejection of the ideas so foreign to Luther's teachings came in the Formula of Concord (1577). Good works, the Formula taught, contribute nothing to our salvation, but neither are they detrimental: "Good works will surely...follow after true faith as the fruits of a good tree" (Formula, IV). On the matter of freedom of the will, the Formula denied any natural power to prepare for the gospel or choose

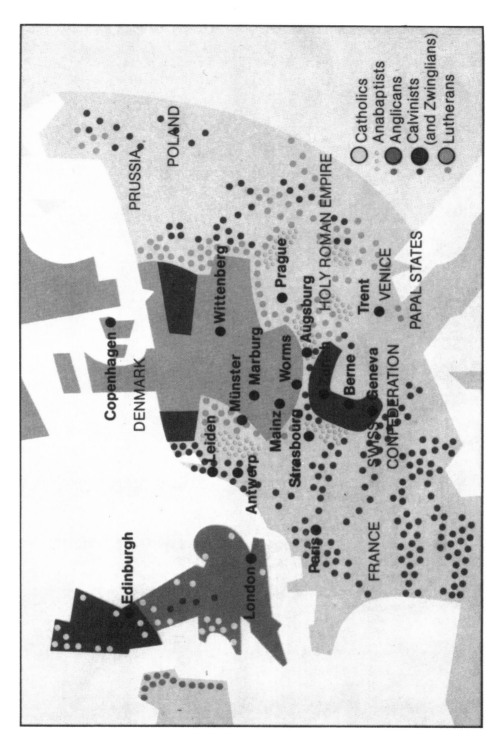

Reformation Europe

Legend:
- ○ Catholics
- Anabaptists
- ● Anglicans
- ● Calvinists (and Zwinglians)
- ● Lutherans

Edinburgh

London

Copenhagen

DENMARK

PRUSSIA

POLAND

Leiden

Antwerp

Wittenberg

Münster

Marburg

Mainz

Worms

Strasbourg

Prague

Augsburg

HOLY ROMAN EMPIRE

Berne

Geneva

SWISS CONFEDERATION

Trent

VENICE

PAPAL STATES

FRANCE

Paris

for Christ. Yet God does work through the will by his Spirit; "Man's will is changed and renewed solely through divine power" (Formula, II). Finally, the Formula rejected both Catholic and Calvinist positions on the Lord's supper, teaching that "the body and blood of Christ are truly and essentially present and received with the bread and wine of Holy Communion" (Formula, VII).

The Formula of Concord gave to the Lutheran movement a degree of cohesive unity; it helped preserve the heritage of Luther as a clear tradition apart from both Calvinist and Catholic.

France

By 1560 some two thousand Calvinist (Huguenot) congregations existed in France. Well organized into regional and national bodies, these churches also had a coherent theological expression of their faith (the Gallican Catechism). Although they comprised only 10 percent of the population, the Calvinists included 40 percent of the nobility and many of the wealthy business class. The Protestants in France were therefore a potent religious and political force.

Then two powerful, noble families seized on this Protestant movement "to reverse the trend toward absolute royal power."[3] Condé and Coligny, both newly converted Calvinists, attempted to kidnap the boy king, Frances II (1559–60), and thus "liberate" him from his Catholic advisors (the noble Guise family).

The plot failed. To prevent civil war the Queen Regent, Catherine de Medici, stopped their execution and called a colloquy of theologians to try to find some basis for religious unity and defuse the explosive religious and political differences. But the colloquy of Poissy failed.

Responding most negatively to the Queen's efforts, the strict Catholic faction murdered an entire congregation of Huguenots at worship. Battles, lootings, and wholesale massacres broke out with both Calvinists and Catholics zealously murdering each other. The zenith of brutality came when Catherine, feeling betrayed by the Huguenots, resolved to destroy their political leaders. The St. Bartholomew's Day Massacre of 1572 was a nationwide slaughter of twenty thousand Calvinist men, women, and children. To celebrate this "victory," Pope Gregory XIII held a mass of thanksgiving, praising God for the destruction of so many heretics.

But Calvinists were still a potent force in France. In 1589 Henry III, a Catholic king, first opposed and later supported by the Calvinists, was assassinated by a monk for allying himself with Huguenots. Then Henry IV (1589–1610), a Huguenot king, discovered he could restore peace only if he renounced Calvinism. He did so, reputedly saying, "Paris is worth a mass." His blatant opportunism may be criticized, but he did establish a religious truce in France with the Edict of Nantes (1598). He guaranteed the Huguenots full

194

Catherine de Medici views the victims of the St. Bartholomew's Day massacre.

civil rights, full access to public office, complete religious freedom in two hundred towns, and the right to worship in their homes throughout France. Such religious freedom, unusual tolerance for that day, restored peace to a war-torn country.

The Netherlands

In the Netherlands the religious issue ignited an explosion. During the rule of Emperor Charles V, this area had enjoyed a high degree of autonomy under local princes. But his son, Philip II of Spain (1556–98), a zealous Catholic, determined to wipe out the Protestant movement in this region while simultaeously gaining more political control. Anti-Protestantism was a good cover for his attempt to consolidate royal power in the Netherlands.

But his efforts only served to identify Protestantism with a struggle for freedom. The Calvinists became stronger. In 1566 they rampaged through the region, committing unspeakable violence in the name of reform and freedom. Philip sent his general, the Duke of Alba, to suppress this revolt. Thousands of Protestants, rebels, and suspected supporters were summarily executed.

These atrocities reunited the fragmented Protestants, as well as some displeased Catholics, under the leadership of William of Orange (1553–84). William strove for a united Netherlands in which Catholics and Protestants could peacefully coexist. But despite some initial successes, his efforts failed. The south (present-day Belgium) chose Catholicism and loyalty to Spain. The Calvinists fled northward. There, thanks to the Calvinist "Sea Beggars" who kept off the Spanish fleet and William's army, the Dutch won independence from Spain and formed a new nation with the Union of Utrecht (1579).

Like the French war, the clash in the Netherlands was a strange mixture of religious and political idealism—with a generous dash of opportunism thrown in. Both sides confused political ends and the kingdom of God. Philip identified Spanish rule with the future of the "true Catholic faith" and William viewed the independence of the northern provinces as necessary for the survival of the "true Protestant faith."

During this frantic period, Calvinism produced some of the great creeds which defined its faith. In 1561 Guido de Bres wrote the Belgic Confession, a beautiful statement of the Reformed understand-ing of the gospel. Somewhat later, in 1563, Prince Frederick III of the Palatinate (a German state) commissioned a catechism aimed at expressing the Reformed beliefs in a manner not offensive to the Lutherans in his realm. The result was the Heidelberg Catechism, a mild, warmhearted document still appealing today—but unacceptable to the Palatinate's Lutherans.

Despite the careful, concise restatement of Calvin's teachings in these two reformed creeds, however, in the early seventeenth century the Netherland's Reformed churches were shaken by a doctrinal controversy concerning God's predestination and human freedom. Because of his views on these matters, Jacob Arminus (1560–1609), a theologian trained by Calvin's successor, Theodore Beza, ran into strong opposition when he left his pastorate in Amsterdam to assume the chair of theology at the University of Leyden (1602). His most outspoken opponent, Gomarus, was a colleague at Leyden. Arminus's death in 1609 delivered him from a bitter debate, but his followers published what was purported to be his position in the Remonstrance of 1610.

The Arminians taught that God chose to save those whom he knew beforehand would choose to believe. The individual's decision for God was thus the basis of God's decision. They also taught that Christ died intending to save all people, but that only those who choose for Christ are actually saved. God's intention is thwarted by human unbelief. People are able to

196

resist God's grace. Finally Arminians taught that through negligence some saved persons may fall away from God and ultimately be damned.

The debates over these issues became entangled with politics: Arminians were identified with the party that favored state control of the church, their opponents with the political group favoring a more independent church. Some opportunist politicians, wholly ignorant of the theology involved, became embroiled in the debates. However, in 1618, the Synod of Dort finally resolved the issue.

Synod of Dort

The Canons of Dort state unequivocally that a person believes because God elects that person, solely out of grace. Does this mean God elects others for reprobation? The Canons avoid making that logical conclusion. Rather they say

God passes by the nonelect, leaving them in their sin and to their deserved reward.

The Canons affirm that Christ's death is "sufficient to expiate the sins of the whole world" (II). Yet Christ's atonement is limited in that God intends it to be effective only in those who "were from eternity chosen to salvation" (II).

The third section of the Canons of Dort deals with human depravity and God's irresistible grace in a way similar to the Formula of Concord. By teaching total depravity, both of these confessions make clear that salvation must be understood wholly as God's work. Human beings have no power or good enabling them to choose, on their own, to follow Christ. Furthermore, since this is wholly God's work and accomplishes God's intention, divine grace is irresistible. People cannot thwart God's purpose.

Finally the Canons teach that God preserves those he chooses so that they do not fall away from his grace. Here also the glory is ascribed to God; we remain in grace through no power of our will but because God graciously "begins, preserves, continues, and perfects his work in us" (IV).

Like Lutheranism, when threatened with teachings that would undermine God's sovereignty in our salvation, Calvinism responded by insisting that every part of our redemption is of God. Yet God works with human hearts through the preaching of the Word and the sacraments. Faced by ideas that threatened to undermine the genius of Protestantism, both of these main wings were able, by God's grace, to produce creeds that were thoroughly biblical—true to the heritage of the reformers—and yet never lost sight of how God works within history.

England

Under Queen Elizabeth, the Puritans (Calvinists in the Church of England) had been a loyal, if dissatisfied, minority. But under her Stuart successors, James I (1603–25) and Charles I (1625–49), they became more numerous and more restless, until in 1640 they finally took up arms against their monarch.

Although some complex political factors were involved, "religion was the single most explosive issue."[4] James was a royal absolutist. He believed he was responsible to God alone, king by divine right. This implied, of course, that he was not answerable to Parliament or to other assemblies of the realm. To make matters worse, James carried on a campaign against the Puritans, insisting that he would "make them conform" or else "harry them" out of England. He was convinced that a Church of England organized along Calvinistic lines would prove uncontrollable. He reputedly said, "No bishop, no king." As a result of his campaign, many Puritan clergy lost their pastorates but—much to James's surprise—the Puritan cause gained support. Many members of Parliament, especially the business classes, were outraged by

the king's behavior and in reaction refused to vote James the funds he needed for his many extravagant activities. Puritan and non-Puritan alike joined in stiff resistance to James's divine-right monarchy.

James's son, Charles I (suspected unjustly of being a secret Roman Catholic), increased the harassment of Puritans. His Archbishop of Canterbury, William Laud (1573–1645), even had the ears of his Puritan opponents cropped. But his action only seemed to increase popular opposition to the monarchy. Then, in an act of utter foolishness, Charles (who was also king of Scotland) and Laud attempted to force the Anglican Prayer Book on the Scottish Presbyterians—leading those hearty Calvinists to rebel and support the Puritan party in England. This ill-thought-out religious policy, when combined with Charles's effort to rule England without Parliament, led to an explosion. For when Charles, desperate for cash, was finally forced to call Parliament, he discovered he had a full-scale rebellion on his hands, a rebellion in which Puritans and other discontents were able to defeat Charles and finally have him beheaded.

That left the way open for the Puritans. The Puritan parliament met little resistance as they set about abolishing the episcopacy in England and reconstructing the church along Presbyterian lines. Charles's policies had been too unpopular. To effect this further reform the Westminster Assembly of divines (1643–49) was called into being. It produced the basic doc-

198

uments of Presbyterianism: the Westminster Confession of Faith, the Westminster Larger Catechism, and the Westminster Shorter Catechism.

Ironically, at just this point the English general and "Independent Puritan," Oliver Cromwell (1599–1658), gained control and rejected a state-enforced Presbyterian church. Rather he proposed toleration for a variety of Puritan churches while proscribing Anglicanism and Catholicism. Cromwell's view was supported by many who feared that a state Presbyterian church would prove as intolerant as the Anglican establishment—that, as John Milton said, "New Presbyter is but priest writ large."

After Cromwell's death the English people, weary of the religious unrest and Cromwell's attempts to regulate moral life, returned to the monarchy. And when Charles II took the throne, the Anglican church was reestablished as the Church of England.

Protestant Scholasticism and the Pietist Reaction

The post-Reformation period also produced a wealth of theological writing. But such works were often speculative, excessively complex, and massive (Johann Gerhard's Lutheran theology ran to twenty-three volumes). It generally lacked the warmth and experiential orientation of the great creeds. Striving to produce a complete and logically consistent theology that would make Reformed or Lutheran beliefs impregnable, theologians used the Bible as a source book for propositions that were speculatively formed into tight, rationalistic systems.

The results for the churches were unfortunate. Faith began to seem merely intellectual assent to given propositions. Pastors, trained in this scholastic approach, preached sermons incomprehensible to laypeople. The moral dimension of the gospel got little attention. All this led to a decline in lay piety, especially in the Lutheran churches. It also led to bitter polemical battles within denominations—like that in the Dutch churches between the Voetian and Cocceijan parties over the nature of the covenant. Many came to view these vitriolic debates as "the rabies of the theologians."

The Pietist reaction to this Scholasticism stressed the practical and subjective elements of Christian faith. In the Reformed churches in the Netherlands, Theodore Gerhard a Brakel (1608–69) was most influential. His handbook for practical Christianity, *The Spiritual Life,* taught that believers must *feel* the presence of God. They must be lifted in their soul to heaven and so overwhelmed by fellowship with God that thoughts of self fall away and God becomes all in all.[5]

Philip Jacob Spener (1635–1705) led the Pietist movement in Germany. Appalled at the theological nitpicking of the Lutheran churches of his day and feeling inadequate to assume pastoral responsibilities, Spener sought a balance between objective theology and subjective experience of God in Christ. He promoted these ideas in an influential book, *Pia Desideria* (*Pious Desires*) which launched a "God-pleasing reform" of the Lutheran churches. Emphasizing the *experience* of justification and rebirth (conversion) rather than these doctrines, *heart* knowledge rather than head knowledge, and the *subjective* certainty that one is a child of God, Spener and the other Pietists helped revive the laity and improve the moral level of Christian life. Pietism served to correct many of the faults of Protestant Scholasticism and, in the case of men like August Herman Francke (1663–1727) and Count Nicholas von Zinzendorf (1700–60), provided a major impetus to Protestant mission activity and led to much work of mercy within society.

Still their gathering into conventicles of true Christians gave the impression of holier-than-thou Christians. The Pietist emphasis on feelings led to some erroneous ideas in both the Reformed and Lutheran churches—the idea, for instance, that if one has proper feelings it doesn't matter what one believes. And finally, excessive Pietism did lead in extreme cases to separation and the establishment of churches for "born-again Christians alone."

In England Pietism led to a new movement in the Christian church—Methodism. The major figures of this pious reaction to the rationalistic Christianity of the church and the low spiritual level of common people were John (1703–91) and Charles (1707–88) Wesley.

While students at Oxford these brothers organized a club that encouraged devotional reading, visiting prisoners, fasting, and other pious practices. One of the club members, George Whitefield (1714–70), urged John, Charles, and the others to preach anywhere—on pulpit or open field. Soon these pious preachers were dubbed the "Holy Club" and members were derisively called "Methodists."

Though profoundly influenced by several encounters with Moravians, the Wesleys decided in 1740 to form a "United Society" of Methodists, a group *within* the Church of England. These societies met in chapels and developed their own officers—"stewards" for finances, "teachers" for Bible schools, and "visitors" to minister to the sick. As the movement expanded beyond a single person's ability to supervise it, societies were placed in "circuits," each with its "superintendent." Methodism became a virtually distinct and independent religious movement giving lip service to union with the Church of England.

As a movement Methodism was extremely successful. The societies grew and spread rapidly for they met the spiritual needs of working-class people. Thousands who otherwise might have remained unaffected found a meaningful faith by which they could live. Not until 1791, after John Wesley's death, did the Wesleyan followers form an independent church. Even then, many Methodists remained in the Church of England, forming an

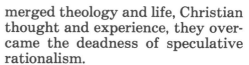

John Wesley preaches in a market square.

merged theology and life, Christian thought and experience, they overcame the deadness of speculative rationalism.

In this period we see again the church's Lord present and working in his church. In spite of the bloody fanaticism of many, the cold speculation of others, the fuzzy subjectivism of still others, the church remained a vehicle of Christ's grace to tens of thousands. Furthermore it began in this period to reach out beyond itself to bring the gospel to all classes of people and to spread to other parts of the world.

evangelical party within the larger body.

****

The post-Reformation period is one in which the churches were threatened by political opponents, fanatical religious enemies, heresy, lethargy, and arid Scholasticism. Yet to each of these threats the Protestant churches responded, not always ideally but nonetheless effectively. Through political alliances and stubborn fighting, they defeated opponents and gained a degree of stability. Through powerful creeds, they upheld the integrity of the Reformers' teachings. Through Pietist movements that

CHAPTER 19
CATHOLICISM COMES
TO THE NEW WORLD

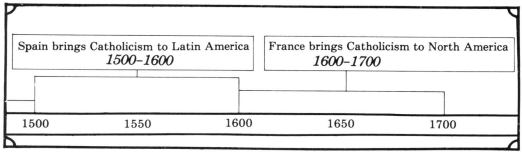

Spain brings Catholicism to Latin America *1500–1600*	France brings Catholicism to North America *1600–1700*

| 1500 | 1550 | 1600 | 1650 | 1700 |

At the time when Luther was beginning his reform, Europe was already entering "an age of discovery without parallel."[1] During this exciting period Europeans explored the coasts of Africa, opened sea routes to the far east, and discovered America (1492). These explorers were soon followed by traders and then settlers. Before long there were European trading posts and settlements in almost every continent on the globe.

This vast enlargement of the European world was a profound challenge to Christianity. The European settlements in North and South America and the trading posts in other parts of the world placed before the church two demanding tasks: first, to follow its European children and minister to them in these new lands, establishing churches and missions; second, to evangelize the native populations that had come under European rule.

In this chapter we will be reviewing the Catholic response to this challenge as it occurred in North and South America. We will focus particularly on Latin America and French North America.

Latin America

Spain and Portugal were the first explorers and colonizers of the New World to the west. Of these two, Spain was the most active and the most successful in this great venture. "The first century of Spanish

203

endeavor in the Americas witnessed the most remarkable series of expeditions of exploration and conquest in the American continent that have...been recorded in any comparable period of written history."[2] By one hundred years after Columbus's initial voyage, Spain had conquered most of South America (excluding Portuguese Brazil), large areas of North America (Mexico, California, Florida, Arizona, New Mexico), and the Caribbean Islands (Cuba, Espaniola, Puerto Rico). The credit for occupying so rapidly this vast empire goes mostly to the Spanish conquistadors, those venturesome soldiers whose military might and political duplicity subdued the vast native population. With relative ease, Hernando Cortes conquered the advanced Aztec nation of Mexico. Pizarro did the same to the highly developed Inca nation in Peru. Lesser conquistadors subdued more primitive peoples in other parts of Latin America. By 1600 Spain was master of a huge empire stretching from California in the north to Argentina and Chile in the south. That vast captive territory made Spain the wealthiest and most powerful country in Europe for over a century.

At the heels of the conquistadors walked the settlers. They flocked to the new world—merchants, planters, ranchers, miners, and also priests. So many poured in that by 1594 over 160,000 Spaniards lived in America in over two hundred chartered towns.[3] With the settlers came churches. Hundreds were established in the new world to minister to the religious needs of settlers, and thousands of additional mission stations were organized in cities and frontier areas to evangelize the approximately five million native Indians. These missions were formed and operated mostly by religious orders—Dominicans, Franciscans, and later Jesuits.

Some of the reasons that sent explorers and settlers scrambling to the exciting New World are obvious and understandable to us: desire for gold, thirst for adventure, and a chance for a new beginning. But there was another motivation that sounds as a recurring theme throughout the contemporary documents. According to the testimony of many Spaniards, including kings and some conquistadors, the reason for all these conquests, the cause of empire, was primarily a desire to win the Indians for the Christian faith. Cortes, for instance, cites this as his major reason for fighting in Mexico and for "the spiritual conquest of the natives."[4]

Yet if, as seems clear, the Spaniards felt a genuine obligation to bring the gospel to unbelieving natives, their methods seem inhumane and at times even barbaric. True, these were quite typical of the methods used in those days by most Christian groups. True also, there were always some among the Spaniards who tried to deal lovingly with the Indians and opposed the barbaric methods of their compatriots. And perhaps truest of all, as evilly as Latin American Indians were treated, it was still better than the treatment given Indians conquered by French, English, and Dutch. At least within the Spanish Empire the native retained (and does retain, even to the present day) a certain identity and kept a numerical, cultural, social, and political significance. In much of North America tribes were virtually eliminated.[5]

In spite of such favorable comparison, however, the Spanish *did* treat the native Indians harshly. A document called "The Require-ment" outlined how the Spanish conquerors were to deal with natives. It contained two stipulations. First, they were to assure Indians that if they acknowledged the church "as the ruler and superior of the whole world" and if they accepted the Spanish ruler as their superior and lord, no war would be made against them. (In other words, Indians must be granted the right of abject surrender). Second, the Indians had to agree to permit the

Cortes held Montezuma hostage while receiving gold and silver from the Indians.

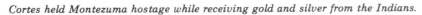

Catholic faith to be preached to them. If on the other hand, the native Indian did *not* accept these conditions, "The Requirement" justified warring against them and allowed conquistadors to "kill [recalcitrant Indians] and enslave those captured in war, precisely as Joshua treated the inhabitants of the land of Canaan."[6] And since most of the native people did refuse to surrender totally, they were in fact attacked and killed or captured.

These captive natives soon served an important function in the Spanish settlement: they became the slave labor force that worked the estates (*encomiendas*) and the mines. The only obligation laid on Spanish masters was to instruct these slaves in the Christian faith and provide for them a place of worship. For this small price Spanish landowners gained a life of relative leisure and wealth built on cheap Indian labor.

It is difficult for us to understand how a genuine concern for the Christian instruction of natives can be paired with such a system of slavery. But most Spaniards regarded the Indians not so much as slaves but as children. Like children, they must be disciplined. Like children, they must be forced to remain and work on the master's estate. Like children, without such controls they would not work and worse would not submit to the church. Like children, this was necessary for their own good.

So as the conquerors advanced, old Indian towns and dwelling places were destroyed. Natives

were housed in special villages on the estates. They were forced to attend church, to receive instruction from the priest, to memorize the Apostles' Creed and Lord's Prayer, to baptize their children, and to wear clothing. They were forced to learn "to govern themselves like Christians."[7] As a result of such forced "Christianizing," hundreds of churches were formed among the Indians. Most Indians did, in fact, accept the Christian faith but often with a heavy mixture of old pagan practices. The task was too great and the methods too faulty for really good results.

Not all Spaniards agreed with the methods promoted by "The Requirement." Among those opposing this enslavement and forced Christianization was a Dominican friar, Bartolomé de Las Casas (1474–1566). Las Casas believed that the Indians were noble people who would respond to methods of "love, gentleness, and kindness."[8] And in his Vera Paz experiment in Guatemala, he practiced such methods. Using Christian ballads in their native language, Las Casas gained an entry and was invited to preach the gospel. Soon the chief and most of his tribe became Christian.

Unfortunately, that good experiment ended most unhappily. Some pagan priests who resented Las Casas's success stirred up anti-Spanish and anti-Christian sentiment by telling the new converts of the harsh treatment other Indians were receiving at the hands of the surrounding Spaniards. As a result thirty Dominican missionaries were killed, one burned on a pagan altar. Las Casas was absent and so survived, but the failure of his attempt reinforced the common Spanish idea that these native Indians could be Christianized only by force.

Fortunately others had Las Casas's vision of nonviolent methods of conversion. In the 1600s the Jesuits established a missionary-nation in Paraguay by such methods. Over one hundred thousand Indians in thirty large missions lived in a highly structured society regulated by the Jesuits. Lands were worked in common and the product distributed according to each worker's contribution while those unable to labor were also given a share. Each Indian was given a cottage and a garden as private property. And each Indian was required to attend mass every morning before work and to receive training in the basics of Christianity from one of the two mission priests.

Indians living in this missionary nation generally seemed content (they worked only four to six hours a day). But one writer notes that in spite of the Jesuits' good intentions, "the Indians were never really taught to be much more than helpless, dependent children."[9] So while avoiding the worst of the "encomienda system," the well-intentioned Jesuit effort ended up by subjecting the Indians to a new form of bondage, a psychological dependence.

Other church leaders, while not opposing the "encomienda system" or trying to find a substitute for it,

did attempt to protect Indians from the worst abuses of their Spanish overlords. Many priests spoke out against the sexual exploitation of Indian women and the sale of alcohol to natives. The church also tried to urge the Spaniards to pay a fair wage to Indians for their labor. So while cooperating with the conquerors, the church tried to soften their harsh methods.

Not all churches were "mission stations" of course. The Catholic church continued to expand quite successfully among the rough settlers as well as the natives. By 1600 there were five archbishops and seven bishops in Latin America. The religious orders were strong, efficient organizations that served the church well. Economically powerful, holding vast tracts of land, the Latin American church grew and prospered until it became one of the largest groupings of Roman Catholics in the world.

How should we evaluate this Catholic presence in the New World? There is much to applaud. The church did work and worked hard to Christianize the Indians. As one author has written, "The role of the missionary martyrs is one of the finest pages in the history of the Spaniards in America."[10]

Yet, embroiled in the "encomienda system," the church itself was often one of the exploiters of the Indians. Too often it hesitated to challenge the unjust system and permitted itself to become a tool of Spanish imperialism. Nor were the efforts to Christianize the Indians

Jesuit missionaries were tortured and killed by Iroquois Indians.

fully successful. Beneath the Christian facade lurked old ideas; using names of saints, the Indians often worshiped forces of nature—and the church was satisfied with their outward conformity.

Finally, the clergy and parish priests who did not belong to the religious orders were often poor examples of the Christian faith. Many drank heavily and had concubines. Some lived luxuriously while parishioners suffered poverty. Overall the level of clergy in Latin America was quite low, and the church suffered from this.

French America

Although French fishermen had earlier fished the waters of the Canadian coast, it was not until Jacques Cartier voyaged there in the early 1500s that these lands were claimed as New France. And it was not until the early 1600s that Samuel de Champlain began to explore the vast areas along the St. Lawrence River. Champlain, the "true founder of French Canada,"[11] established the settlement at Quebec and cleared the area that later became Montreal. He also brought (in 1615) the first Catholic missionaries (Reformed Franciscans or Recollects) to Canada to convert the Huron and Algonquin Indians.

During the seventeenth century Frenchmen explored and claimed lands far west and south of Quebec, including Detroit, the eastern coastal areas of Lake Huron, parts of Michigan and Wisconsin, and the Mississippi Valley as far as New Orleans. But though these areas were explored and eventually dotted with military and missionary outposts, New France was thinly populated. In 1689 there were but 10,000 French settlers in Canada compared to 200,000 English settlers in what became eastern United States. In 1756 the comparative figures were 70,000 French Canadians to 1,500,000 English settlers. Yet despite this numerical inferiority and even after the English conquest of Canada in 1759, the French Catholics kept their identity and, thanks to a phenomenal birthrate, grew rapidly into the present major force in Canadian life.

The French settlements are also important for understanding the development of Christianity in Canada. Like the Spanish settlements to the south, the explorers and settlers were accompanied by priests and missionaries who came both to minister to the spiritual needs of settlers and to evangelize the native Indians. But unlike the Spaniards, the French never viewed religion as a central reason for their presence in the New World. The French came to exploit the rich coastal fisheries, to search fruitlessly for a "Northwest Passage" to the Indies, to seek rich mines comparable to those found in Latin America, and, above all, to engage in the fur trade. Efforts to convert the Indians were an afterthought, not a primary motivation.

Samuel de Champlain established a settlement at Montreal, Quebec.

Yet missionaries did come in large numbers, risking life and health for the gospel. First came Recollects, later Jesuits. Both groups played important roles in the life of New France, and when the Jesuit Francois Laval was appointed bishop of Quebec—religious leader of all French America— the Jesuit influence on life in French Canada became enormous.

The Catholic church in the French colonies was largely a missionary church. The spiritual welfare of "the savages" was considered at least as important as that of colonists. Mission stations were established from Quebec to the farthest reaches of the French Empire in America.

Unlike the Spanish, the French

209

did not enslave Indians or compel them to become Christian. The most force they used was a threat to stop trading for furs with tribes that refused to let missionaries live among them. Actually this economic compulsion was not trifling since the fur trade became very important to most Indians.

The French missionaries tried to protect Indians by gathering them in compact mission villages, isolated from uncouth French fur trappers and unconverted Indian tribes. They also tried to protect Indians from the use of alcohol since it was pointed out that Indians drink "only to become drunk" and excessive use of alcohol by Indians produces "many grave and dangerous diseases, for their vitals are scorched by the brandy and injured by the quantities of wine...with which they gorge themselves for several days at a time."[12] In 1660 Bishop Laval threatened to excommunicate those who sold alcohol to Indians. That helped somewhat, but since "the trade in spirits" was economically important to France and to the colonists, the church was unable to stop it completely.

The church in the French colonies was very well organized. Through the Quebec Seminary which trained the priests, collected tithes, distributed funds to priests scattered through New France, and cared for them in old age, Bishop Laval was able to establish authority over the whole church. Since that seminary was answerable only to the bishop, the church in New France was relatively autonomous and had great freedom of action over against secular powers.

Though under the bishop's control, local parishes also had some autonomy. Each parish had a "fabrique," that is, a board of trustees. The members of this board were laypeople elected by local parish members and responsible for providing and maintaining a church building, rectory, cemetery, and a local parochial school. This system, unique in Catholicism, worked reasonably well, although at times some "fabriques" had to be chastised for inadequately providing for local needs.

The church tried, through education, to produce Christian citizens and a society more Christian in character than the one found in Old France. To that end Jesuits founded a college in Quebec, the Sulpicians established schools in Montreal and Arcadia (and among Indian tribes), and the Recollects started schools in Detroit, Isle Royale, Three Rivers, and Montreal. Soon there were also "fabrique schools" that provided education in rural areas. Although these schools were not able to form the hoped-for ideal Christian society, they did improve literacy, teach basic Christian morality, and markedly improve life in New France.

The church in New France also operated all the public welfare programs and ran the hospitals—caring for sick, paupers, orphans, and illegitimate children. If unable to cure disease or stem the frequent epidemics of typhus and smallpox, the church at least was able to provide loving care for the sick and dying.

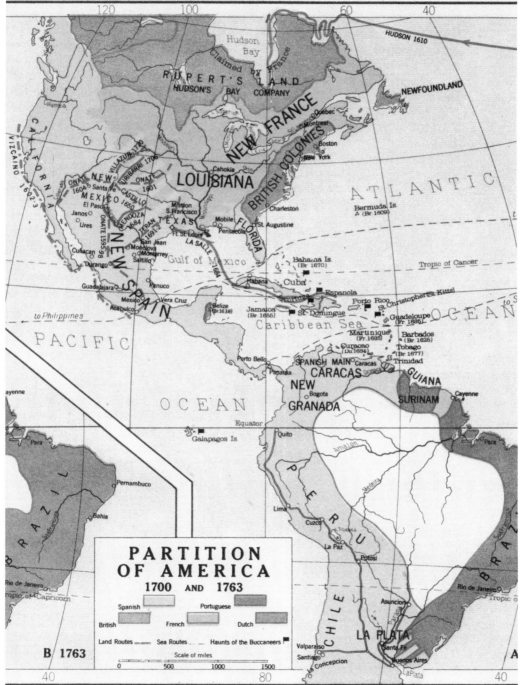

PARTITION OF AMERICA

1700 AND 1763

Spanish	Portuguese	
British	French	Dutch

Land Routes _____ Sea Routes _____ Haunts of the Buccaneers ∎

Scale of miles

0   500   1000   1500

European settlements in the New World

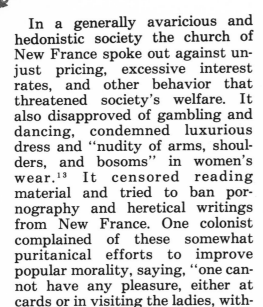

In a generally avaricious and hedonistic society the church of New France spoke out against unjust pricing, excessive interest rates, and other behavior that threatened society's welfare. It also disapproved of gambling and dancing, condemned luxurious dress and "nudity of arms, shoulders, and bosoms" in women's wear.[13] It censored reading material and tried to ban pornography and heretical writings from New France. One colonist complained of these somewhat puritanical efforts to improve popular morality, saying, "one cannot have any pleasure, either at cards or in visiting the ladies, without the [priest] being told of it, and without his denouncing it from the pulpit."[14]

If the church demanded good manners and morals, the clergy also generally set a good example. They were "singularly well behaved and disciplined, dedicated and devout."[15] Their moral and spiritual level was far higher than that of clergy in Latin America. Yet, in spite of the good example of its clergy, the church was not very successful in its attempts to enforce its strict codes on the settlers. Evidence from this period suggests that the lifestyle of the settlers left much to be desired.

After 1759 French Canada became part of the British Empire. But the French there, and to a lesser degree the French in New Orleans and southern Louisiana, retained their religious and ethnic identity. "French Canada," as one author notes, "has a sense of tradi-

tion unique in North America... and lives in and on her past to a degree which...is difficult for English-speaking North Americans to appreciate."[16]

Of other Catholic settlements in North America, notable is the experiment in Maryland. In 1634 Lord Baltimore, an English Catholic, established this colony as a refuge for English Catholics, a place where they could practice their religion without impediments. From the outset Catholics were a minority in the Maryland colony and religious toleration was granted to all Christian groups.

However, after Catholics were "guilty" of supporting the wrong side in the English Civil War, that religious freedom was negated. By 1702 the Anglican church had become the established church in Maryland, and Catholics (now one fourth of the population) could only practice their religion as inconspicuously as possible. In the part of colonial America that became the United States, Catholics did survive but only as a rather insignificant minority.

****

Through Spanish and French imperialism, Catholicism came and established itself in the New World. Its efforts at evangelism among the native Indians were fairly successful, although its methods were often highly questionable.

Although it ministered well to the settlers' religious needs, the church was not very effective in improving their behavior. In Latin America this was partly due to the clergy's own moral laxity, but even in New France where the clergy gave a high example, the church was not very capable of forming and reforming the daily lives of its members. Still it is certainly true that, had the church not been present and active, conditions in Latin America and New France would have been far worse.

CHAPTER 20
PROTESTANTISM COMES TO THE NEW WORLD

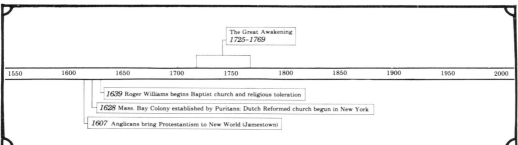

The Great Awakening
1725–1769

| 1550 | 1600 | 1650 | 1700 | 1750 | 1800 | 1850 | 1900 | 1950 | 2000 |

1639 Roger Williams begins Baptist church and religious toleration

1628 Mass. Bay Colony established by Puritans; Dutch Reformed church begun in New York

1607 Anglicans bring Protestantism to New World (Jamestown)

Not long after Catholic Spain and France had laid claim to huge portions of North America, Protestants began to arrive in the New World. Like the Catholics before them, they immigrated for a number of reasons. Many were driven by economic motives, by the desire to seek their fortune in a new land. But many others had religious reasons for becoming settlers. They came to counteract Catholicism's spread by claiming part of the New World for the "true" religion. They came to escape religious persecution in Europe. And they came to bring the Christian faith to the native Indians.

In almost every one of these Protestant settlements one religious expectation was strongly present—the desire to establish a godly society. Many believed, like William Strachey of Virginia, that "God had kept America hidden for a purpose," that he had "sifted a whole nation" (England) in order to plant his "choice grain" in America. These settlers came as those with an "errand into the wilderness"—to create in the New World a righteous society of the sort that the unfaithful servants of God in Europe had been unable to establish.[1] That kingdom-of-God-on-earth motivation placed a unifying mark on the diverse forms of Protestantism that came to the New World.

The Anglicans (Episcopalians)

The established religion of England was the first form of Protestantism to arrive in North America (Virginia in 1607). Rev. Robert Hunt, the chaplain who traveled with that first shipload of settlers, administered the sacraments to a congregation sitting on "unhewed logs" and spoke from a pulpit made of "a bar of wood nailed to two neighboring trees."[2] Unfortunately the service he must have performed most during those early years was the funeral: 460 of the 500 original colonists died of disease between 1608 and 1610.

Other colonists arrived in Virginia, but most of them were not devout Christians; they came for economic reasons. The parishes were too large (some were sixty by twenty miles) for good pastoral care, and lay vestrymen controlling the parishes often removed clergy whom they felt interfered with their personal lives by protesting their moral conduct. Nominally they were under the distant bishop of London, but actually there was no effective ecclesiastical control in the church. There was no local seminary until 1693 (when William and Mary College was founded) and the clergy, lured to America by the twenty pound bounty offered, were often misfits. Not surprisingly the Anglican Church in Virginia did not prosper, and by 1700 only an estimated one twentieth of the populace were church members.

The same poor conditions existed in Maryland, Georgia, and North and South Carolina—other colonies where Anglicanism became the official religion. But in spite of this weak base, Anglicanism did spread in the New World: churches were founded in New England, New York, Pennsylvania, and New Jersey. No doubt the most dramatic instance of the spread of Anglican influence took place in New England where in 1722 Timothy Cutler, president of Puritan Yale University, and three other Puritan ministers converted to Anglicanism.

Cutler's conversion and most of Anglicanism's success in New England, the other northern colonies, and later Canada can probably be attributed to the "superior caste among the Anglican Clergy"[3] that emerged after the Society for the Propagation of the Gospel became active (1701). Although these dedicated clergymen were only a minority, they served the cause of Christ with idealism and devotion and helped improve the Anglican church's witness to the gospel in the New World.

The Puritans (Congregationalists)

While not the first to arrive, the Puritans played the most formative role in shaping American Protestantism. They exerted "a powerful influence upon the religious, social, and political life of the whole nation."[4]

The first settlers in Plymouth, Massachusetts, were Separatists driven out of England because they had refused to conform to the Anglican church. From the Netherlands they boarded the Mayflower and traveled to Plymouth. There they established a congregational church, believing that independent

On December 21, 1620, the Pilgrims came ashore on a rocky ledge which was to become known as Plymoth Rock.

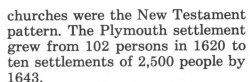

churches were the New Testament pattern. The Plymouth settlement grew from 102 persons in 1620 to ten settlements of 2,500 people by 1643.

More numerous and more important were the Puritans of the Massachusetts Bay Colony (1629). The initial group came for economic reasons, but later colonists were mostly people who had come to escape the active hostility of Charles I. Yet, as one of them said, "We do not go to New England as Separatists from the Church of England, though we cannot but separate from its corruptions."[5]

Once in New England these Puritans adopted the same congregational church pattern as the Plymouth colony separatists. Shortly the two groups "became joint representatives of what was to be a single denomination"[6]—the New England Congregationalists.

In contrast to the Anglicans, the Congregationalists had a plentiful supply of educated clergy. Between 1620 and 1650 some one hundred thirty ministers trained in Oxford and Cambridge came to serve in New England. They were joined by many others who were educated at Harvard College, established in

On Sunday, January 21, 1621, the Pilgrims held their first public worship in a rough blockhouse at New Plymouth.

1636 to train Congregational ministers.

In the freedom of the New World, the Congregational churches were able to develop their own simple style of worship. Gathering in plain but beautiful "meeting houses" and seated according to sex, the believers sang from the *Bay Psalm Book,* were led in prayer and Scripture reading, and heard one- or two-hour sermons.

These New England churches were also able to create their own form of government, the Cambridge Platform (1648). While Calvinistic in doctrine (it accepted the Westminster Confession as the basic creed), this document declared each congregation autonomous; they were to depend on each other only for advice and fellowship. Furthermore each congregation—and this idea came to characterize American Protestantism—was made up of those who voluntarily joined together. Not everyone in a given locale would automatically be considered a church member; only those who had had a religious experience and publicly professed their faith could be part of the congregation. Such members then elected the officers—pastor, teachers, elders, and deacons. (Later when tax money supported the church all voters in a township, including nonchurch members, could vote on church officers.)

One problem that quickly arose in New England was lack of toleration. The Congregational churches initially allowed no other denominations to practice in their territories. Thus when Roger Williams, an outspoken Separatist, arrived in Boston in 1631 and refused to join the Boston congregation because it had never formally separated from the Church of England, the General Court of the colony refused to let him become pastor of a congregation in Salem. Later, when he was permitted to serve there, his vigorous promotion of separation of church and state in his sermons got him into further trouble with the authorities. Fleeing to Rhode Island, Williams purchased land from the Indians and established Providence colony. There, in 1638, he founded the first Baptist church in the New World. But shortly convinced that he could not find the true church in *any* visible structure, Williams gave up leadership of the congregation, saying that "only by a new apostolic dispensation" could the true church be restored.[7]

Williams had ideas that, while repugnant to the Puritans, are widely accepted today. He rejected the common notion of his day (shared by the Puritans) that a state must have uniformity of religion. Instead he advocated a religiously pluralistic society that would include even the "most Paganish, Jewish, Turkish [Muslim], or other anti-Christian consciences."[8] Toleration, he believed, was the best pattern for the state and for Christianity.

Unfortunately, few agreed with him. It became obvious just how far the New England Congregationalists were from toleration when they dealt with the case of Mrs. Anne Hutchinson. This "woman of ready wit and bold spirit" was disturbed by some Puritan preaching that seemed to give human beings too important a role in "preparing for salvation" and seemed to require good works as "evidence for salvation." To her that appeared a return to salvation by works, a departure from the Calvinist teaching of salvation by grace alone. Mrs. Hutchinson held meetings in her home to discuss these sermons. There she developed the idea that the justified believer is directly inspired by the Holy Spirit (a concept threatening to pastors' and elders' authority) and came to reject any place of works in salvation.

Before long Mrs. Hutchinson was banished as a threat to the religious unity of the colony. She fled to Rhode Island and then to Rye, New York, where she and her five children were later massacred by Indians. Her case indicates that New England Puritanism already in the 1630s was developing into a modified form of Calvinism with a far greater stress than traditional on human preparation and striving.

The next crisis in New England Puritanism was occasioned by the growing number of people who, although baptized as infants, could relate no personal religious experience that would qualify them for full church membership. The crucial question became: should the church baptize children of such "unregenerate" persons? The dilemma was clear. "If baptism were denied to children of unregenerate parents, the integrity of the churches as gathered communi-ties of convinced believers would be preserved, but an increasing proportion of the population would be removed from the discipline of the church, and the effort to fashion a holy commonwealth... would be brought to naught. If [on the other hand] baptism were granted, the churches would be in danger of becoming 'mixed multitudes' of the regenerate and unregenerate."[9] The unhappy solution to this insolvable problem was the so-called Halfway Covenant of 1662. Children of "only-baptized" parents were granted baptism. Later the churches even allowed those baptized persons (who could relate no salvation experience) to take part in the Lord's supper. These two compromises contributed to a growing laxity in New England Congregationalism.

When in 1699 the Brattle Street Church in Boston went so far as to allow those who could not testify to a religious experience to become church officers, the Congregational churches in Connecticut reacted strongly against such growing "liberalism." They founded Yale College to counter liberal Harvard. They also, in 1708, adopted the Saybrook Platform which altered their church government to a kind of Presbyterianism. They had come to believe that Congregational church policy left individual churches too vulnerable to all sorts of new ideas with no denominational controls or checks.

The story of these years is the tale of the erosion of the Puritan pure church ideal. As unbelievers came to be included in church life

220

and foreign ideas intruded, the once warm religion of the Puritans turned cold and unemotional with an emphasis on human means rather than miraculous divine grace.[10] Even the revival under Jonathan Edwards's preaching was only a brief check to the movement of New England religion into cold rationalism.

The Presbyterians

Two streams of Presbyterianism entered the New World: New Englanders (of English descent) who migrated from other colonies to Pennsylvania, New York, and the Carolinas, and Scotch-Irish followers of Knox who immigrated directly to these same areas. Frances Makemie, of this latter group, can be called "father of American Presbyterianism." From 1684 he served as "missionary at large," establishing churches throughout the colonies.[11] By 1706 Makemie had helped form the Presbytery of Philadelphia which together with three other presbyteries became the Synod of Philadelphia.

Very significant in the history of American Presbyterianism was the Adopting Act of 1729. It required all ministers and licensed preachers to subscribe to the Westminster Confession of Faith. This was a victory of the conservative Scotch-Irish over the more liberal English element and was intended to protect the new denomination from "many pernicious and dangerous

corruptions in doctrine [which have] grown so much in fashion."[12]

American Presbyterianism was never an established church supported by tax revenues. It was a dissenting body in the New World, without official govenmental support. Yet probably because of its centralized church government it was more successful than Congregationalism in remaining true to its Old World heritage. It had problems. Some ministers were disciplined for bigamy, drunkenness, cursing, lying, and "folly and levity unbecoming a minister."[13] Still Presbyterianism had far fewer problems settling into the New World than Puritanism did.

The Baptists and Quakers

The early Baptists in America were an offshoot from Separatist Puritanism. Churches were founded when men like Roger Williams or (in 1665) Henry Dunster, president of Harvard, became Baptist and organized congregations. Although by 1707 there was a Philadelphia Baptist Association including churches in a number of colonies, they remained a rather small group until the Great Awakening in the mid-eighteenth century. With the Great Awakening they began a period of rapid growth which made them the largest Protestant body in the New World.

The Quakers also came out of Puritanism. Founded by George Fox during the Puritan Revolution

The Quakers are sent away from Massachusetts, 1660.

in England and strongly persecuted there, many Quakers began to immigrate to the New World. There also they were strongly opposed. The first to arrive, Mary Fisher and Ann Austen in 1656, were thrown into prison by the Boston authorities and examined for witchcraft. After their books were burned, these two women were deported from the colony.

This became the pattern for treating Quakers for several decades. Congregationalists were alarmed by the Quaker advocacy of toleration, their public rejection of a theocratic state, and their indifference to doctrinal issues.[14] Yet Quakers kept coming. Finally, in 1661, Congregationalists took the harsh step of executing four of them. But that approach backfired. In response Charles II of England ordered New Englanders to stop all further proceedings against the Quakers. And in 1681, after all anti-Quaker legislation was suspended, Quaker "meetings" sprang up throughout New England.

The most famous Quaker in the New World was William Penn. Granted a large section of the New

World as payment for a debt, this wealthy and influential English Quaker founded a religiously tolerant colony, Pennsylvania. This colony attracted many Quakers who were finding life difficult in England, but it also attracted many other types of Protestants who wished to live in a more tolerant environment.

Though never numerically strong, the Quakers—with their toleration, silent meetings where members waited to be led by the "inner light," and simple honesty and integrity—were very influential in the New World. They spoke eloquently against slavery and other practices they deemed inappropriate to a Christian society.

The Reformed

Three branches of the Reformed church came to the New World. Earliest were the Dutch Reformed who accompanied Dutch East India Company traders to present-day New York and northern New Jersey in the early 1600s. The first minister, Jonas Michaelius, came in 1628 to take up ministry to the settlers from the earlier two "lay comforters." By 1664, when the English captured the New Amsterdam colony and renamed it New York, there were six Dutch ministers and thirteen congregations. By 1776 there were one hundred Dutch Reformed churches in the area. These formed the nucleus for what today is the Reformed Church in America.

As a result of the persecution in France by Louis XIV, many Huguenots fled to the New World. By 1700 there were five French Reformed churches in the New York area, several in the Carolinas, and a scattering in Massachusetts and Virginia. But eventually these congregations were absorbed by Anglicans in the south and the Dutch Reformed in the New York area.

When Louis XIV of France conquered the Palatinate and tried to impose Catholicism in the late 1600s, many German Reformed people immigrated to the New World. Settling in Pennsylvania, these people wished to form a church but lacked a minister. They pressed a farmer, John Boehm, son of a minister, into becoming their pastor. He served three congregations and was finally, on the advice of Michael Weiss, a German Reformed minister who arrived somewhat later, ordained by the Dutch Reformed Church in 1729.

By 1749 the German Reformed churches were able to form a classis subject to the Synod of Netherlands. As they continued to grow they became independent of the Dutch Reformed and formed their own denomination, the Reformed Church in the United States, now part of the United Church of Christ.

The Lutherans

Swedish Lutherans were the first to arrive. They settled in Pennsyl-

vania and Delaware in the mid-1600s. Later came German Lutherans.

One nominally Lutheran group that arrived in the early 1700s were the Moravians under the leadership of Count Nicholas von Zinzendorf. These German Pietists settled first in Georgia and then in Bethlehem, Pennsylvania, and Salem, North Carolina. In the New World they evolved into an independent denomination with little place for their old-country Lutheran confessional heritage. They tried to form in America a "Church of God in the Holy Spirit" that would unite the various German Protestant groups—Pietist, Lutheran, and Reformed—into one single body.

But that effort was resisted by other German Lutherans. Led by Melchoir Muhlenberg, a Pietist who was also self-consciously Lutheran, these people were able to unite most Lutherans into the "Ministerium of Pennsylvania" (1748). This was the first permanent Lutheran Synod in America and became the center for Lutheran development in later years.[15]

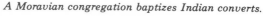
A Moravian congregation baptizes Indian converts.

The Great Awakening

The most profound religious movement in North America during the colonial period was the Great Awakening. Rooted in English Methodism and German Pietism, this revival brought many unchurched into the body of Christ and revitalized many church members. It did much to overcome American religious diversity and "to mold the various denominations [of the New World] to a common pattern, to subordinate differences, and...make possible wide-ranging cooperative efforts."[16]

The Great Awakening began in two distinct areas and three religious groups. In the Raritan Valley of New Jersey, Theodore Frelinghuysen, a Pietist-trained Dutch Reformed minister, began to preach renewal among his parishioners. Large numbers in the surrounding Dutch communities were converted.

Soon Gilbert Tennent, a Presbyterian minister in New Brunswick, New Jersey, joined Frelinghuysen's efforts. Both preached the need for awareness of sin, a personal conversion experience, and a sanctified Christian life. By the 1730s other pastors had joined in and the New Jersey churches had experienced eight or ten local revivals.[17]

Somewhat later the Congregational minister, Jonathan Edwards, preached a series on the religious complacency of the day, Arminianism, and justification by faith apart from works. Revival swept his congregation and spread to neighboring congregations. What occurred is recorded in Edwards's essay, "Faithful Narrative of the Surprising Work of God in the Conversion of Many Souls in Northampton." That work, in turn, became the basis for revival in other parts of colonial America.

But it was the Englishman, George Whitefield, who made the Great Awakening a North American phenomenon from Nova Scotia to Georgia. A Calvinist who had broken with the Wesleys because of their Arminianism, Whitefield came to America in 1739 at the age of twenty-four. His magnificent sermons had dramatic effect. Huge crowds came to hear him when he preached, not only in churches but outdoors, in public halls, and wherever people would gather. He introduced the revival enthusiasm to every major religious group in America—excepting only the Catholic.

Yet there was opposition. When Tennent urged Presbyterians to "forsake the ministry of natural men" and seek truly converted preachers,[18] that stirred a controversy that resulted in the expulsion of the revival party from the Presbyterian church. Charles Chauncey, a Congregationalist minister, was outraged both by Tennent's sermon and by the derogatory things Whitefield was saying about New England clergy, Harvard, and Yale. Fuel was added to the fire when James Davenport, an extreme revivalist, promoted sobbing, swooning, and crying out at revival meetings. Davenport furthermore claimed he could distin-

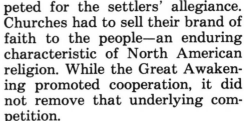

guish the elect from the damned—and in general behaved in a way that gave the Awakening a bad name. He later apologized for this erratic behavior, but the damage had been done: the Congregationalist church split into Old Lights (anti-Awakening) and New Lights (pro-Awakening). Eventually many New Light churches became Baptist congregations. In fact, in both the United States and Canada, the Baptists were the group that benefited most from the discord caused by the Great Awakening.

All in all the Great Awakening had profound influence on American Protestantism. It gave the thirteen colonies a national consciousness, a sense of special destiny that distinguished them from corrupt Europe. It led many to enter the ministry and generated an essential Pietist orientation in American religion. Finally, it weakened denominational ties by instilling a sense of shared experience between "awakened" Christians of very different denominational fellowships.

****

Protestantism in the New World was marvelously diverse. That pluralism undermined various attempts at religious establishment and led inevitably to growing religious toleration. The lack of established churches in turn fostered lay power since clergy had to "compete for the allegiance of the people through their powers of persuasion and the force of their example."[19]

But that pluralism also led to competition. Several religious bodies in a given area often competed for the settlers' allegiance. Churches had to sell their brand of faith to the people—an enduring characteristic of North American religion. While the Great Awakening promoted cooperation, it did not remove that underlying competition.

Thus the coming of Protestantism to the New World produced a new and unique religious situation quite different from anything the church of Christ had experienced in the Old World.

CHAPTER 21
A NEW ERA BRINGS NEW THREATS TO CHRISTIANITY

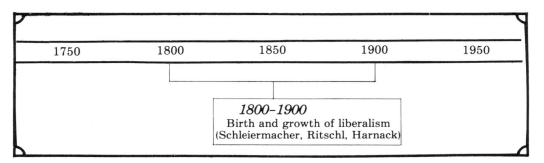

1750	1800	1850	1900	1950

1800–1900
Birth and growth of liberalism
(Schleiermacher, Ritschl, Harnack)

The Christian church, as it confesses the truth and proclaims the gospel it received, has never been impervious to its earthly environment. It has never been a disembodied voice in a vacant wilderness. And rightly so. Because the church lives and witnesses within an active, challenging society, there is and always must be a certain dialogue between the church and its age, an exchange of reflections between the church's faith and society's thought.

Sometimes that dialogue threatens the faith. During the earliest centuries of the church's history, for example, the opinions of the age caused perversions and misunderstandings of the Christian truth—dangerous heresies. The great early creeds were in many ways the church's reply to the age's voice. But the dialogue wasn't over. As the seventeenth century brought the modern era of Western civilization, new and strong thought currents moved within society—and also within the church. Again the era's perversions and misunderstandings became a serious threat to faith in Christ.

It is in the eighteenth-century Enlightenment period that a new, "final" arbiter of truth arose—human reason. In the name of reason all the old authorities, especially the church and the Bible, were questioned. Euphoric over the achievements of such human geniuses as Isaac Newton—"God said, let there be Newton, and all was light," said the poet, Alexander Pope—modern thinkers began to suppose that unfettered human reason could explain everything: the physical universe, human nature, society, and religion. If people would only dare to know, said the philosopher Immanuel Kant, they could, without revelation and the church's authority, explain the soaring mysteries of human existence and advance "with a firm and sure step along the path of truth, virtue, and happiness."

Such a modern faith and trust in reason became, in the new era, a serious threat to the church's faith and trust in Jesus Christ.

Deism and Rational Christianity

In reaction to the disruptive theological debates and corrosive religious wars of the time, some of those who trusted in human reason tried to construct a new, natural religion, a faith that would be acceptable to all reasonable people. The "father" of this rational religion, called Deism, was Lord Herbert of Cherbury (1583–1648), an Englishman.

Deism was a religion without a church and, in a sense, without God. It viewed God as a clockmaker who created the universe, set it working by natural laws, and let it run on its own. Deism was also a religion without miracles and supernatural revelation. Humankind, it said, can know truth and live virtuously by reason alone. In *De Veritate* (*Concerning Truth*) Lord Herbert outlines what be-

came the basic articles of this Deist faith:

God exists.

God ought to be worshiped.

The practice of virtue is the chief part of the worship of God.

Humans should repent of their evil ways and other crimes.

Humans will be rewarded or punished after death.

This skeletal religion spread rapidly, profoundly influencing the educated classes—especially in England, France, and the United States. Just a few of its eminent devotees were Voltaire, Thomas Jefferson, and Benjamin Franklin.

Even many of the Christians who spoke against Deism were influenced by some of its basic tenets. For example, English philosopher John Locke (1632–1704) argued against Deism—but did so in a rationalistic way. In *The Reasonableness of Christianity,* Locke attempted to demonstrate that his faith was eminently reasonable. While agreeing with Cherbury that much religious truth can be gained through reason, Locke insisted on the necessity for the supernatural revelation the Bible provides. But he used reason to "prove" his point. As any reasonable person can see, Locke pointed out, the messianic promises of the Old Testament were fulfilled in Jesus Christ. Furthermore, he argued, the miracles of Jesus support the Bible's claims about Jesus' person and work. Therefore, said Locke, it's only rational to accept the biblically revealed truths.

Another Englishman, Bishop Butler (1692–1752), answered

228

Deism in quite a different way. In *The Analogy of Religion*, Butler pointed out to the Deists that their rational religion requires just as much faith as does Christianity's revealed religion. Both the natural world and the moral (religious) world contain puzzles and mysteries; both require faith. Deists deceive themselves in supposing all is clear and lucid in their natural religion. Both worlds are plausible; miracles and life after death are as believable as Deist tenets. In recognizing the role of faith and mystery in seeking life's meaning, Butler's reply to Deism was truer to Christianity's genius than was Locke's.

Ironically it was not such Christian apologies, but rather two rationalistic philosophers, David Hume (1711–76) and Immanuel Kant (1724–1804), who destroyed the "religion of reason." They demonstrated by reason that reason cannot move from the observation of nature to the concept of a divine being who wishes people to live virtuously. Reason can neither establish nor falsify religious beliefs. So Deism died, "in a sense consumed in the fires of its own analysis."[1]

Liberal Christianity

It was in the context of Hume's and Kant's rejection of a rational basis for religion that Friedrich Schleiermacher (1768–1834), a German pastor and professor at the University of Berlin, became the "father of liberal theology." Brought up in a Pietist home and educated early in Pietist Moravian schools, Schleiermacher developed "the mystic tendency...which," he writes, "has been of so much importance to me, and has supported and carried me through all the storms of skepticism."

As a university student he became involved in another movement which, while not explicitly Christian, emphasized the role of feeling as the best path to truth. The movement, known as Romanticism, was an intellectual rebellion against the Enlightenment belief that all knowledge, religious and otherwise, could be gained from reason. To understand the universe

David Hume

229

and God we must not dissect life by reason but feel a oneness with these realities. As the poet Wordsworth wrote:

One impulse from a vernal wood
May teach you more of man,
Of moral evil and of good,
than all the sages can....

Enough of Science and of Art;
Close up those barren leaves;
Come forth, and bring with you
  a heart
That watches and receives.

Under these dual influences (Pietism and Romanticism) Schleiermacher came to base religion (and Christianity) not on reason or moral experience but on religious feeling. Religion, he said, grows out of an "immediate self-consciousness" that one has being and life through a higher being, God. It comes from a feeling of dependence on God. The Bible and Christian creeds are then little more than inspiring monuments that remind us of a great spirit those writers possessed. For us they have no objective truth, no final authority. We must produce *our own* reflections from *our own* religious feelings, *our own* insights based on *our own* religious experiences while still respecting these insights of earlier generations.

Christianity, said Schleiermacher, is unique among religions only in that it is "a deeper, more sublime and universal religion than [any] which have preceded it" and in that it possesses "the consciousness of redemption accomplished by Jesus."[2] Jesus is only a man, like any of us, but one whose "God consciousness" was fully devel-

oped. He is our model, for God would have us possess a like consciousness. Since the feeling of absolute dependence generally does not occur in isolation, but rather in "that community of persons [which] has been formed by the mind of Christ," the church functions to communicate Jesus' God-consciousness to later generations.

Schleiermacher's thinking might be called a Copernican Revolution in Christian theology. Adam's fall, he said, is only a myth that reflects every person's struggle with sin. Sin is just "an arrestment of the God-consciousness due to the preponderance of flesh over spirit."[3] The Trinity makes no sense in terms of human experience of God. Schleiermacher's God often seems to have become more of an impersonal force in the world (Pantheism) than the Christian creator and sustainer of heaven and earth.

These ideas—the emphasis on God's imminence, on Christ's humanity, and on human potential—did not die with Schleiermacher. They became part of the liberal movement that radically altered traditional Christian teaching. Like Schleiermacher, the liberals who followed him taught that the Bible and the creeds are nothing more than the fruit of past religious experiences. Each believer's present inward experience becomes the final court of appeal, the standard of truth.

One of these followers, Albrecht Ritschl (1822–89), played a major role in establishing and disseminating the liberal tradition. He practiced a thoroughly practical Christianity centered on the idea of moral freedom. Look at the critically accepted accounts of Jesus' life, said Ritschl, and you will see a man who demonstrated how a person may be delivered from the bondage of the natural world and become morally free to live out an ethical calling directed to realizing the kingdom of God. This kingdom is "the organization of humanity through action inspired by love." Following Christ's moral lead, we too can experience redemption from nature, can discover God's kingdom.

Ritschl turned liberal Christianity toward social reform of this evil world. He pointed to the task of the church and Christian individuals to establish a just and moral society in which other people can, like Jesus, overcome their bondage to blind fate.

Another prominent liberal, Adolph Harnack (1851–1930), popularized Ritschl's theology in his book, *What Is Christianity?* And in his great work, *History of Dogma,* Harnack developed several key liberal themes. "The history of dogma," he said, "furnishes the most suitable means for the liberation of the church from dogma," for through it we come to see that church dogma is but a dispensable husk added to the original kernel of Christian truth. In *What Is Christianity?* Harnack tries to define that kernel. It has, he said, three elements: the kingdom of God and its establishment, God the Father and the infinite value of the human soul, and the higher righteousness and the commandment of love. All

else, the Bible's miracle accounts and the claims that Christ is God's eternal Son, are all "later accretions." Jesus, taught Harnack, did not preach a gospel concerning himself. He preached only the Father. We call Jesus divine only because of the special way he knew the Father and because he can kindle such knowledge even in present-day people as "fire is kindled by fire." Jesus is thus an example, an inspiring force, nothing more.

Like Ritschl, Harnack believed the gospel called us to establish a just social order based on love. "[The gospel] is profoundly socialistic....Its object is to transform the socialism which rests on the basis of conflicting interests [Marxism] into the socialism which rests on the consciousness of spiritual unity." Such ideas produced the Social Gospel movement of the late nineteenth and early twentieth centuries.

Though somewhat chastened in its optimistic view of human abilities by two world wars, this gospel according to the liberal theologians is still present and very influential in many Protestant denominations today. It is a form of Christian theology that in trying to make the gospel acceptable to its era, lost that gospel. Yet it did perceive that an otherworldly Pietism in the church had come to deny the social implications of the gospel so clearly perceived by Calvin, generations earlier. And in a distorted way it did remind the church that Jesus was a truly human person—really one of us. And finally it reminded the church that truly "God himself is with us," active in the world and in human hearts. Never again could the church fall into the error of thinking of God as only "out there," far distant from his world.

Radical Biblical Criticism and Darwinism

For centuries Christians have used literary techniques to determine the most reliable Bible texts, when and by whom Bible books were written, and the relation of the Bible to other contemporary writings. But the radical biblical criticism of the nineteenth and twentieth centuries was of a very different character. Carried on by liberals who disbelieved miracles and viewed the Bible as just another, though venerable, religious book, this critical work threatened to destroy the credibility of the writings on which the Christian religion was based.

Julius Wellhausen (1844–1918) and other radical critics of the Old Testament rejected the traditional view of Israel's history. They argued, on the basis of evolutionary presuppositions, that the prophetic books must have been written prior to the books on law (the Pentateuch). Why? Because, they said, a frozen static religious form (law) must necessarily have come after the more dynamic, prophetic form. Many of these critics regarded Abraham, Isaac, and Jacob as mythological figures invented by the Israelites to explain their national origins and, in general, had little confidence in the historical reliability of the Old Testament.

The New Testament was treated similarly. David Friedrich Strauss (1808–74), in his controversial *The Life of Jesus,* argued that Jesus was not, in his own day, viewed as the Messiah. Instead, after his death, as a tribute to his greatness, his followers attributed to Jesus the widespread Jewish ideas about a future Messiah. The supernatural accounts of his birth, the stories of his miracles, even the account of Jesus' resurrection should be regarded as unhistorical since, as Strauss said, we cannot accept accounts "when the narration is irreconcilable with the known and universal laws which govern the course of events."

In dismissing the biblical authors as merely children of their own time who used myth to express Jesus' impact on their lives, Strauss and other radical critics failed to perceive that they themselves also were being children of their own time. Radical criticism, though it did yield some profound insights into the Bible, canonized many modern presuppositions: that miracles are impossible, that prophecy is never fulfilled, that Christianity is but one of several world religions, and that the Bible is just another human book. Didn't such presuppositions threaten the essence of Christianity? The liberals said no. Religion, they argued, is located not in historical documents but in present human experience.

Briefly we should mention one

Charles Darwin was attacked and ridiculed for his theory of evolution.

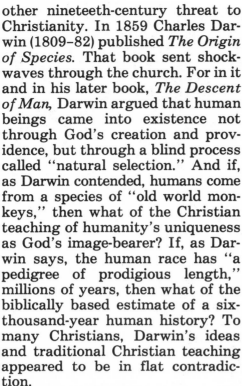

other nineteeth-century threat to Christianity. In 1859 Charles Darwin (1809–82) published *The Origin of Species*. That book sent shockwaves through the church. For in it and in his later book, *The Descent of Man*, Darwin argued that human beings came into existence not through God's creation and providence, but through a blind process called "natural selection." And if, as Darwin contended, humans come from a species of "old world monkeys," then what of the Christian teaching of humanity's uniqueness as God's image-bearer? If, as Darwin says, the human race has "a pedigree of prodigious length," millions of years, then what of the biblically based estimate of a six-thousand-year human history? To many Christians, Darwin's ideas and traditional Christian teaching appeared to be in flat contradiction.

But more liberal men like Tyman Abbott (1835–1922), pastor of the Plymouth Congregational Church in New York City, thought Darwin's evolutionary teaching could be "Christianized." God, Abbott taught, dwells in nature fashioning it in an evolutionary progressive way. God is an imminent force who works through natural selection. Rejecting the doctrine of the fall, Abbott found in the Bible a record of humanity's evolution from bestiality to a higher state. Christ is the epitome of the human spiritual evolution.

Abbott and others like him failed to see the basically contrasting values of Darwinism and Christianity. To Darwin all change comes through a "war of nature," through violence, competition, and death. Christianity teaches love and concern for the neighbor. To reconcile these two views is to pervert both.

Opposition to Liberal Christianity

By 1920 liberal theology had gained a great following in much of Europe, England, and North America. Many universities and seminaries had adopted and were teaching the ideas of Schleiermacher, Ritschl, and Harnack. But many people still opposed those ideas. A few men, often at great personal cost, tried to stem the tide of liberalism.

Ernst Wilhelm Hengstenberg (1802–69) was a preacher and professor in Berlin. He was one of "a self-conscious minority seeking to defend the Church against the dominance of rationalist and idealist [liberal] views."[4] With others he founded an influential journal, the *Evangelical Church Times*, dedicated to defending biblical Christianity. In this and other writings, Hengstenberg defended the uniqueness of the Bible and the reality of Jesus Christ's messianic work. He accused liberalism of being human centered and of robbing Christian dogma of its truth by making it only the fruit of religious experience. By influencing key appointments to church positions and theological faculties, Hengstenberg was able to slow the spread of liberalism somewhat.

In the twentieth century Karl

Barth (1886–1968), a European, became an outstanding opponent of liberalism. Educated under the greatest liberal theologians in Germany, including Adolph Harnack, Barth began his pastorate in a Reformed church in Switzerland, convinced of the truth of liberal Christianity. But in his pastoral work he soon began to find this theology inadequate in its understanding

Karl Barth

of human sinfulness and its dealing with Scripture. The brutality

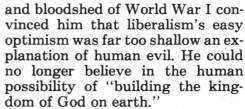

and bloodshed of World War I convinced him that liberalism's easy optimism was far too shallow an explanation of human evil. He could no longer believe in the human possibility of "building the kingdom of God on earth."

Reading the Bible, as Barth said, "without the spectacles of liberalism," he rediscovered the Christian faith. He expressed this discovery in his *Commentary on Romans* (1919), "the theological bombshell which shook liberalism to its foundations." In this and in many subsequent writings Barth taught, in flat contradiction to Schleiermacher's immediate intuition of the divine, that we human beings never know God immediately. "Nothing can lead us to God but God." Only Jesus Christ, mediated to us through the Bible, gives us true knowledge of God, and then only when by God's grace the Bible becomes God's Word for us.

In rejecting liberalism's religious experience of God, Barth also rejected Protestant orthodoxy's idea that the Bible is a book of self-evident propositions about God, available to all who read it. Because of this and because Barth accepted much radical biblical criticism of the Bible, many in the orthodox Protestant tradition have been uncomfortable with him. Still Barth's attack on liberalism had great impact in Europe and North America, forcing many to take seriously the reality of human sin and the uniqueness of Jesus Christ. For this, evangelical Christians can be grateful.

The outstanding opponent of

Princeton University

liberalism in North America was probably J. Gresham Machen (1881–1937). Like Barth, Machen was educated under liberal theologians in Germany and only after an intense personal struggle concluded liberalism was no true Christianity at all. In his *Christianity and Liberalism* he calls this modern version of the Christian faith a wolf in sheep's clothing which uses traditional Christian terminology to express another faith. In trying to relate Christianity to modern culture, it has, he said, lost the very essence of the faith.

While a professor at Princeton Theological Seminary, Machen began to struggle against liberalism in his own Presbyterian church. His efforts were not very successful. In 1929 Princeton Seminary, until then a solidly orthodox institution, was reorganized to allow representation to all elements in the Presbyterian church. Refusing to join this compromise, Machen left and founded Westminster Theological Seminary as an institution that would carry on the tradition of "Old Princeton." Finally in 1936, after he was expelled from the Presbyterian church because of a controversy over the support of liberal missionaries, Machen established the Orthodox Presbyterian Church.

****

It is unwise for us to attack or impugn the intentions of the Deists and liberals. Many were genuinely seeking to dialogue with modern thought, to maintain the validity of religion, to express what they conceived to be their faith in the new modes of thinking. But in that process they undermined the faith they sought to protect. Their perhaps well-meant but misled at-

236

tempts to create a "relevant Christianity" resulted in something that was no longer the faith confessed by generations of followers of Jesus Christ.

As in earlier centuries, God led his church to respond. Many in the church came to see the inadequacy of liberalism. Valiant men and women opposed the heresy involved and held to the gospel of Christ. Liberalism is still with us today, but its irrelevancy has become clearer in the light of twentieth-century events. In contrast the gospel of orthodox Christianity approaches more realistically the human conditions and speaks more clearly to human spiritual needs.

CHAPTER 22
THE CHURCH FACES THE CHALLENGE OF MISSIONS

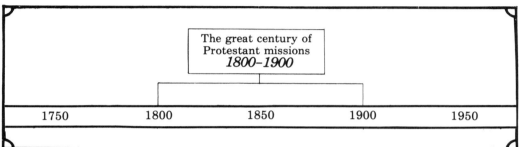

The great century of Protestant missions *1800–1900*

| 1750 | 1800 | 1850 | 1900 | 1950 |

The church is the band of people who have been *sent* by Jesus Christ to carry out a certain task in the world. The risen Lord said to his worshiping disciples, "Go...and make disciples of all nations" (Matt. 28:19). Again, just before his ascension, Christ told those who were to form his church, "You shall be my witnesses in Jerusalem and in all Judea and Samaria and to the end of the earth" (Acts 1:8). Since the term *missionary* comes from the Latin word meaning "to send," it would be fair to define the church as the company of missionaries, those sent to witness.

The earliest church carried out this mission to all the lands bordering on the Mediterranean Sea. And when these first apostles died, there were others to continue their work. During the late Roman Empire and into the Middle Ages the church grew rapidly. Recall the story of Pope Gregory's interest in spreading the gospel to England, of St. Boniface's missions to the German tribes, of the thousands of committed monks who often paid with their lives to bring the gospel to the pagans of northern Europe.

Even after the evangelization of Europe was completed (around the year 1000), the Roman Catholic church continued to feel the call to do mission work among non-Christian people. The Dominicans, the Franciscans, and later the Jesuits worked among the Muslims in Africa, the Indian tribes in South America and Canada, and many people in the Far East. The years 1300 to 1700 were a period of great

239

missionary activity for the Roman Catholic church.

Protestants took up the task of mission in a serious way only after 1700, eventually sending out the same number of missionaries as the Catholic church. Never in the history of Christianity, with the possible exception of the first century, has the church of Christ committed such a large portion of its resources to the spread of the gospel as it has in the years from 1700 until the present. Not even the threats posed by liberalism, biblical criticism, Darwinism, and the Enlightenment were able to divert the church from its calling to "be a light to the nations" (Isa. 49:6).

Many aspects of this mission endeavor could and should be criticized. Yet all in all it is an exciting, even at times heroic, story of men and women who at great personal cost brought the gospel of Christ's forgiving love to people who had never heard it. The net result was a truly universal church; in every nation on the globe today live those who confess Jesus Christ as Savior and Lord.

Roman Catholic Missions

The Roman Catholic church had some distinct advantages in pursuing its missionary work. In its religious orders, first of all, the church possessed a ready-made "army of servants" which it could send "to any part of the habitable globe."[1] And in its *Sacred Congregation for the Propagation of the Faith* (1622) it had a well-worked out set of missionary goals:

—Missions should be controlled by Rome rather than by the colonial nations (such as Spain and Portugal).

—Mission churches with native clergy should be developed wherever possible and as quickly as possible. Native priests and bishops are more effective than foreign missionaries.

—People need not be Westernized to be Christianized. "Do not bring any pressure on the people to change their manners, customs, and uses, unless they are evidently contrary to religion and sound morals. What could be more absurd than to transport France, Spain, Italy, or some other country to [the mission field]?"

Although this policy was not strictly followed in every case, in general Catholic missions were less guilty of exporting Western culture and more successful in building churches on the foundation of existing cultures than Protestant missions were. On the other hand, Catholic missions were also more liable to accommodate Christianity to the local religions. To illustrate these points and the story of Catholic missions, we'll look briefly at a few representative fields: India, the Philippines, China, and Africa.

The first Catholic missionaries in India accompanied the Portuguese conquerors in the sixteenth and seventeenth centuries. In spite of the resentment they naturally encountered because of that association, they were still able, by 1800, to win several hundred thousand converts.

Other missionaries notably Robert de Nobili (1577–1656) disassociated themselves from the Western imperialists. This Jesuit tried to convince higher caste, Brahmin Indians that Christianity was an Oriental religion (rooted in Palestine) and could be adapted to Indian culture. To make Christianity appear less foreign, Nobili adopted the Indian way of life, mastered Hindu scriptures, and held public discussions on theological issues in a way that was understandable to an educated Indian. His work was very successful among the Brahmins and later, as he had hoped, many lower caste people followed the Brahmins into the church. For forty-two years Nobili remained in India; after his death others continued his work so that by 1700 there were over 150,000 Indian Christians in the Madura area of India.

After a decline in the eighteenth century, Catholic missions in India took on new vigor in the nineteenth and twentieth centuries. It was in this period that many Indians were ordained priests and consecrated bishops, and a genuinely Indian Catholic church developed under Indian leadership. The church also established several colleges which, by training many who later became government officials, greatly spread the Christian influence.

However, the Indian mission field was not without its problems. One major difficulty was the papal insistence that Indian priests learn Latin and celebrate mass in that language. That insistence continued to stamp Christianity as a European import. Not until the Second Vatican Council of 1963 was this stumbling block finally removed.

In spite of such difficulties, the Indian Catholic church of today has more than a million members. Impressive though this number sounds, however, it is a minute fraction in a population of six hundred million and illustrates the resistance to the gospel invariably found in lands like India that have an ancient and advanced civilization.

Such resistance was not a problem in the Philippines. The primitive animism on these islands was no match for sophisticated Catholic theology. The Jesuits who began work there in 1521 established a network of schools among these illiterate people and encouraged them, wherever possible, to integrate the new faith with their old culture. The foreignness of Christianity was further lessened by the high amount of intermarriage between Spanish conquerors and native peoples.[2] Under such circumstances it's not surprising that by 1800 the vast majority of Philippine people had accepted the Christian faith.

China was more like India, a vast land with huge numbers of people and an advanced civilization. The greatest of the early Catholic missionaries to the Chinese was another Jesuit, Matteo Ricci (1552–1610). Like Nobili in India, Ricci tried to build a Chinese Christianity on the foundation of local beliefs, in this case Confucianism. To Ricci Confucian rites seemed more civil

Matteo Ricci (left) adapted his religious teachings to the native Chinese customs.

than religious. The Chinese, he argued, honored Confucius essentially as a great lawgiver—just as people in the West honor heroes from the past for their great achievements. He allowed the Chinese converts to participate in rites honoring both Confucius and dead ancestors, failing to recognize that for many Chinese these rites were closely tied to a belief in the need to placate the spirits of the dead.

Such accommodation was probably necessary at the time, but after Ricci's death a major debate broke out among China's missionaries. Many non-Jesuits considered such concessions a blatant selling out to paganism. And ultimately these non-Jesuits prevailed: in 1704 the papacy ruled, forbidding Chinese Christians to honor Confucius and dead ancestors. Most missionaries who disagreed were forced to leave.

In retrospect one must agree with the pope's decision. It's true, of course, that forcing Chinese Christians to make a radical break with their families and culture made winning converts far more difficult. But the alternative was worse; it would probably have led to an acculturated Christianity that included much of the old religions of China.

Partly because of these problems over Confucianism and ancestor worship, the eighteenth century was a difficult time for Catholic missions in China. Only after 1840 were they revitalized—and then mainly because of Western imperialistic power which required the reluctant government to permit missionaries to work in the land. So when Jesuits, Dominicans, Franciscans, and other orders poured in "a fatal link was . . . forged between imperialistic penetration and the preaching of the gospel."[3] In spite of this "fatal link" many converts joined the church, some of them for questionable reasons. "Word began to get around that it was a good thing to have a missionary on your side,"[4] especially if you got into trouble with the Chinese authorities.

As the nineteenth century progressed, however, more and more Chinese priests were ordained and the number of Chinese Christians continued to grow. When the Communists took over in 1949 the Chinese Catholic church numbered some three million. How many defected under Communist rule is not known. But it is probable that the church today is but a small fraction of its earlier size.

At the same time that Ricci was working in China and Nobili was spreading the word in India, other Catholic missionaries began work in Africa. By 1700 over 600,000 converts had been baptized in the Congo, Angola, and surrounding regions. But here, as in China and India, the eighteenth century was one of ebbing efforts; many converts, improperly catechized, relapsed into their native religions. The nineteenth century brought renewed efforts and great successes, especially in the Congo and among the Ibo tribe in Nigeria. Today in much of Africa the Catholic church is a strong presence that has weathered the storm of independence movements and can count its members in the millions.

Orthodox Missions

From 1700 to 1917 Orthodox missionaries worked primarily in Siberia to evangelize the native tribes there. These efforts, begun by Czar Peter, were closely tied to the crown's desire to promote government control of this vast region. Yet it can't be denied that Orthodox missionaries were sincerely concerned for the souls of the people they worked with. Men like Cyril Suchanor (1741–1814) and John Veniaminor (1797–1879) spent much of their life bringing

the gospel to Siberia and beyond to the Alaskan island.

Too often, however, Orthodox missionaries were satisfied with a superficial, outward allegiance to the Russian state religion. As a result the "converted" tribespeople who were "heathens before their baptism were still heathens after it."[5] Still many did truly choose to follow Christ and after conversion destroyed all remnants of their non-Christian past.

Protestant Missions

Protestants were relative latecomers on the mission fields. There were a few efforts made prior to 1700 by French Huguenots in Brazil, by Dutch Calvinists in Indonesia, and by white settlers in North America, but these were sporadic and rather unsuccessful. As a widespread, organized movement, Protestant missions were begun by Pietists who taught that such a worldwide endeavor was a necessary prelude to Christ's return.

The first Pietist mission (the Danish-Halle Mission) began when King Frederick IV of Denmark wished to evangelize his Indian subjects in the Danish colony at Tranquebar on the southeast coast of India. When no Danes would serve, he asked help of the great German Pietist, August Herman Francke in Halle. Francke found two volunteers, Bartholomew Ziegenbalg and Henry Plutschau. These, the first non-Roman Catholic missionaries to India, arrived in

1706. They began working and "at point after point...made the right decisions, and showed the way that has been followed ever since by the best and most successful among Protestant missions."[6] The pattern they set involved:

—closely relating church and school, teaching new Christians to read and understand the Bible

—translating the Bible as quickly as possible into the native tongue

—trying to understand the culture and mindset of the local people

—emphasizing personal conversion and setting high standards for church membership

—quickly training local ministers who could become church leaders

Soon another Pietist group, the Moravians, set up mission stations in the Virgin Islands in 1732, in Greenland in 1733, in Africa and South America in 1739. At one point, one out of every twelve members of this Moravian church was on the mission field.[7]

These Pietist efforts soon inspired others. Reading of them, William Carey (1761–1834), an English Baptist shoemaker, wrote a very influential book (in 1792), *An Enquiry into the Obligations of Christians to Use Means for the Conversion of the Heathens*. The next year Carey himself went to India and, following the pattern of the Danish-Halle Mission, began working there. He also wrote letters back to England, fanning a fire of enthusiasm and leading the or-

ganization of a number of mission societies to support foreign missionaries. The stage was set for "the great century" of Protestant missions in the nineteenth century.

Various factors occasioned and sustained this explosion of mission interest. Bolstering the challenging excitement of the Pietists' and Carey's work was Europe's growing awareness of new areas of the globe. Europeans were consciously reaching out around the world. In fact during this century Western powers literally forced many nations to accept missionaries and continued to protect them as they worked abroad. Also, because of the Industrial Revolution, there was enough wealth in the churches to support a large-scale, far-reaching missionary enterprise. And finally, thanks to Pietism and other evangelical movements, Protestants were able to work together on foreign fields in a way which had been unthinkable earlier. Comity agreements established territories that each group respected and, regardless of denomination, Protestant missionaries saw themselves as cooperating in a great, common task.

The work begun in India by the Danish-Halle Missions and by William Carey was continued by other Protestants. One figure who stands out in this continuing epic is Alexander Duff (1806–78), a Scottish Presbyterian. Like Nobili, Duff directed his ministry to the elite Brahmin class, hoping through them to reach the masses. His method eventually led to a large and very influential group of highly

244

William Carey translates the Bible into one of the Indian languages.

educated Christians in India.

Thanks to the efforts of Duff and others like him, after 1850 the Protestant churches in India grew rapidly and began to develop indigenous leadership. As large numbers of lower caste people entered the church (especially after 1914), many feared the upper classes would come to see Christianity as a religion only for the poor and unworthy. But instead, educated classes were impressed by the improved behavior of lower class converts and began to receive Christian instruction themselves.[8]

For a long time many Indians were hostile to Christianity, viewing it as a sort of remnant of Western imperialism. That hostility has been partly overcome today by the dominantly Indian leadership of the various churches—a leadership outspokenly critical of many Western ways and actively involved in the national political life. Furthermore, the Ashram Movement founded by the Indian Christian, Sundar Singh, has adapted Christianity to the Indian scene by forming religious communities which are outwardly very similar to the local Hindu communities. Christian Ashrams are a group of men and women who live together and carry on a work of mercy among the poor. They have helped make Christianity seem less foreign to many.

The total number of Christians in India today, including both Protestants and Roman Catholics, add up to several million. While constituting only 2.5 percent of the population, these believers form some vital and independent churches that serve as a light in India and a means by which many others may eventually be brought to Christ.

Protestant missions, of course, were not limited to India. Like the Catholic church, Protestants wanted to reach China, and Africa, and "the ends of the earth." It was not until the Treaty of Nanking in 1842, however, that Protestant missionaries were able to enter the Chinese heartland. Unfortunately this forcible entry "in the wake of gunboats and artillery" created resentment and bitterness among many Chinese.[9] But in spite of that bitterness, dozens of missionary societies began work—mostly in the larger cities of the more easily accessible provinces.

It was Hudson Taylor (1832–1905), an Englishman, who after 1865 brought Christianity to *all* the provinces of China. Earlier missionaries tended to congregate in the more accessible provinces. He established the China Inland Mission, an agency headquartered in China rather than in England— open to all missionaries who would

Christian baptism among the people of Northern India

sign its conservative doctrinal statement. This mission required little formal education from its missionaries but did insist they wear Chinese dress and identify as much as possible with the Chinese people. While not opposed to educational and medical work, the primary focus of the China Inland Mission was evangelistic preaching. This mission had great success in recruiting missionary workers and in carrying on work throughout China.

There were also dozens of other mission agencies representing various denominations. Each agency founded churches, provided medical missions, and established schools. By 1900 it is estimated that over one million Chinese had become converts. That year the anti-Western Boxer Rebellion resulted in the death of scores of missionaries and thousands of Chinese Christians, yet the following years were good ones for China missions. Thousands of young Chinese eagerly entered Christian schools and most emerged at least nominal believers. Yet many joined the church searching for a way to remake China into a modern nation state rather than for personal salvation. "The question was not 'how can I be saved' but 'how can China live anew.' "[10] Sun Yat-sen, the president of the new Chinese Republic that followed the Revolution of 1910, expressed these same goals when he said he hoped through Christianity to bring to China the "ideals of religious freedom" and "a knowledge of Western political freedom."

Such hopes were dashed. Sun Yat-sen could not rule the country. When the real power passed into the hands of contending "war lords," anti-Western and anti-Christian feeling grew stronger. Even under Sun's Christian successor, Generalissimo Chiang Kaishek, mission work was dangerous in an unsettled country. The Japanese occupation from the late thirties, the civil war of the late forties, and the Communist takeover in 1949 all hampered evangelistic work further.

While many Chinese Christians welcomed the Communist victory because of the great improvement in economic, social, and political conditions, Christian missionaries were soon expelled (by 1953) and the existence of the church was seriously threatened. To be a Christian in China became, for many years, equivalent to being a traitor, a "running dog" of the Western imperialists. Yet today it seems the church has survived both as an organization that cooperates with the Communist government (Three-Self Movement) and in the form of independent House churches.

Although thousands of Christian missionaries gave years and lifetimes to the task of building churches in India, China, and other parts of Asia, even more people and more lives were poured into bringing the gospel to Africa. In African missions the name that stands out is David Livingstone (1813–73). Though kind and patient with the natives and outspoken in his opposition to the slave trade and Western exploitation of Africans,

Madonna and child from the East

he was quite willing to use Western imperialism to advance the spread of Christianity. Like so many missionaries of the nineteenth century, Livingstone often confused evangelization and Westernization, desiring to "make an open path" in Africa "for commerce and Christianity."

The earliest years of Protestant missions in Africa were physically difficult. They were "an amazing tale of adventure, endurance, privation, sickness, weakness, and death."[11] Nearly half of the early missionaries died within a year or two of their arrival in Africa.

The first fifty years were also difficult evangelistically. Few natives converted and many who did reverted to native religions. But later people began to pour into the churches, and today there are 70 million Protestant and 75 million Roman Catholic Christians in Africa, about half the total population.

This major success (especially when compared to missions in Asia) cannot fully be explained by human factors, yet it is worth noting some of these. The number of missionaries in proportion to the population was far greater in Africa than anywhere else. Also the Africans generally had no developed religion (only primitive animism) or advanced cultures. They were unable to resist the Western ideas that poured in and the resulting religious vacuum was filled by the Christian faith.[12]

Very briefly, Protestant missionaries also visited other areas of the globe. In Latin America today there are millions of Protestant Christians, mostly Pentecostals. In Korea the membership of Presbyterian and Methodist churches includes 15 percent of the population. In Japan, despite strong resistance, Catholic and Protestant missionaries have established churches whose membership (around one million) makes up close to 1 percent of the total population. But in Muslim nations, despite sustained efforts, results have been negligible. Not only is the idea of a divine Christ "utterly and completely abhorent" to these strict monotheists;[13] but converts to Christianity are treated as defectors from Islam and national traitors. Islam has proven more resistant to the gospel than any other religion.

****

The tale of Christian missions in the modern period is an impressive one. Committed believers, Catholic and Protestant, sacrificed much to bring the gospel to unbelievers in true loving concern for these people's physical and spiritual well-being. Yet many mistakes were made. The gospel was too closely tied to Western culture and imperialism: many missionaries lacked adequate sensitivity to local cultures and customs—they were loving, but patronizing in their evangelism.

In the twentieth century we have paid for those mistakes. Nationalistic movements have often brought rejection of Christianity and charges that the followers of Christ were also guilty of exploiting native peoples. We must pray that as time passes and native leadership

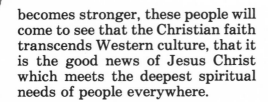

becomes stronger, these people will come to see that the Christian faith transcends Western culture, that it is the good news of Jesus Christ which meets the deepest spiritual needs of people everywhere.

CHAPTER 23
THE ROMAN CATHOLIC CHURCH
(1600–1965)

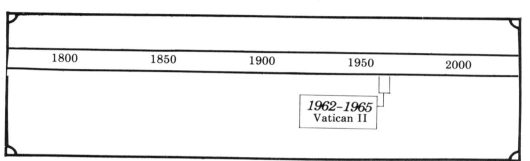

| 1800 | 1850 | 1900 | 1950 | 2000 |

1962–1965
Vatican II

Traditionally, most Protestants have tended to see the Roman Catholic church as a colossal, monolithic structure—a sort of ecclesiastical pyramid. Like those ancient Egyptian monuments, the Catholic church seemed to tower, weathered but enduring, above the multitude of smaller, more changeable, Protestant institutions. Like the pyramids and in contrast to Protestant volatile divisiveness, it seemed to stand solid, made of the same unchanging rock throughout; it seemed to stand united, admitting one authority, the pope, and bound to absolute agreement by his infallible teaching voice (when he spoke *ex cathedra*). That at least has been the image of the Catholic church among many of the Reformation's children.

Only recently have Protestants begun to see that this image is very false and has always been false— that the Roman Catholic church really is not so different from other churches. It is larger perhaps, more structured and authoritarian, but it is still split by internal tensions and subject to historical changes. Especially since the visible alterations and stresses of Vatican II, non-Catholics have begun to see that church more realistically.

For in actual fact, although the Council of Trent (1546–62) asserted papal supremacy, from 1600 to 1800 popes were not supreme. They continued to meet a great deal of resistance within their church. Capable bishops struggled against them to retain some freedom within their own countries.

Catholic kings and princes, for political reasons, tried to control affairs in their own realms. So the Italian popes had to struggle for the power they claimed to have at Trent.

This power struggle exceeded personal contests between popes and certain strong rulers or bishops. It produced a division into and tension between two distinct parties within the church—the Ultramontanists, who supported an absolute papacy, and the Gallicans, who wanted only nominal papal control.* Not until the nineteenth century was this struggle finally resolved by an Ultramontanist victory. The signal of that victory was the dogma of papal infallibility.

And the story does not end there. In recent years there have been further, remarkable changes in the Catholic church. The Second Vatican Council (1962–65) is a witness to that. Not only does the locus of power seem again to be shifting, but it would appear that, as someone has remarked, the Catholic church has finally come into the modern world.

In the Age of the French Revolution

Until the last decade of the eighteenth century, the Roman Catholic church enjoyed many special privileges in the Catholic nations of Europe. It remained the only tolerated religion. It was entrusted with most of the education of the youth. It enjoyed many financial concessions. Its officers held many high government positions.

This special status began to slip during the French Revolution. First in France—then in Germany, Italy, Spain, and Portugal—privileges were progressively curtailed or revoked. In many of these countries religious toleration increased. Church and state became separated. Protestants openly practiced their faith, and atheists were openly irreligious. Before long non-Catholics were holding public office. To Catholic leaders it appeared as if the rising democratic spirit were undermining the Catholic influence in Europe.

Even more of a threat were actions taken by anticlerical forces within the new secularized governments of France, Germany, and even Italy. Attempting to break the church's power, government officials often confiscated church lands, making the Catholic charges dependent on the state treasury. Frustrated Catholic bishops realized the danger of this new dependency: a government which paid clergy one day could withhold payment the next.

Equally threatening were the frequent attacks on the monastic orders. On the insistence of secular rulers, the papacy disbanded the

---

*Note: Ultramontanist means literally "beyond the mountain" and is the name given those who favored control by a pope who resided on the other side of the Alps from France and Germany. Gallican means French and is the name given the movement which sought relative freedom for the French Catholic church.

strongly Ultramontanist Jesuit Order. Many other orders lost their holdings. There was even a law passed in France (1789) forbidding the taking of new monastic vows—a law which proved impossible to enforce but showed the anticlerical spirit of the time.

A final threat came in the movement to secularize education. After 1800 the Catholic countries of Europe attempted to replace church education by establishing state-run schools with lay teachers. This move particularly threatened the hold of the Catholic church over the masses of these nations.

What impact did this movement toward secularization have upon the Roman Catholic church? In what must be one of the supreme ironies of history, these attacks and threats became the catalyst that enabled the papacy to tighten its hold on the Catholic church. Bishops, no longer able to rely on the privileges granted by their governments, had to turn to the pope for support. Monastic orders and clergy lost their financial independence with the confiscation of church lands. In Canada and the United States, Catholics faced a developing anti-Catholic fanaticism that drove them to Rome and the popes for guidance and help. In a hostile world, members of the Roman Catholic church found solace in being part of a cohesive, worldwide religious movement under strong leadership.

In summary, the setbacks that the Catholic church experienced in the age of the French Revolution actually led to a consolidation of papal power. The ideal of papal supremacy enunciated at Trent became a reality in the new hostile environment. What popes could not accomplish when Catholic princes were favoring the church, they were able to do when that favor had been replaced by secular indifference or opposition. It seems that the principle of earlier church history was again being proved true—persecution and suffering often strengthen the church rather than weaken it.

Pope Pius IX (1846–78)

The achievements of Pius IX, one of the most influential popes in Roman Catholic history, vividly display the new papal ascendancy. Yet his reign also demonstrates the papal inability to cope with the rising nationalism, secularism, and democracy.

In 1857 Pius IX proclaimed the dogma of the "Immaculate Conception of Mary." This teaching, that from the moment of her conception the Virgin Mary was "immune from all taint of original sin," now became binding on all Roman Catholics—under threat of excommunication. The promulgation of this doctrine was a clear indication of papal dominance because it was the first time in history that a pope had defined doctrine independent of any council of bishops. Also it was a declaration that the pope was above the Bible and Catholic tradition, for neither the Bible nor the great theologians and earlier popes had ever hinted at such a dogma.

In 1864 Pius made another powerful move by publishing a Syllabus of Errors. By this document he set himself and the Catholic church solidly in opposition to all forms of modernity. Eighty "errors of the day" were listed, errors that by papal injunction must be rejected by all Catholics. Among these so-called errors were separation of church and state, religious tolerance, secular education, trial of Catholic priests in secular courts, the notion that Protestants are Christians (just a different kind from Catholics), the Marxist teaching that social change comes from class struggle, and the democratic teaching that political authority rests with the people.

Binding all Catholics to an antidemocratic world view and suggesting that their task was to restore the church to its former dominant role in influencing policy of state, this document was an embarassment to Catholics living in democracies. It caused many, both Catholics and non-Catholics, to see the papacy as a threat to the modern state. It caused Catholic political figures in Europe and North America to be viewed suspiciously by many people as possible conspirators against democratic government. A clear legacy of this Syllabus of Errors was the difficulties Roman Catholic candidates experienced during the American presidential campaigns of 1928 and 1960. Many feared that a Catholic president would be loyal first to the papal church and only second to the United States. If the Syllabus were the official stance of the Catholic church, it seemed logical to suppose that loyal Catholics like Al Smith and John Kennedy would feel bound by its teachings and not truly dedicated to the democratic ideals of their country.

Pius's third and culminating demonstration of papal power—forcing the dogma of papal infallibility through the First Vatican Council (1870)—had far-reaching effects. Those who opposed the dogma argued that at least one pope, Honorius, was condemned as a heretic by three church councils and could not, therefore, have spoken infallibly on matters of doctrine. Others maintained that traditionally infallibility had been ascribed to papal pronouncements only when these were made in conjunction with church councils. Ignoring such views, Pius pressured the majority of bishops to state that "the present mind of the church overrules history and tradition."[1] To his opponents he said, "I am tradition." Finally, recognizing the inevitability of approval, sixty bishops left the council early to avoid displeasing the pope with their negative votes, and those who remained approved the dogma of papal infallibility, 533 votes to 2.

These three actions by Pope Pius convincingly demonstrated papal supremacy within the Roman Catholic church. Yet these victories were bought at a price. They further widened the gulf between Roman Catholic Christians and believers in Protestant and Eastern Orthodox churches. They were a virtual declaration of war with the

254

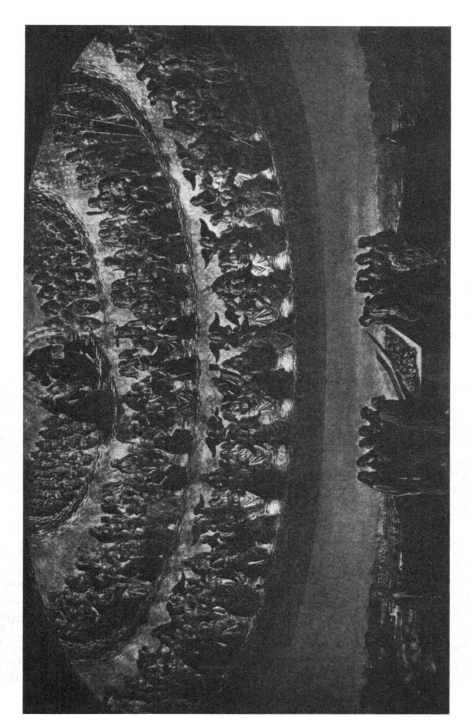

BOTTICELLI, The Assumption of the Virgin

modern world, a rejection of most of the political and religious movements from the Reformation to that time. Finally, they led to a church split. Already disturbed by earlier actions, several leading scholars and several thousand other Catholics took the proclamation of papal infallibility as an occasion to leave and form the Old Catholic church. Though a small group, this church had as one of its supporters Johann Döllinger (1799–1890), perhaps the greatest Catholic scholar of that age.

So despite his successes within the church, Pius was responsible for further alienating the Roman Catholic church from the rest of the world. He was also the pope who lost the papal states. The national unity which the papacy had so long feared and opposed finally became a reality. Italy became a nation state and in 1870 Italian troops made Rome and the papal states part of the unified nation. The new leaders offered the pope a substantial payment for this loss and guarantees of his independence, but Pius IX (and several of his successors) refused to surrender claims to these territories. They chose instead to become "prisoners of the Vatican." It was not until fifty years later, during the Mussolini regime, that the papacy finally recognized the new state of affairs and accepted a large payment for the lost papal territories. At that same time the area known as Vatican City (about 100 acres) gained the status of an independent and sovereign state.

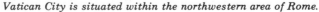

Vatican City is situated within the northwestern area of Rome.

Pope Leo XIII (1878–1903)

Pope Leo XIII, Pius's successor, was more willing to face modern realities. Although unwilling to approve democracy in principle, he did accept the status quo (except in Italy) and attempted to make peace with Europe's democratic states. He was ready to compromise enough to make the best of what he considered a bad situation.

Leo is best known for his encyclical, *Rerum Novarum* (*Concerning New Matters*). By this document he tried to place the papacy and the Catholic church solidly on the side of the working people in industrial society. While categorically rejecting Socialism and Marxism (two movements that were attracting many from the Catholic working class), he advocated the right of workers to organize unions—although he intended these to be Catholic labor unions for Catholic workers. He demanded that employers cease forcing employees to work excessive hours, thereby allowing enough time for healthy family life and religious practices. At a time when the social welfare state was still only the dream of a few, he pleaded with modern governments to properly house, clothe, and feed workers and to stop child labor.

In spite of this socially progressive teaching, Leo was very conservative in other areas, having little sympathy for democracy, religious toleration, or secularized education. Yet, more realistic than Pius IX, he recognized that the Catholic church must learn to live with these modern "evils."

Catholic Modernism

The Roman Catholic church, despite its entrenched conservatism, was not immune to modern intellectual currents of thought. During the nineteenth century some Catholic scholars adopted critical attitudes toward the Bible and church doctrines similar to those of liberal Protestants (chapter 21).

One of the Catholic modernists, Alfred Loisy (1857–1940), began to question much of the New Testament. We cannot be sure, he said, that Jesus actually said much of what is ascribed to him in the Gospels. The New Testament is really a tradition which purports to relate the life and teachings of Jesus. But, Loisy said, it is really "a mosaic of divine truths and human errors." It is the scholar's task to distinguish between these and thereby arrive at what is authentic. Only in that way can Christ become "historically available" to the believer.

Loisy went on to critically study the history of the development of Catholic dogmas. These are also, he claimed, like the New Testament, relative and historically conditioned. Loisy tried to distinguish between the historical, transient statement of the dogmas and the abiding truth these dogmas were trying to relate. Like many liberal Protestant scholars, he was attempting to draw a line between the Christian truth that transcends any particular form and the historical form or mode in which such truth came to expression.

Unlike Protestant liberalism, Catholic modernism did not prosper. Pope Pius X (1903–14) read it out of the church. In two encyclicals he declared that the Bible is inerrant and may not be studied critically like other books. He also rejected any distinction between the abiding truth and the historical form of a dogma. Dogma, he asserted, is not historically conditioned; it is as binding in its original form in the present day as it was originally. Finally Pius required all priests and teachers to sign an anti-Modernist oath, excommunicating any such as Loisy, who refused to do so. All forms of Catholic Modernism were either driven out of the church or forced to go underground to wait a more favorable day.

The Second Vatican Council (1962–65)

Many had assumed that the Vatican Council of 1870 would be the last such gathering in the Roman Catholic church. What need for councils of bishops when the church had adopted a dogma of papal infallibility? Hadn't the church "placed its own future into the guaranteed guidance of the 'vicar of Christ'?"[2]

Yet Pope John XXIII (1958–63) chose to convene a Second Vatican Council in 1962. We can only speculate about his reasons, but G. C. Berkhouwer has suggested some plausible possibilities:

—John was concerned that for too long the Catholic church's stance had been negative, *against* new developments in the world; it was time to be *for* something.

—John felt the need for a more positive approach to other Christian churches, Protestants and Eastern Orthodox; one that did not simply dismiss them as "sects" or "heretical groups."

—John wished the teaching of the church to directly address the modern world rather than merely repeating what had been said in the past; he said "we must distinguish between the inheritance of faith itself...and the way in which these truths are formulated" (a statement almost identical to those of the excommunicated modernist, Loisy)"[3]

Made up of bishops from around the world, the Second Vatican Council was called with the hope that it might bring the Roman Catholic church into the modern world, might bring forth a more vital Catholicism that would deal with twentieth-century issues. That hope and intent were no mere aberrations of Pope John. His successor, Pope Paul VI (1963–78), continued the council after John's death, encouraging it to make Christ's message understandable to the contemporary world.

Vatican II will undoubtedly rank

as one of the most influential councils in Roman Catholic history. In a relatively short time it has already effected a virtual revolution in that church. Its final results are yet unclear, for the Catholic church is still in the process of absorbing its implications and adjusting to the new life situation it produced.

Concretely, Vatican II substantially changed the practice of worship in Catholic churches. Formerly worship was conducted in Latin and monopolized by clergy. Laypeople were passive observers, "no more than clientele."[4] Now the worship service is conducted in the language of the people. The laity sometimes receive both bread and wine in communion and participate in congregational singing (including many "Protestant" hymns). No longer does the priest say the mass alone with his back to the audience. Now he faces the congregation who also say parts of the mass. All these changes reflect the teaching of Vatican II that not only the clergy but also laypeople are part of "the people of God."

This Council also radically changed the attitude of Catholics toward Protestants. For the first time since the Council of Trent, Protestant denominations were called "churches" rather than "heretical sects." Vatican II still affirmed that the Roman Catholic church is the truest approximation of "apostolic fullness," but it regarded Protestants as actually participating in the body of Christ, though in an inferior way. The results have been new dialogues with Protestants and joint services

of prayer and worship. How radical a change this embodies is only seen when one remembers that before Vatican II Roman Catholics were forbidden to even enter a Protestant church.

Equally revolutionary is the new stance on religious liberty. In a radical about-face, the Council endorsed religious toleration, maintaining that people should follow their own consciences in religious matters without outside interference and that there should be an "amicable separation of church and state." It would seem that "for the first time in history the Roman Catholic church...officially relinquished her religious monopoly."[5]

Vatican II also modified the extreme papalism of Vatican I, stressing the important role of church councils. The new ideal is one of councils cooperating with popes to formulate the tenets of the faith. It would seem reasonably certain that the Catholic church will never again be governed by an autocratic ruler like Pius IX, answerable to no one, but rather that bishops will once again play vital roles in directing the church's life.

Last, but not least, Vatican II called for a return to the study of the Scriptures, the vital source of Catholicism. It encouraged scholarly study of the Bible, study unfettered by dogmatic restrictions. That call has produced a flowering of biblical studies in the Catholic church. But with that new scholarship has also come, among some, a new uncritical adoption of the methodology of radical biblical

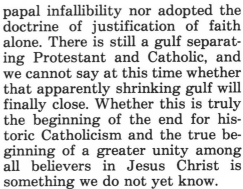

criticism so common in liberal Protestant circles. Hans Küng and some other Catholic scholars are questioning the authenticity of the miracles recorded in the Gospels and of much else in the New Testament. It is a pertinent question whether a return to the study of Scripture, if carried on in such a critical spirit, might not prove ultimately more destructive than constructive.

One thing is overpoweringly clear—Vatican II opened the Catholic church to new currents of thought. The fresh air of freedom has led Catholics in some unanticipated directions. Many clergy are now acting as if there are virtually no differences remaining between Catholics and Protestants. Some Catholic theologians are trying to show that the doctrine of the mass is really quite compatible with the Protestant Lord's supper. Hans Küng is attempting to demonstrate that the decrees of the Council of Trent, properly understood, are in harmony with Luther's doctrine of justification by faith. Advocates of clerical marriage are trying to show that the ideal of clergy celibacy is "historically conditioned" and should not be binding in this modern age. Educated Catholics are attacking indulgences, saints, and other forms of popular Catholic piety. Due to Vatican II the Catholic church is in a state of flux, which has made many faithful Catholics extremely nervous.

Still the final verdict on the post-Vatican II Catholic church is not in. That council neither rescinded papal infallibility nor adopted the doctrine of justification of faith alone. There is still a gulf separating Protestant and Catholic, and we cannot say at this time whether that apparently shrinking gulf will finally close. Whether this is truly the beginning of the end for historic Catholicism and the true beginning of a greater unity among all believers in Jesus Christ is something we do not yet know.

****

This chapter has sketched an amazing story. In what seems a complete reversal of basic direction, the Roman Catholic church changed from a movement toward ever greater centralization, control by the papal authorities, and rejection of anything modern to a church seeking decentralization with more lay involvement in worship, a greater role by bishops in church government, and a new openness to modern thinking. The story of that radical reversal illustrates the vitality of a church that not so many years ago would have been dismissed as dead by most Protestants. When the long avoided contact with the broader world finally occurred, it resulted in a church far healthier than before.

CHAPTER 24

THE CHURCH
AND SOCIAL CHALLENGES
(1800–1979)

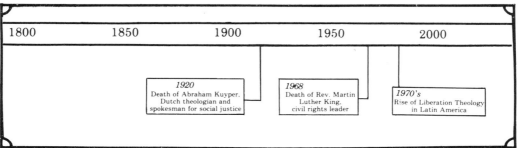

1800	1850	1900	1950	2000

1920
Death of Abraham Kuyper,
Dutch theologian and
spokesman for social justice

1968
Death of Rev. Martin
Luther King,
civil rights leader

1970's
Rise of Liberation Theology
in Latin America

"Am I my brother's keeper?" Cain's question (Gen. 4:9) should be echoed by Christians in every age and answered in biblical terms, "Yes, you are!" For Old Testament laws required concern for "the strangers that sojourn among you," the prophets sternly reproved the rich who exploited their helpless brethren, our Lord told the story of the Good Samaritan as a shining example of how we should be brothers and sisters to needy fellow humans, and James rebuked those who neglect the works of faith: "If a brother or sister is ill-clad and in lack of daily food, and one of you says to them, 'Go in peace, be warmed and filled,' without giving the things needed for the body, what does it profit?" (James 2:15, 16).

Church history records the church's frequent, if imperfect, attempts to be faithful to these biblical teachings. The early church cared for its widows and orphans, fed the hungry, and established hospitals. During the reign of the first Christian emperor, Constantine, new laws improved the lot of slaves, prisoners, and poor and prohibited abortion. Even during and after the barbarian invasions, monasteries were havens for the homeless, refuges for those fleeing vengeance, and medical centers for the sick. St. Francis of Assisi and those of his order dedicated themselves totally to serving the urban poor of the twelfth and thirteenth centuries. And Calvin's Geneva tried to establish a Christian social order that would protect the poor

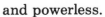

and powerless.

The church has a long tradition of caring for the needy brother or sister. Even in those ages when most believers seemed rather to reflect Cain's indifference, there have been at least a few who recognized that the good news means "freedom to the captive," "relief for the poor," and "justice for those who suffer injustice."

In the nineteenth and twentieth centuries many Christians have made continued attempts to be their "brother's keeper." In this chapter we will be detailing how they have done that.

Christianity and Slavery

Those of you who saw the television series *Roots* would probably have little difficulty condemning the entire slavery system portrayed in that film as self-evidently unchristian. From the horrible conditions in the slave ships, where captives were stacked like cordwood in the cargo holds, to the slave auctions, where families were torn apart and human beings were sold like cattle or hogs, the injustice and inhumanity seems clearly indefensible. Yet many of the early slave traders who owned and operated the slave ships were devout New England Puritans. The slave buyers and owners, both in the North and South, were Christians, often devout Methodists, Presbyterians, or Baptists. In 1776 there were over six thousand slaves in New England; even the great Calvinistic evangelist, Jonathan Edwards, was a slaveholder.

These Christians justified the system of slavery in several ways. They pointed to the apostle Paul, citing how he admonished slaves to obey their masters and sent the runaway slave Onesimus back to Philemon. They recalled that slavery had never been totally condemned in the Christian Roman Empire or in Christian Europe. But they failed to note that slaves in Roman and medieval times were usually treated humanely and could hope for emancipation for themselves and certainly for their children. They justified making slaves of Africans (and Indians) because these were subhuman or inferior beings, incapable of living freely. And tracing incorrectly the ancestry of the black people to Ham, they explained slavery as a result of the curse on that son of Noah. For all these reasons, though Christian in belief and profession, many people in Christian nations were able to live with the system of slavery and enjoy its benefits for themselves.

But by the late 1700s a change of heart and thinking began to occur. Some Christians in the southern half of the United States and many in the northern states and Canada began to condemn slavery. Movements developed seeking to abolish the slave trade and even slavery itself.

No clear and simple reasons can be given for this change of heart. Some historians point out that slavery had ceased to be economically beneficial in the North. Others credit the great religious revivals of this period with releasing an outpouring of concern for exploited fellow humans—prisoners, the insane, victims of the liquor traffic, and slaves. Still others argue that the humanitarian principles of the American Declaration of Independence were beginning to take effect and people were realizing the disparity between enslaving blacks and stating that "all men are created equal" and have an "inalienable right" to life, liberty, and the "pursuit of happiness."

Regardless of the reasons, the 1800s saw the emergence of many antislavery societies. Some were quite secular; others clearly Christian. Some demanded instant abolition of slavery regardless of the political, economic, and social consequences; others, the vast majority, favored a gradual approach.

Among the Christian leaders of the antislavery movement was the evangelist Charles G. Finney (1792–1875), later president of Oberlin College. To Finney slavery was an abomination for any Christian nation. Finney's disciples in this cause included Theodore Dwight Weld (1803–95) who, with his followers, made the antislavery cause a crusade, an emotional issue throughout the East and Midwest. By revivalistic methods they won many passionate converts to this cause especially among the churches in the North.

Other leaders included Charles Tappan, a wealthy Christian industrialist in New York who financed and published many antislavery books and newspapers, and Francis Wayland (1796–1895) of New En-

gland. Wayland, as a Baptist pastor and later as president of Brown University in Rhode Island, gave the antislavery movement an intellectual respectability.

The Christian antislavery people argued strongly that slavery is a denial of the Christian principles that we must be "our brother's keeper" and "love our neighbor as ourselves." In response to those who contended that the New Testament condones slavery, they replied that Paul temporarily tolerated it only because conditions in the Roman Empire were not conducive to living out Christian principles. But that same excuse cannot be used eighteen hundred years later in a supposedly Christian nation. We are obligated, they insisted, to live by Christian principles—and therefore to abolish slavery. No Christian, they argued, can justify the present brutal and dehumanizing forms of slavery that tear husband from wife (in clear violation of the Christian ideal of marriage: "What God has joined together, let not man put asunder"—Matt. 19:6) and children from parents. And how can Christian masters who keep their slaves "in a state of . . . mental imbecility . . . fulfill Christ's injunction to bring the gospel to all peoples if the black slaves are kept so ignorant that they cannot really grasp the meaning of the gospel?" Slavery, said those crusaders, is theft, stealing another person's labor, and thus a clear violation of God's law.

But antislavery people did more than preach against this institution. First, they urged churches to speak out against slavery with united voices. That resulted in many church splits. In 1843 six thousand Northerners left the Methodist church because they felt it was too timid in speaking out against slavery; they formed the Wesleyan Methodist church. Then, just two years later, a group of Southerners withdrew because the Methodist church ordered a Southern bishop to either get rid of his slaves or desist as bishop; they formed the Southern Methodist denomination. The Baptists were also affected: in 1845 when the national Baptist church refused to endorse a Georgia slaveholder for missionary service abroad, the Southern Baptist Convention withdrew in protest. The Presbyterians split for similar reasons, forming the Southern Presbyterian church. Remarkably, although the Methodists reunited in the 1920s, the other divisions still persist today.

Second, many antislavery people became active in the "underground railroad," helping slaves escape to Canada. Charles Torrey, a New England pastor, moved to Virginia and helped four hundred slaves to flee north. Harriet Tubman, a black woman called "the Moses of her own people," made nineteen trips from her base in Canada to rescue over three hundred slaves. As she and the newly freed slaves crossed the bridge at Niagara Falls they would sing:

Glory to God and Jesus too,
One more soul is safe!
Oh, go and carry de news,
One more soul got safe!

Canada was the land of refuge. Even though the majority in the North were opposed to slavery, runaways weren't safe there. The Fugitive Slave Law applied in the North as well as the South, meaning runaways captured anywhere in the states could be returned to their owners.

In spite of, and perhaps because of, the continued enforcement of such laws, the rift over slavery continued to grow. Although they read the same Bible and professed the same faith, Christians in the United States were totally divided on this important question. Besides the proslavery and antislavery split there were other divisions. Some wished to help all slaves back to Africa—Liberia was the result of such efforts. Some wanted immediate abolition, even if it meant war. Others were grad-

Harriet Tubman, "The Moses of Her People"

ualists. But a significant number of Northern Christians believed slavery to be a crucial issue in living out the gospel and regarded the war between the states as a Christian crusade to liberate the slaves.

The Civil War did not really solve the problem. For those emancipated, there continued to be indignities and a new form of bondage. The final chapter on slavery has yet to be written. The Civil Rights movement of the 1950s and 60s, led by Rev. Martin Luther King, has shown, first, that the United States does not yet treat its black people justly and, second, that Christian principles can be a powerful force for change in this century too.

Martin Luther King, Jr.

Christianity and the Industrial Revolution

In recent years we have come to see the Industrial Revolution as a mixed blessing. While providing for the majority of those in industrial nations a standard of convenient and comfortable living that is the envy of those in nonindustrial nations, it has also polluted the air and water, eaten up much of the earth's limited energy resources, and produced frightening weapons of war and destruction. It has divided our world into rich and poor, producing restlessness and hatred among those in the nonindustrial world who see the wealth others derive from their raw materials.

These are modern problems. But, as a matter of fact, from the very beginning the Industrial Revolu-

tion created massive social problems that cried for Christian responses.

Imagine yourself a farmer in Germany in 1850. Your family has farmed the same plot of land for over five hundred years. Although this land is owned by a nobleman, you fully expect it to be farmed by your children and grandchildren. This is your family's way of life.

One day the nobleman's representative appears at your door and tells you that because of the new fertilizers and farm machinery fewer farmers are needed. You and your family must leave. What can you do? You know only farming and have no other way to support your wife and five children. Others in the same situation are moving to the city, to Berlin, to work in the new factories there; so you and

265

The Industrial Revolution drastically changed transportation patterns with the invention of steam engines and locomotives.

your family move also. In the crowded city you manage to find a hovel with two small rooms and an outhouse shared with several neighbors. Although there are three people for every available job, you're fortunate enough to find employment in a textile mill.

But in this job you must work fourteen hours a day, seven days a week, on a dangerous machine where a wrong move means a lost finger, or arm, or life. The wages are not nearly enough to support your family. When you talk to the foreman about this, he suggests that your wife and children should also work. At first you are reluc-

tant. Your oldest child is fifteen, your youngest eight, and they should be in school while your wife runs the home. But poverty leaves no options and your family joins you working in the dangerous, noisy, unventilated factory.

Even with the entire family working, however, there are uncertainties. You could be laid off in one of the recurrent recessions; you could become ill or be injured. There is no unemployment or health insurance, no social security with retirement. There are few laws governing factory safety, working hours, and child labor—and those that do exist are usually ignored.

To join a protest group or workers' organization would mean losing your job or being beat up by company thugs. With a family to care for, you are trapped in a boring job and feel (to quote Karl Marx) "like an appendage of a machine." Family life is poor because you're all exhausted at the end of the day. Christian life is difficult for you work on Sunday. Even when you do get to church occasionally you're too tired to truly participate. Unfortunately this pathetic scenario is more than a story. Conditions like these were commonplace for millions of families in nineteenth-century Europe and North America. As a result, the dawn of the industrial age was a living hell for those who manned the factory machines.

The sheer speed of industrialization was partly to blame, for it made social upheavals, inadequate housing, and poor conditions in the factories inevitable. But blame must also be shared by ideologies that justified the horrible conditions and stifled reform efforts.

One of these ideologies was the Laissez Faire Economic Theory developed by Adam Smith in his *Wealth of Nations* (1776). This free enterprise approach opposed all government regulation of industry as interference with natural laws of competition. On such principial grounds it opposed child labor laws and rules regarding working conditions and wages. It was Smith's notion that "labor is a commodity" just like iron ore or coal. That idea encouraged factory owners to buy labor as cheaply as possible with

no regard for fair dealings with employees and no Christian concern for their workers' welfare.

Another ideology that supported the worst of the Industrial Revolution was Social Darwinism. Using Charles Darwin's concept of "survival of the fittest," supporters of this ideology said that poor and suffering factory workers were obviously "unfit" and deserved to perish. To help them would only keep the weak alive and impoverish the race. On the other hand, the social Darwinists pointed out, the rich were obviously the most "fit" and deserved whatever they acquired.

Unfortunately, many Christians accepted these ideologies, adding a small smattering of Christian concern. Russell Conwell, a Baptist preacher, gave some popular lectures entitled "Acres of Diamonds." Everyone has in their own backyards, he said, acres of diamonds—if they only have the will and drive to mine them. It is the Christian's "duty to get rich." Poor people just lack proper strength of character.

Along much the same lines Andrew Carnegie (1835–1919), founder of United States Steel and a "self-made multimillionaire," preached a Gospel of Wealth. Unimpeded competition is sacred, he declared, and the free accumulation of wealth a right. The struggle for wealth is a "basic law of life" (presumably from God) which assures "the survival of the fittest, and thereby benefits the race."[1] The rich should give generously "for public purposes," but excessive charity, he warned, will only "en-

Child labor contributed to the Industrial Revolution.

courage the slothful, the drunken, the unworthy."[2]

Since attitudes like these of Conwell and Carnegie were widespread in Christian churches during the nineteenth century, it was not surprising that workers became disenchanted with Protestant churches. In Berlin (around 1870) fewer than 10 percent of the working class had any association with the church, and in New York and Toronto under 20 percent participated regularly in church life. By taking sides with the ownership class and displaying a decided lack of interest in the weak, poor, and exploited, the church contributed to the "de-Christianization" of the working class.

There were, however, Protestants and Catholics who challenged this system that forced millions to become wage slaves, living and working in grim conditions. One of the largest of these reform groups, the Social Gospel movement, operated in Canada and the United States. To most conservative Christians the term *social gospel* triggers images of liberalism, of perversions of the good news of salvation into schemes for world improvement by social engineering. Whether such images are valid or not, the Social Gospel movement did understand, with John Calvin and other earlier Christians, that the gospel of Christ teaches not only "salvation of souls" but also "redemption of social structures."

The Social Gospel was proclaimed in several Protestant denominations through the leadership of clergymen like the Baptist Walter Rauschenbusch (1861–1918), the Episcopalian W.D.P. Bliss (1856–1926), the Congregationalist George Herron (1862–1925), and the Disciples of Christ pastor Shailer Matthews (1863–1941). It was propagated partly by students from such seminaries as the University of Chicago Divinity School, Union Theological Seminary, and Colgate-Rochester.

The Social Gospel movement vigorously attacked many aspects of industrial society—such as unrestrained competition (rejected as "magnification of selfishness into a universal principle"), the accumulation of vast wealth by a few (condemned as theft from low paid workers), the idea that poverty is the result of moral weakness, and the notion that God loves the rich and shows disfavor toward the poor. It called for establishing the kingdom of God on earth, a kingdom that would come to expression in a just society that respected the wealth of all, workers as well as owners. Most Social Gospel people pictured this "kingdom" as a socialistic society in which workers as well as employers would have a part in policy decisions. As George Herron said, "Pure socialism becomes the only form through which religion can express itself in life and progress."

The Social Gospel movement helped establish institutional churches in city ghettos where medical care, cooking classes, saving associations, athletic programs, and the like were available to the poor. These churches often advocated political action to bring change and Social Gospel leaders were active in the Socialist or Democratic parties. Involved also in the labor movements, the Social Gospel leaders almost all encouraged workers to organize for political strength and, when necessary, to strike.

On the positive side this movement recognized the effects of sin and the need for redemption in social structures, promoted justice in society, and forced the church to realize that Jesus Christ, for the most part, identified with the poor, neglected, and oppressed in society rather than with the rich and influential. On the negative side this movement optimistically believed that by law, moral preachments, and organized labor, the kingdom of God could be approximated on earth. They had "little sense...of the depth and stubbornness of sin and evil."[3] They tended to identify God's kingdom with specific social movements, not seeing the sin also in these. Yet, whatever its flaws, the Social Gospel movement was a prophetic voice calling Christians to recognize that they are their brother's and sister's keepers.

A more conservative criticism of industrial society, and one very influential in the Netherlands and in some Reformed churches in North America, was voiced primarily by Abraham Kuyper (1837–1920). This churchman, theologian, professor, and prime minister of the Netherlands shared the Social Gospel movement's conviction that Christianity has to do with all aspects of life, including politics and social structures. He addressed the problems created by industrial society in his book *Christianity and the Class Struggle* (1891).

Kuyper agreed with the Social Gospel movement that Christ "never takes his place with the wealthier, but always stands with the poor." He shared its criticism of "the mercantile gospel of *laissez faire*" in which the law of life became "the law of the animal world,...dog eat dog." He also condemned the existing social order for its unjust exploitation of the working class and the thoroughly unchristian "selfish individualism" of owners. In a just and Christian society, he believed, the welfare of all is protected, for "we are members of each other."

But Kuyper vigorously opposed

Abraham Kuyper

270

Socialism's essentially materialistic view of life. He sought a society ordered according to God's laws, a society that looks to God as the source of all good and recognizes the vacuity of material comfort apart from God.

Through the Antirevolutionary party, a Christian political group he helped form, and often in conjunction with the Roman Catholic political party, Kuyper promoted laws regulating working hours, abolishing child labor, and providing insurance for injured or retired workers. He promoted the right of labor to organize, encouraging Christian labor unions. In all this he tried to establish structures in which labor, owners, and government could work out a just relationship, each group respecting the other's rights and dues. He played a key role in developing a truly "mutualistic society" that respected the rights and responsibilities of each segment of the population.

In general it should be admitted that Christian churches of the late nineteenth century were not vocal or active enough in combating the unjust conditions created by industrial society. Yet there were those in the church who, in the name of Christ, called and worked for a society in which justice would reign and their brothers and sisters would receive proper care.

The Theology of Liberation

Liberation Theology is the name given to a contemporary movement that seeks a more just world order. It is a predominantly Roman Catholic movement headed by strong Latin American leaders, but it does include a number of Protestant leaders in Africa and Asia.

Liberation Theology teaches the radical injustice of the present political and economic world orders in which a few rich nations consume nearly all the world's resources, leaving the majority of humanity to live in poverty and hunger. It finds it Christianly incomprehensible that followers of Christ in rich nations contentedly enjoy incomes often one hundred times greater than those of people in less developed nations and that rich, supposedly Christian governments can support the oppressive, self-serving dictatorships that rule so many developing nations.

The present situation, says Liberation Theology, is the collective fruit of sin, for sin is "evident in oppressive structures, in the exploitation of man by man, in the domination and slavery of peoples, races, and social classes."[4] In this sinful world order Christianity should bring a message of liberation, liberation from sin and the consequences of sin. The exodus of the Israelites is a symbol of such liberation, for God led his people from slavery in order to create through them "a just and fraternal order."[5] In Christ, God now wishes to lead all oppressed peoples out of slavery into a just social order. In an unjust world a true believer must be unwilling to accept an otherworldly salvation; rather, "to be converted is to commit oneself

271

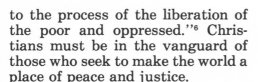

to the process of the liberation of the poor and oppressed."[6] Christians must be in the vanguard of those who seek to make the world a place of peace and justice.

In general, considering the causes of the present maldistribution of wealth and power, Liberation Theology blames capitalism. The capitalist emphasis on accumulating wealth has caused rich to exploit poor and rich nations to exploit poor nations. Socialism, oriented to the needs of the community, would distribute wealth according to need, Liberationists claim, thus producing a more just society.

But such a society can never be attained by the rich individuals or nations voluntarily surrendering their privileged positions. That will never occur. We must turn to the poor, God's chosen people, "the privileged recipients of the gospel."[7] Only when the poor grasp the radical implications of the gospel can justice be restored in the world.

In order to bring about this better world, Christians must become subversives and revolutionaries— or so some of the writings and actions of people involved in Liberation Theology seem to say. At the very least that possibility must be faced, for "liberationists . . . must accept the class struggle both as an undeniable fact and as a starting point for devising strategies of change."[8] Violence may be part of rousing the "class consciousness" of the oppressed and may be required to bring about a better order that radically alters social structures. But such violence is a re-

sponse to violence already carried out against the oppressed. In South America this has meant that some Catholic priests have supported urban guerillas, social revolutionaries, and revolutions against the government.

In evaluating Liberation Theology we must first agree with its idea that Christian redemption is more than personal salvation; Christian redemption is related to social, economic, and religious structures. We should also sympathize with its demands that Christians work to change evil and oppressive structures. Both of these reflect Calvin's teaching and work in Geneva and have been echoed by Calvinists in many lands and times.

But while praising these goals of Liberation Theology, we must criticize it on several other points. Like the Social Gospel movement, the Theology of Liberation places nearly all its emphasis on the this-worldly establishment of the "kingdom of God." While we can agree with Antonio Fragoso that "the struggle for justice is also the struggle for the Kingdom of God,"[9] we must recognize that Liberation Theologians frequently seem to think that such a kingdom is fully attainable this side of the grave. That view is not biblical: Scripture teaches that only when Christ returns will his kingdom become a reality. Also, Liberation Theologians tend to identify Christian efforts with such secular movements as Socialism and Marxism. As a result they have rather uncritically adopted notions of class struggle, violence, and subversion as legiti-

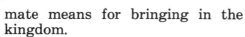

mate means for bringing in the kingdom.

Finally in its emphasis on salvation as an active seeking for just society, Liberation Theology seems to have lost sight of individual conversion and belief. Justification of the individual sinner before God is a foundational, if not the final, part of Christian faith. Liberation Theology seems singularly uninterested in such conversion.

****

Whatever our criticisms might be, we should recognize that the antislavery crusades, the Social Gospel movement, and the Theology of Liberation all remind us of our Christian obligation to correct injustices and inequities in our world. As Christians we are called to be keepers of our brothers and sisters, including the millions who have been oppressed and dehumanized. If we are truly God's children and if we are truly praying that his kingdom come "on earth as it is in heaven," we must be ready to point out the injustices in our world and work with others, using proper means, to create a more just world order.

CHAPTER 25
THE CHURCH
IN A SECULARIZED WORLD

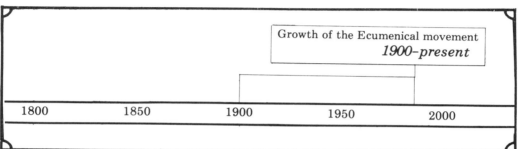

1800	1850	1900	1950	2000

Growth of the Ecumenical movement
1900–present

At the end of almost two thousand years of history, the church of Jesus Christ still exists—but in a vastly changed world. In the secularized society that covers most of the earth, the church's future seems distressingly grim. There are those within the church who expect its influence and support to continue to wane with the century. There are those outside the church who predict its increasing irrelevance as a relic of an earlier age, unneeded by those modern people with courage to live in a world without God.

How should we as Christians react to such dismal projections? By recognizing certain realities. The sharp decline during this century of the church's influence in state and society is indisputable. Equally obvious is the loss of the active support of the majority of people in (what used to be called) Christendom. In England only 20 percent of the people participate in worship at all and only 5 percent with some regularity. In Germany, France, and the Scandinavian countries, the situation is very similar. Only in North America, it seems, does a substantial part of the populace still faithfully take part in the church's life.

But there are other realities. In many non-Western parts of the world, the church still grows and shows a vital life. In Africa, for example, the response to the gospel has been so enthusiastic that by the end of this century possibly half of the continent's population may be Christian. And there remains the abiding reality of the Lord whose body the church is, the one who has received all power and authority and rules the history of all people, the one who has promised to be with his church to the end of time.

In this chapter, keeping those realities in mind, we will consider several factors that have contributed to the weakening of Christianity's influence, especially in the Western world. We will also discuss the church's disunity and the efforts people have made to promote a unified and therefore more credible witness of the church of Christ in the modern world.

Forces Contributing to the Church's Loss of Influence

The Industrial Revolution, some of the effects of which were discussed in the last chapter, resulted in a virtual de-Christianization of the masses. This rejection of Christianity was partly due to the new social situation: long working hours and impersonal city life (without the village's pressures to conform) encouraged many to become lax in church attendance. But it was also due to the church's neglect. Promoting the values of factory owners and ignoring the real needs of factory workers, the church alienated many of the working class. Especially Protestant churches failed to establish new church fellowships in the working class neighborhoods.

Only in recent decades have churches in Europe and North America tried to re-Christianize the masses. But despite valiant efforts, success has been limited. There are still millions of workers in the West who simply ignore Christianity, content to live "without benefit of clergy or church."

A second factor detrimental to the church's influence is the non-Christian mindset arising from modern science and technology. As humanity has seemingly gained control over the forces of nature, many Westerners have concluded that God is an unnecessary hypothesis and the church is irrelevant. The myth of "autonomous man," which began among eighteenth-century Deists, has spread rapidly during the last two centuries as more and more people come to believe that humanity is "slowly but surely refashioning the world" into a place where people can, by their own power, achieve happiness.[1]

The late Bertrand Russell, an English philosopher, was a major spokesman for this viewpoint. In *Why I Am Not a Christian*, he contended that humankind will achieve a happier and more just world not by depending on God, but by the greater and wider use of human intelligence. Though painfully aware of the two World Wars, the Holocaust, and the atomic weaponry of this century, Russell was still convinced that human beings have the rational and technical means to create a just and happy society on earth and that the church, by turning people away from this world, hampers the resolution of human problems.

This myth of "autonomous man," nurtured by intellectuals, has filtered down to more ordinary people. Millions today are practical atheists. The church to them functions only to preach personal piety and morality. It has nothing to do with the human problems of world hunger, atomic warfare, or economic injustice. Such problems, they suppose, must be resolved by reason and technology.

The otherworldliness of much of evangelical Christianity and its almost exclusive emphasis on personal salvation has encouraged this myth. Many Christians have concluded that "the church is so heavenly that it is no earthly good" and that the great human problems can be handled best by secular specialists and scientists who approach life from a purely humanistic perspective.

A variant of this "autonomous man" myth is found in Marxism. Marxists have vigorously attacked the Christian church for promising "pie in the sky in the sweet bye and bye" and thereby encouraging suffering workers to accept mistreatment by their social and economic exploiters. Besides, adherents of this atheistic system have a deep faith that through class struggle and revolution humankind will attain redemption in history. They believe that eventually a classless society will emerge in which each person will work according to ability and receive according to need. History, according to the Marxist faith, is moving inexorably toward a day when war, greed, exploitation, hunger, and such evils will be abolished through human effort and a truly just society will be a reality.

In nations like Russia and China, where Marxists have gained control, the church operates under severe disabilities. Atheism is the official doctrine and foundation of the educational system. The church and all religion are expected to fade as the classless society emerges. While Christian churches have continued to exist, and in a few cases like Poland even to prosper, Christians generally remain a persecuted minority with little opportunity to influence the state or shape society. But what these churches have lost in influence and numbers, they may possibly have gained in quality: only sincerely committed followers of Christ now belong to the church in these countries.

Marxism has attracted many disciples, especially in areas where exploitation and gross injustice are common. In such lands Marxist propaganda stridently attacks the Christian church, accusing it of always siding with the wealthy and privileged against the downtrodden, and charging Christian missionaries with being, unwittingly perhaps, agents of Western imperialism.

In reply the church must first admit that such accusations are often true. Next, it must demonstrate concretely its unity with the exploited and its genuine concern for justice. Finally, it must declare clearly that God alone gives meaning and purpose to human life and that apart from God no one can gain ultimate happiness. Only then will the church be able effectively to counter Marxist propaganda.

The myth of "autonomous man" and attempts in the name of that myth to create an ideal society have led only to creating hells on earth. The experience of Stalinist Russia, of Pol Pot's Cambodia, and of Mao's China would all seem to support Dostoevski's assertion that "if God does not exist, then everything is permitted."

Still another factor in the church's waning influence has been the rise of nationalism. In many cases the state has become almost a substitute god, and a secular religion that worships people has displaced the Christian faith. Dis-

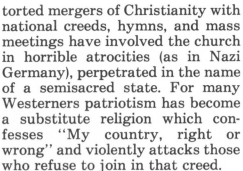

Karl Marx

torted mergers of Christianity with national creeds, hymns, and mass meetings have involved the church in horrible atrocities (as in Nazi Germany), perpetrated in the name of a semisacred state. For many Westerners patriotism has become a substitute religion which confesses "My country, right or wrong" and violently attacks those who refuse to join in that creed.

Today in Third World countries nationalism is a major threat to the churches. As African and Asian nations achieve freedom from their colonial European masters, many in these nations have rejected Christianity as the religion of the conqueror. To be a good Tanzanian or Ugandan, many feel they must give up Christianity. A related phenomenon is the revival of the religions of Africa and Asia such as Islam, Hinduism, and Buddhism. Often such revivals are related to a sense of national pride and identity and are a fruit of the feeling that to be a good Indian, for example, one must identify with an authentically Indian religion.

So the rise of nationalism in the Third World has made both the task of Western missionaries and the life of national Christians more difficult. The church today must strive to convince non-Western peoples that Christianity is a religion of oriental origins, a religion that truly transcends Western culture and genuinely practices the belief that "in Christ there is neither Jew nor Greek."

A final factor that has eroded the church's position has been the rise of pessimistic atheism. These atheists not only disagree strikingly with Humanists and Marxists on humanity's ability to make the world good but often boldly assert the essential meaninglessness of life. As Friedrich Nietzsche said already in the nineteenth century: an athiest recognizes that life can have no meaning except that which he himself chooses to give it. Nietzsche made "might" his ultimate. The Russian, Dimitri Pisarev, asserted that since for the atheist there is no difference between good and evil, one should ignore traditional moral standards and live only for personal self-indulgence. Jean Paul Sartre, the French atheist, concluded that each person should choose freedom, the freedom to be what he or she wants to be for "every man is his own first norm."[2] Truly, as Hans Küng, the Catholic theologian, has said, those who deny God "decide against an ultimate reason, [an ultimate] support, an ultimate end of reality."[3]

A similar hopelessness is reflected in much of modern literature and in Edward Albee's "theater of the absurd." It is also found in the novels of Ernest Hemingway and in T. S. Eliot's early poem, *The Waste Land.* God has departed and life is left chaotic, filled with despair and empty of meaning.

This pessimism sprang at least partially from the failure of liberated human beings (liberated from religious superstition) to achieve the promised great things. Utopia has not come. "Autonomous man" has not created the good society. Science has not produced the brave new world. Instead "progress" has proved destructive and modern technological society, rather than making the world more humane, has dehumanized humanity.[4] Science has proved no source of redemption, for while providing constructive things like smallpox vaccine and computers, it has also produced destructive things like poison gasses and hydrogen bombs.

Similarly many who gave allegiance to Marxism have experienced the police state and stifling of human freedom and creativity that came with Marxist control. In despair they have concluded that their material gains were purchased at the price of human freedom and dignity.

So while some today still trust in humanity's ability to create utopia, others are left without any hope—no hope in human beings and no hope in the Christian faith. The twentieth-century church must address especially this latter group with the good news of hope in Jesus Christ. But the manner of that address has not yet been determined by the church.

The Problem of Christian Unity

The church today, as we have seen, faces some formidable challenges. Unfortunately it faces them in a fragmented state. Confessing a "holy Catholic church" and singing "we are not divided, all one body we," the church is actually divided into hundreds of separate denominations. While some of these maintain good mutual relations, many are so busy bickering with each other, they lack the energy to face the forces that oppose Christianity.

Granted diversity is not in itself bad and there are often good reasons for the different denominational groupings. A spirit of Christian cooperation can transcend these separations. Yet in actual fact, denominational pride, mutual competition, and exaggeration of differences have often hindered the ministry and witness of Christ's church in this century.

The developing awareness of these divisions as a problem that must be overcome stems from varied sources. First, there is the missionary experience. When Christians are a minute minority facing a gigantic evangelistic task, competition appears absurd. Missionaries have often questioned the need to import the results of doctrinal wars of the West into these new emerging churches: when real Christian fellowship is experienced on a lonely mission field, denominational differences fade. The result has been not only cooperative arrangements on most fields but also a spirit of mutual respect that undoubtedly has slowly spread back to the sending churches.

Pietism, with its tendency to minimize doctrine and emphasize the oneness of those who have "experienced" Jesus Christ, has been another influence for unity. This was apparent in North America already during the nineteenth-century revival when Baptists, Congregationalists, Presbyterians, and Methodists often worked together to bring the gospel to the frontier folk. It is the Pietist influence that leads people of various denominations to support great evangelists like Dwight L. Moody, a Congregationalist leader of the late nineteenth century, and Billy Graham, a contemporary Baptist. It is also the Pietist influence that helps form transdenominational organizations like InterVarsity, Campus Crusade, Wycliffe Bible Translators, and so on. Pietism, especially in North America, has been a powerful force to overcome a confusingly divided Christianity.

Protestant liberalism has also played a significant role in encouraging Christian cooperation. It too minimizes doctrinal differences, though on moralistic rather than experiential grounds. Following the lead of theologians like Adolph von Harnack, many liberals sought a common kernel of belief, such as "the fatherhood of God, the brotherhood of man, and the example of Jesus of Nazareth" that would give them a basis for Christian unity.

Through all of these means, recent years have brought a growing awareness of the biblical injunction for oneness. "As theologians recovered the idea of the mystical body of Christ, the church of the Pauline epistles, they began to have a Pauline horror of divisions within the body."[5] Many Christians began to understand that mutual love must be the visible sign of discipleship (John 13:35) and that the endless, bitter splintering of the church violates the oneness of Christ's body and gives a poor witness to the world.

Billy Graham

The twentieth century has witnessed some decided efforts to overcome divisions—first of all within denominational families. The Lutherans are an outstanding example. From some nineteen different bodies as late as 1960, it has united into four groups—Lutheran Church in America, American Lutheran Church, Lutheran Church (Missouri Synod), and Lutheran Church (Wisconsin Synod). The first two of these manifest a great deal of cooperation, but the last two differ markedly from the others on questions of scriptural authority and creedal subscription.

A similar though less spectacular movement toward institutional unity has occurred among Calvinistic churches. In the 1950s the old United Presbyterian Church and the Presbyterian Church, USA merged and the so-called Southern Presbyterians appear to be moving toward unification with the United Presbyterian Church, USA. More conservative Presbyterians are also negotiating for a merger that would include the Reformed Presbyterian Church, Evangelical Synod, the Orthodox Presbyterian Church, and the Presbyterian Church in America. Additionally, a number of the Protestant Reformed congregations which left in 1924 have rejoined the Christian Reformed Church. While institutional merger is unlikely, the Reformed Church in America and the Christian Reformed Church have in recent years been trying to heal the wounds inflicted when the Christian Reformed Church left in 1857; the two churches have instituted pulpit exchanges, common worship, and cooperation in a number of church agencies.

This century has also brought a significant number of interconfessional mergers. One of these, the Church of South India, took place as a conscious "challenge to the the whole of divided Christendom."[6] Seeking to present a unified Christian witness in southern India, this group united Episcopal, Presbyterian, Congregational, and Methodist groups into a single church. It was especially remarkable as the first occasion that an Episcopal church, believing in the apostolic succession of bishops, has joined with non-Episcopal bodies.

Still another example of interconfessional merger is the United Church of Canada, formed in 1925. This church is mainly the fruit of local unions; for as the western frontiers of Canada were settled between 1880 and 1920, local Christians often formed community (union) churches. By 1920 there were three thousand such congregations made up mostly of Methodists, Congregationalists, and Presbyterians. These Christians were instrumental in establishing the nationwide United Church of Canada.[7]

Perhaps the most remarkable development in twentieth-century church history is the ecumenical movement culminating in the World Council of Churches. That movement developed through several ecumenical organizations

Delegates to the World Council of Churches

formed in the late nineteenth and early twentieth centuries.

The first of these was a student movement. In 1886 Dwight L. Moody called a nondenominational conference at Mt. Herman, Massachusetts, in order to get volunteers for missionary service abroad. Out of this conference came the Student Volunteer Movement (1888) led by Dr. John R. Mott. Thousands of college and university students were recruited under the motto "the evangelization of the world in our generation" and sent out with a vision for a unified church. In 1895 this movement expanded worldwide as the World Student Christian Federation formed under Mott's leadership. This federation, impatient with church divisions, "became the most important, and probably the indispensable, nursery of the personnel of the ecumenical movement."[8]

The second significant ecumenical organization arose from the World Missionary Conference held in Edinburgh, Scotland, in 1910. The resultant International Missionary Council brought together many representatives of various Protestant missionary agencies to discuss together the theology of missions. The council resulted in a number of cooperative mission efforts and reminded Christians of various churches that they served

283

a common Master and should proclaim his gospel in a spirit of unity.

Not long after the Edinburgh Conference, Bishop Brent, an Episcopalian participant, feeling with others that missionary cooperation raised a number of pertinent theological issues, began to work for a conference "for the purpose of considering those things in which we differ, in the hope that a better understanding of divergent views of faith and order will result in a deepened desire for reunion and in official action on the part of the separated communions themselves." At this first Faith and Order Conference at Lausanne, Switzerland (1927), there were representatives of Protestant, Episcopalian, and Eastern Orthodox churches. It was "the first time in church history that the churches considered together the deepest ground of their divisions and had departed without condemnation or excommunication."[9] Conspicuous by its absence was the largest church, the Roman Catholic, which had maintained that any desiring unity should return to the Roman fold.

Though they met regularly after 1927 and became a constitutive part of the World Council of Churches in 1948, the Faith and Order Conference did not resolve the deeply established differences dividing the various communions. Nor did it seek to do so by way of some lowest common-denominator solution. But it did give member churches a deeper appreciation of their own traditions and a deeper understanding of the Christian traditions of other denominations.

Still another ecumenical organization was formed by the Lutheran Archbishop Soderblom of Sweden. This was the Universal Christian Conference on Life and Work which sought to unite many denominations for a common witness in Christian ethics. It was able to arrange joint works of mercy through agencies such as Church World Service.

In 1937 Life and Work invited Faith and Order to join with it in forming the World Council of Churches (WCC). The union, delayed by World War II, was finally effected in Amsterdam in 1948. In 1961, at New Delhi, India, the International Missionary Council also joined.

The World Council of Churches is not, nor does it seek to become, a super church. It does not legislate to member churches. "Each member church remains...free to decide to what extent and in what means it should cooperate with the WCC." It is an organization intended to facilitate contacts between Christian churches and thereby promote mutual understanding and hopefully greater cooperation between Christians throughout the world. But the World Council does assume that the church of Christ is one, that all member churches are "in some way" members in Christ's church, a part of the "holy Catholic church," and it does believe that this oneness should come to institutional expression.

Many churches, including the Roman Catholic, Southern Baptist, Missouri Synod Lutheran, and

284

Christian Reformed, have chosen not to participate in the World Council of Churches. Many reasons have been given for these deliberate abstentions. The Roman Catholic church sees itself as the only road to unity. Some Protestant churches fear that participating will imply approval of the views of Liberal theologians who have been very influential in the WCC, theologians whose ideas they consider antithetical to Christian faith. Other Protestants fear the WCC, like some ecclesiastical leviathan, will swallow up their own denominations. Still others are offended by the involvement of related organizations in radical political activity or even violent revolutions. Finally some believe that especially the Life and Work segment of the WCC identifies God's kingdom with present movements and ideologies, totally neglecting the aspects of the kingdom that will only be realized with Christ's return.

Yet despite such apprehensions and reservations on the part of some churches, the World Council of Churches is a significant force in the Christian church today. Those who remain aloof from it must face the question of what they are doing to overcome the church's fragmentation and whether they are seeking the unity that Jesus Christ enjoined when he prayed to the Father "that they may become perfectly one, so that the world may know that thou hast sent me and hast loved them even as thou hast loved me" (John 17:23).

****

The contemporary situation of Christ's church is a frightening threat for many believers. The alternatives it seems to force upon them—remaining isolated denominational groups with diminishing numbers and waning influence or joining in an eventual super church that would probably ignore the distinctive traditions born out of our histories—are equally unattractive.

But a study of the church's history through the last millennia should remind us that the church is Christ's and that even at the time when it seems most lost, when its future is dimmest, it remains his church and he cares for it.

The church is born of faith and it must live and work by faith. It must continue to carry out the missions entrusted to it with the confident belief that the God who so faithfully guided his people through the past centuries will continue to be with them "to all generations."

Footnotes

NOTES TO CHAPTER 1

1. S. G. De Graaf, *Promise and Deliverance,* volume I (St. Catharines, Ontario: Paideia Press, 1977), p. 47.

2. Shakespeare, *Macbeth.*

3. Langdon Gilkey, *Shantung Compound* (New York: Harper & Row, Publishers, Inc., 1966), pp. 240-1.

4. Geerhardus Vos, *Biblical Theology* (Grand Rapids, Michigan: Wm. B. Eerdmans Publishing Company, 1948), p. 119.

5. Daniel-Rops, *Israel and the Ancient World,* trans. K. Madge (London: Eyre and Spottiswoode, 1949), p. 147.

NOTES TO CHAPTER 2

1. Philip Schaff, *A History of the Christian Church,* volume I (Grand Rapids, Michigan: Wm. B. Eerdmans Publishing Company, 1950), p. 84.

2. Martin E. Marty, *A Short History of Christianity* (New York: Meridian Books, 1959), p. 16.

3. H. Boer, *A Short History of the Early Church* (Grand Rapids, Michigan: Wm. B. Eerdmans Publishing Company, 1976), p. 19.

NOTES TO CHAPTER 3

1. Joseph Gaer, *The Lore of the New Testament* (Boston: Little, Brown & Company, 1952), pp. 133-4.

2. J. Stevenson, ed., *A New Eusebius* (London: SPCK, 1965), p. 187.

3. *Ibid.,* p. 109.

4. Bernhard Lohse, *A Short History of Christian Doctrine* (Philadelphia: Fortress Press, 1966), p. 41.

5. Stevenson, *A New Eusebius,* p. 268.

6. *Ibid.,* pp. 346-7, 351.

7. Jaroslav Pelikan, *The Emergence of the Catholic Tradition,* The Christian Tradition, volume I (Chicago: University of Chicago Press, 1971), p. 198.

NOTES TO CHAPTER 4

1. Stevenson, *A New Eusebius,* p. 48.

2. *Ibid.,* p. 12.

3. *Ibid.,* p. 118.

4. *Ibid.*

NOTES TO CHAPTER 5

1. Stevenson, *A New Eusebius,* pp. 33-4.

2. *Ibid.,* p. 36.

3. *Ibid.,* p. 40.

4. *Ibid.,* pp. 56-7.

5. *Ibid.,* pp. 172-3.

6. *Ibid.,* p. 62.

7. *Ibid.,* p. 64.

8. *Ibid.,* p. 32.

9. Eusebius of Caesaraea, *Life of Constantine,* book I, chap. XXVIII, found in *The Nicene and Post-Nicene Fathers,* volume I (Grand Rapids, Michigan: Wm. B. Eerdmans Publishing Company, 1976), p. 490.

10. Eusebius of Caesaraea, *Church History,* book X, chap. IX, found in

The Nicene and Post-Nicene Fathers, volume I (Grand Rapids, Michigan: Wm. B. Eerdmans Publishing Company, 1976), p. 387.

11. Eusebius of Caesaraea, *Life of Constantine,* book IV, chap. XXIV, found in *The Nicene and Post-Nicene Fathers,* volume I (Grand Rapids, Michigan: Wm. B. Eerdmans Publishing Company, 1976), p. 546.

12. *Ibid.,* book IV, chap. LVI, p. 555.

NOTES TO CHAPTER 6

1. Clyde Leonard Manschreck, *A History of Christianity* (Englewood Cliffs, New Jersey: Prentice-Hall, Inc., 1962), p. 81.

2. Augustine of Hippo. *Confessions* (Grand Rapids, Michigan: Sovereign Grace Publishers, 1971), book III, chap. VI, section 11.

3. *Ibid.,* book V, chap. X, section 19.

4. *Ibid.,* book V, chap. VI, section 10.

5. *Ibid.,* book V, chap. VII, section 12.

6. *Ibid.,* book VII, chap. XVI, section 22.

7. *Ibid.,* book VIII, chap. XII, section 28.

8. *Ibid.,* book VIII, chap. XII, section 29.

9. Lohse, *A Short History of Christian Doctrine,* p. 94.

NOTES TO CHAPTER 7

1. Herbert Workman, *The Evolution of the Monastic Ideal* (London: The Epworth Press, 1913), p. 45.

2. *Ibid.,* p. 43.

3. Brian Tierney, *The Crisis of Church and State* (Englewood Cliffs, New Jersey: Prentice-Hall, Inc., 1964), p. 13.

4. Venerable Bede, *A History of the English Church and People* (Middlesex, England: Penguin Books Ltd., 1955), chap. 26.

5. Williston Walker, *A History of the Christian Church,* 3d ed. (New York: Charles Scribner's Sons, 1970), p. 181.

NOTES TO CHAPTER 8

1. Tierney, *The Crisis of Church and State,* p. 2.

2. *Ibid.,* p. 9.

3. *Ibid.,* p. 20.

4. Gerd Tellenbach, *Church, State, and Christian Society at the Time of the Investiture Contest,* trans. R. F. Bennett (Oxford: B. Blackwell, 1940), p. 59 (hereafter cited as *Church, State, and Christian Society*).

5. Tierney, *The Crisis of Church and State,* pp. 49–50.

NOTES TO CHAPTER 9

1. John B. Christopher, *The Islamic Tradition* (New York: Harper & Row, Publishers, Inc., 1972), p. 23.

2. Koran, Sura 88.

3. William R. Cannon, *History of Christianity in the Middle Ages* (Nashville: Abingdon Press, 1960), p. 169.

4. *Ibid.,* p. 171.

NOTES TO CHAPTER 10

1. Geoffrey Barraclough, *The Medieval Papacy* (New York: Harcourt, Brace, and World, 1968), p. 103.

2. Workman, *The Evolution of the Monastic Ideal,* p. 272.

3. *Ibid.,* p. 282.

4. *Ibid.,* p. 281.

5. *Ibid.,* p. 309.

NOTES TO CHAPTER 11

1. Bernd Moeller, *Geschichte des christentums* (Göttingen: Vanden Hoek & Ruprecht, 1965), p. 201.

2. *Ibid.,* p. 202.

3. *Ibid.,* p. 208.

4. *Ibid.,* p. 209.

NOTES TO CHAPTER 12

1. Moeller, *Geschichte des christentums,* p. 243.

2. John Dolan, *History of the Reformation* (New York: Mentor-Omega Books, 1965), p. 97.

3. *Ibid.,* p. 99.

4. *Ibid.,* p. 124.

5. Gordon Leff, *Medieval Thought: St. Augustine to Ockham* (Baltimore: Pelican Publishing Company, Inc., 1958), p. 258.

6. Dolan, *History of the Reformation,* p. 185.

7. *Ibid.,* p. 209.

8. *Ibid.,* p. 219.

9. John Baillie, John T. McNeill, and Henry P. Van Dusen, gen. eds., The Library of Christian Classics, volume XIV, *Advocates of Reform: From Wyclif to Erasmus,* ed. Matthew Spinka (Philadelphia: Westminster Press, 1960), p. 26.

10. *Ibid.,* p. 30.

NOTES TO CHAPTER 13

1. Lewis Spitz, *The Renaissance and Reformation Movements* (Chicago: Rand McNally & Company, 1971), p. 326.

2. *Ibid.*

3. Erik Erikson, *Young Man Luther* (New York: W. W. Norton & Company, 1958), p. 251.

4. Roland Bainton, *Here I Stand* (Nashville: Abingdon Press, 1950), p. 41.

5. Spitz, *The Renaissance and Reformation Movements,* p. 335.

6. Erikson, *Young Man Luther,* p. 233.

7. Roland Bainton, *Women of the Reformation in Germany and Italy* (Boston: Beacon Press, 1971), p. 26.

8. *Ibid.,* p. 42.

9. *Ibid.,* p. 26.

10. Spitz, *The Renaissance and Reformation Movements,* p. 355.

NOTES TO CHAPTER 14

1. Franklin Littell, *The Origin of Sectarian Protestantism* (New York: Macmillan, Inc., 1964), p. 32.

NOTES TO CHAPTER 15

1. J. I. Packer, "The Faith of the Protestants," in *Eerdmans Handbook to the History of Christianity,* ed. Tim Dowley et al., p. 374.

2. Hierosme H. Bolsec, *Historie de la vie, moeurs, actes, doctrine, constance et mort de Jean Calvin,* in *The Reformation,* ed. H. J. Hillerbrand, pp. 205-6.

3. H. J. Hillerbrand, ed., *The Reformation,* (Grand Rapids, Michigan: Baker Book House, 1978), pp. 205-6.

4. Francois Wendel, *Calvin, The Origins and Development of His Religious Thought* (New York: Harper & Row, Publishers, Inc., 1963), p. 20.

5. John Calvin, *Commentary on the Book of Psalms,* volume I, trans. Rev. James Anderson (Grand Rapids, Michigan: Wm. B. Eerdmans Publishing Company, 1949), Preface.

6. Kenneth Scott Latourette, *A History of Christianity* (New York: Harper & Row, Publishers, Inc., 1953), p. 752.

7. Spitz, *The Renaissance and Reformation Movements,* p. 416.

8. Calvin, *Commentary on the Book of Psalms,* volume I, Preface.

9. Robert Kingdon, *Transition and Revolution* (Minneapolis: Burgess Publishing Company, 1974), p. 69.

10. John Calvin, "Letters II," 7th April, 1549, in *The Reformation,* by H. J. Hillerbrand, p. 204.

11. Kingdon, *Transitional Revolution,* pp. 69-70.

12. W. Fred Graham, *The Constructive Revolutionary* (Richmond: John Knox Press, 1971), p. 167.

13. *Ibid.,* p. 63.

14. Roland Bainton, *Reformation of*

the Sixteenth Century (Boston: Beacon Press, 1952), p. 116.

15. *Ibid.*

16. *Ibid.*, p. 117.

17. Jean Cadier, *The Man God Mastered*, trans. O. R. Johnston (Grand Rapids, Michigan: Wm. B. Eerdmans Publishing Company, 1960), p. 105.

NOTES TO CHAPTER 16

1. Latourette, *A History of Christianity*, p. 745.

2. T. M. Parker, *The English Reformation to 1558* (London, New York: Oxford University Press, 1950), p. 18.

3. *Ibid.*, p. 46.

4. *Ibid.*, pp. 40-1.

5. Bainton, *Reformation of the Sixteenth Century*, p. 198.

6. Parker, *The English Reformation to 1558*, p. 150.

7. Bainton, *Reformation of the Sixteenth Century*, p. 183.

8. *Ibid.*, p. 209.

9. John T. McNeill, *The History and Character of Calvinism* (New York: Oxford University Press, 1967), p. 307.

NOTES TO CHAPTER 17

1. Thomas S. Kepler, ed., *The Table Talk of Martin Luther* (Grand Rapids, Michigan: Baker Book House, 1979), p. 37.

2. John Baillie, John T. McNeill, and Henry P. Van Dusen, gen. eds., The Library of Christian Classics, volume XX, *Calvin: Institutes of the Christian Religion*, ed. John T. McNeill, trans. Ford Lewis Battles (Philadelphia: Westminster Press, 1960), book IV, chap. vii, paragraph 23, p. 1142.

3. Dolan, *History of the Reformation*, p. 318.

4. S. Harrison Thomason, *Europe in Renaissance and Reformation* (New York: Harcourt, Brace, and World, 1963), p. 612.

5. Dolan, *History of the Reformation*, p. 352.

6. Thomason, *Europe in Renaissance and Reformation*, p. 625.

7. Dolan, *History of the Reformation*, p. 355.

8. Thomason, *Europe in Renaissance and Reformation*, p. 618.

9. Richard Dunn, *The Age of Religious Wars* (New York: W. W. Norton & Company, 1970), pp. 9-10.

NOTES TO CHAPTER 18

1. Frank C. Roberts, *The Reformation* (Grand Rapids, Michigan: Christian Schools International, 1976), p. 15.

2. John Osborne, *Luther* (New York: Signet Books, 1961), p. 105.

3. Dunn, *The Age of Religious Wars*, p. 24.

4. *Ibid.*, p. 145.

5. Heinrich Ludwig Julius Heppe, *Reformed Dogmatics Set Out and Illustrated from the Sources*, ed. Ernst Bizer, trans. G. P. Thomson (London: Allen and Unwin, 1950), p. 181.

NOTES TO CHAPTER 19

1. Hans Gatzke, E. Harris Harbison, and Joseph Strayer, *The Mainstream of Civilization* (New York: Harcourt Brace Jovanovich, Inc., 1974), p. 393.

2. Arthur Aiton, *Colonial Hispanic America*, ed. Curtis A. Wilgus (New York: Russell & Russell, Publishers, 1963), p. 148.

3. *Ibid.*, p. 159.

4. Lewis Hanke, *The Spanish Struggle for Justice in the Conquest of America* (Boston: Little, Brown & Company, 1965), p. 133.

5. Philip Means, *Colonial Hispanic America*, ed. Curtis A. Wilgus (New York: Russell & Russell, Publishers, 1963), p. 67.

6. Lewis Hanke, *The Spanish Struggle for Justice in the Conquest of America*, pp. 32–3.

7. *Ibid.*, p. 25.

8. *Ibid.*, p. 126.

9. C. H. Haring, *The Spanish Empire in America* (New York: Oxford University Press, 1947), p. 186.

10. *Ibid.*, p. 182.

11. Mason Wade, *The French Canadians* (Toronto: Macmillan Company of Canada, Ltd., 1967), p. 9.

12. Cornelius Jaenen, *The Role of the Church in New France* (Toronto: McGraw-Hill Ryerson Ltd., 1976), p. 78.

13. *Ibid.*, p. 129.

14. Wade, *The French Canadians*, p. 24.

15. Jaenen, *The Role of the Church in New France*, p. 120.

16. Wade, *The French Canadians*, p. 1.

NOTES TO CHAPTER 20

1. Winthrop Hudson, *Religion in America* (New York: Charles Scribner's Sons, 1965), pp. 19–20.

2. William Warren Sweet, *The Story of Religion in America* (Grand Rapids, Michigan: Baker Book House, 1973), p. 27.

3. Hudson, *Religion in America*, p. 35.

4. Philip Schaff in *Religion in America*, by Winthrop Hudson, p. 8.

5. Frances Higginson in *Religion in America*, by Winthrop Hudson, p. 37.

6. *Ibid.*

7. Hudson, *Religion in America*, p. 44.

8. Sweet, *The Story of Religion in America*, p. 71.

9. Hudson, *Religion in America*, pp. 39–40.

10. Sweet, *The Story of Religion in America*, pp. 64–5.

11. Hudson, *Religion in America*, p. 42.

12. Sweet, *The Story of Religion in America*, p. 124.

13. *Ibid.*, p. 122.

14. *Ibid.*, p. 95.

15. Hudson, *Religion in America*, p. 56.

16. *Ibid.*, pp. 59–60.

17. *Ibid.*, p. 64.

18. *Ibid.*, p. 69.

19. *Ibid.*, p. 13.

NOTES TO CHAPTER 21

1. James C. Livingston, *Modern Christian Thought: From the Enlightenment to Vatican II* (New York: Macmillan, Inc., 1971) p. 40.

2. *Ibid.*, p. 104.

3. *Ibid.*, p. 107.

4. Claude Welch, *Protestant Thought in the Nineteenth Century*, volume I (New Haven: Yale University Press, 1972), p. 195.

NOTES TO CHAPTER 22

1. J. Herbert Kane, *A Concise History of the Christian World Mission* (Grand Rapids, Michigan: Baker Book House, 1978), p. 58.

2. *Ibid.*, p. 62.

3. Stephen Neill, *Twentieth Century Christianity* (New York: Doubleday & Company, Inc., 1961), p. 409.

4. *Ibid.*

5. *Ibid.*, p. 448.

6. *Ibid.*, p. 228.

7. Charles Henry Robinson, *History of Christian Missions* (New York: Charles Scribner's Sons, 1920), p. 50.

8. Neill, *Twentieth Century Christianity*, p. 481.

9. *Ibid.*, pp. 282–3.

10. *Ibid.*, p. 355.

11. Kane, *A Concise History of the Christian World Mission*, p. 138.

12. J. H. Bavink, *An Introduction to the Science of Missions*, trans. David Hugh Freeman (Philadelphia: Presbyterian & Reformed, 1960), p. 103.

NOTES TO CHAPTER 23

1. James Hastings Nichols, *History of Christianity* (New York: Ronald Press, 1956), p. 215.

2. G. C. Berkhouwer, *The Second Vatican Council and the New Catholicism* (Grand Rapids, Michigan: Wm. B. Eerdmans Publishing Company, 1965), p. 11.

3. *Ibid.*, pp. 16–22.

4. Eduard Schillebeeckx, *The Real Achievement of Vatican II* (New York: Herder and Herder, 1967), p. 28.

5. *Ibid.*, p. 60.

NOTES TO CHAPTER 24

1. Hudson, *Religion in America*, p. 304.

2. *Ibid.*, pp. 304–5.

3. John C. Bennett, *The Social Gospel*, ed. C. Howard Hopkins and Ronald White (Philadelphia: Temple University Press, 1976), p. 285.

4. Gustavo Gutierrez, *Liberation Theology* (Maryknoll, New York: Orbis Books, 1973), p. 175.

5. *Ibid.*, p. 155.

6. *Ibid.*, p. 205.

7. Enco Gatti, *Rich Church = Poor Church?* (Maryknoll, New York: Orbis Books, 1973), p. 43.

8. Rene Visme Williamson, "The Theology of Liberation," *Christianity Today*, August 1975, p. 8 (1080).

9. Gutierrez, *A Theology of Liberation*, p. 168.

NOTES TO CHAPTER 25

1. Neill, *Twentieth Century Christianity*, p. 289.

2. Clyde Leonard Manschreck, *A History of Christianity* (Englewood Cliffs, New Jersey: Prentice-Hall, Inc., 1962), p. 353.

3. Hans Küng, *On Being a Christian*, trans. Edward Quinn (New York: Doubleday & Company, Inc., 1976), p. 75.

4. *Ibid.*, p. 42.

5. Barry Till, *The Church's Search for Unity* (Baltimore: Penguin Books, 1972), p. 21 and Stephen Neill, op. cit., p. 335.

6. Till, *The Church's Search for Unity*, p. 32.

7. Neill, *Twentieth Century Christianity*, p. 349.

8. H. H. Walsh, *The Christian Church in Canada* (Toronto: Ryerson Press, 1956), pp. 289–90.

9. Nichols, *History of Christianity*, p. 347.

10. *Ibid.*, p. 444.

Bibliography

Augustine of Hippo. *Confessions.* Grand Rapids, Michigan: Sovereign Grace Publishers, 1971.

Baillie, John; McNeill, John T.; and Van Dusen, Henry P.; gen. eds. The Library of Christian Classics. Vol. XIV. *Advocates of Reform: From Wyclif to Erasmus.* Edited by Matthew Spinka. Philadelphia: Westminster Press, 1960.

—————. *Calvin: Institutes of the Christian Religion.* Edited by John T. McNeill. Translated by Ford Lewis Battles. Philadelphia: Westminster Press, 1960.

Bainton, Roland. *Here I Stand.* Nashville: Abingdon Press, 1950.

—————. *Reformation of the Sixteenth Century.* Boston: Beacon Press, 1952.

—————. *Women of the Reformation in Germany and Italy.* Boston: Beacon Press, 1971.

Barraclough, Geoffrey. *The Medieval Papacy.* New York: Harcourt, Brace, and World, 1968.

Bavink, J. H. *An Introduction to the Science of Missions.* Translated by David Hugh Freeman. Philadelphia: Presbyterian & Reformed, 1960.

Bede, Venerable. *A History of the English Church and People.* Middlesex, England: Penguin Books Ltd., 1955.

Bennett, John C. *The Social Gospel.* Edited by C. Howard Hopkins and Ronald White. Philadelphia: Temple University Press, 1976.

Berkhouwer, G. C. *The Second Vatican Council and the New Catholicism.* Grand Rapids, Michigan: Wm. B. Eerdmans Publishing Company, 1965.

Boer, H. *A Short History of the Early Church.* Grand Rapids, Michigan: Wm. B. Eerdmans Publishing Company, 1976.

Bolsec, Hierosme H. *Historie de la vie, moeurs, actes, doctrine, constance et mort de Jean Calvin.* Lyon: N. Scheuring, 1875.

Cadier, Jean. *The Man God Mastered.* Translated by O. R. Johnston. Grand Rapids, Michigan: Wm. B. Eerdmans Publishing Company, 1960.

Calvin, John. *Commentary on the Book of Psalms.* Vol. I. Translated by Rev. James Anderson. Grand Rapids, Michigan: Wm. B. Eerdmans Publishing Company, 1949.

—————. *Golden Booklet of the True Christian Life.* Translated by Henry J. Van Andel. Grand Rapids, Michigan: Baker Book House, 1952.

Cannon, William R. *History of Christianity in the Middle Ages.* Nashville: Abingdon Press, 1960.

Christopher, John B. *The Islamic Tradition.* New York: Harper & Publishers, Inc., 1972.

Daniel-Rops. *Israel and the Ancient World.* Translated by K. Madge. London: Eyre and Spottiswoode, 1949.

De Graaf, S. G. *Promise and Deliverance.* Vol. I. St. Catharines, Ontario: Paideia Press, 1977.

Dolan, John. *History of the Reformation.* New York: Mentor-Omega Books, 1965.

Dowley, Tim, organizing editor; with Briggs, John H. Y.; Linder, Robert D.; and Wright, David F.; consulting editors. *Eerdman's Handbook to the History of Christianity.* Grand Rapids, Michigan: Wm. B. Eerdmans Publishing Company, 1977.

Dunn, Richard. *The Age of Religious Wars.* New York: W. W. Norton & Company, Inc., 1970.

Erikson, Erik. *Young Man Luther.* New York: W. W. Norton & Company, Inc., 1958.

Eusebius of Caesaraea. *Church History and Life of Constantine.* Both found in *The Nicene and Post-Nicene Fathers.* Vol. I. Grand Rapids, Michigan: Wm. B. Eerdmans Publishing Company, 1976.

Gaer, Joseph. *The Lore of the New Testament.* Boston: Little, Brown & Company, 1952.

Gatti, Enco. *Rich Church = Poor Church?* Maryknoll, New York: Orbis Books, 1973.

Gatzke, Hans; Harbison, E. Harris; and Strayer, Joseph. *The Mainstream of Civilization.* New York: Harcourt Brace Jovanovich, Inc., 1974.

Gilkey, Langdon. *Shantung Compound.* New York: Harper & Row, Publishers, Inc., 1966.

Graham, W. Fred. *The Constructive Revolutionary.* Richmond: John Knox Press, 1971.

Gutierrez, Gustavo. *Liberation Theology.* Maryknoll, New York: Orbis Books, 1973.

Hanke, Lewis. *The Spanish Struggle for Justice in the Conquest of America.* Boston: Little, Brown & Company, 1965.

Haring, C. H. *The Spanish Empire in America.* New York: Oxford University Press, 1947.

Heppe, Heinrich Ludwig Julius. *Reformed Dogmatics Set Out and Illustrated from the Sources.* Edited by Ernst Bizer. Translated by G. P. Thomson. London: Allen and Unwin, 1950.

Hillerbrand, H. J., ed. *The Reformation.* Grand Rapids, Michigan: Baker Book House, 1978.

Hudson, Winthrop. *Religion in America.* New York: Charles Scribner's Sons, 1965.

Jaenen, Cornelius. *The Role of the Church in New France.* Toronto: McGraw-Hill Ryerson Ltd., 1976.

Kane, J. Herbert. *A Concise History of the Christian World Mission.* Grand Rapids, Michigan: Baker Book House, 1978.

Kepler, Thomas S., ed. *The Table Talk of Martin Luther.* Grand Rapids, Michigan: Baker Book House, 1979.

Kingdon, Robert. *Transition and Revolution.* Minneapolis: Burgess Publishing Company, 1974.

Küng, Hans. *On Being a Christian.* Translated by Edward Quinn. New York: Doubleday & Company, Inc., 1976.

Leff, Gordon. *Medieval Thought: St. Augustine to Ockham.* Baltimore: Pelican Publishing Company, Inc., 1958.

Littell, Franklin. *The Origin of Sectarian Protestantism.* New York: Macmillan, Inc., 1964.

Livingston, James C. *Modern Christian Thought: From the Enlightenment to Vatican II.* New York: Macmillan, Inc., 1971.

Lohse, Bernhard. *A Short History of Christian Doctrine.* Philadelphia: Fortress Press, 1966.

Manschreck, Clyde Leonard. *A History of Christianity.* Englewood Cliffs, New Jersey: Prentice-Hall, 1962.

Marty, Martin E. *A Short History of Christianity.* New York: Meridian Books, 1959.

McNeill, John T. *The History and Character of Calvinism.* New York: Oxford University Press, 1967.

Moeller, Bernd. *Geschichte des christentums.* Göttingen: Vanden Hoek & Ruprecht, 1965.

Neill, Stephen. *Twentieth Century Christianity.* New York: Doubleday & Company, Inc., 1961.

Nichols, James Hastings. *History of Christianity.* New York: Ronald Press, 1956.

Osborne, John. *Luther.* New York: Signet Books, 1961.

Parker, T. M. *The English Reformation to 1558.* London, New York: Oxford University Press, 1950.

Pauck, Wilhelm. *The Heritage of the Reformation.* Glencoe, Illinois: Free Press, 1961.

Pelikan, Jaroslav. *The Emergence of the Catholic Tradition.* The Christian Tradition. Vol. I. Chicago: University of Chicago Press, 1971.

Roberts, Frank C. *The Reformation.* Grand Rapids, Michigan: Christian Schools International, 1976.

Robinson, Charles Henry. *History of Christian Missions.* New York: Charles Scribner's Sons, 1920.

Schaff, Philip. *A History of the Christian Church.* Grand Rapids, Michigan: Wm. B. Eerdmans Publishing Company, 1950.

Schillebeeckx, Eduard. *The Real Achievement of Vatican II.* New York: Herder and Herder, 1967.

Spinka, Matthew, ed. *Advocates of Reform.* Library of Christian Classics. Vol. XIV. Philadelphia: Westminster Press, 1953.

Spitz, Lewis. *The Renaissance and Reformation Movements.* Chicago: Rand McNally & Company, 1971.

Stevenson, J., ed. *A New Eusebius.* London: SPCK, 1965.

Sweet, William Warren. *The Story of Religion in America.* Grand Rapids, Michigan: Baker Book House, 1973.

Tellenbach, Gerd. *Church, State, and Christian Society at the Time of the Investiture Contest.* Translated by R. F. Bennett. Oxford: B. Blackwell, 1940.

Thomason, S. Harrison. *Europe in Renaissance and Reformation.* New York: Harcourt, Brace, and World, 1963.

Tierney, Brian. *The Crisis of Church and State.* Englewood Cliffs, New Jersey: Prentice-Hall, 1964.

Till, Barry. *The Church's Search for Unity.* Baltimore: Penguin Books, 1972.

Vos, Geerhardus. *Biblical Theology.* Grand Rapids, Michigan: Wm. B. Eerdmans Publishing Company, 1948.

Wade, Mason. *The French Canadians.* Toronto: Macmillan Company of Canada, Ltd., 1967.

Walsh, H. H. *The Christian Church in Canada.* Toronto: Ryerson Press, 1956.

Welch, Claude. *Protestant Thought in the Nineteenth Century.* Vol. I.

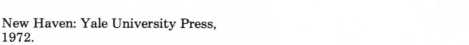

New Haven: Yale University Press, 1972.

Wendel, Francois. *Calvin, The Origins and Development of His Religious Thought.* New York: Harper & Row, Publishers, Inc., 1963.

Wierwille, Victor Paul. *Jesus Christ Is NOT God.* New Knoxville, Ohio: The American Christian Press, 1975.

Wilgus, A. Curtis, ed. *Colonial Hispanic America.* New York: Russell & Russell, Publishers, 1963.

Williamson, Rene Visme. "The Theology of Liberation." *Christianity Today,* August 1975.

Workman, Herbert. *The Evolution of the Monastic Ideal.* London: The Epworth Press, 1913.

Index

G

H

I

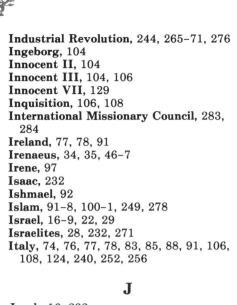

World Missionary Conference, 283
World Student Christian Federation, 283
World War I, 235
Worms, Germany, 89
Worship, 19, 41-2, 44, 47, 48, 74, 95, 97, 98, 155, 174, 176, 219, 223, 259. *See also* church; hymns; liturgy; prayer; sacraments
    buildings of, 22, 74, 78, 96, 210, 219
    current participation in, 275
    Sunday service, 29
Wycliffe, John, 130-1, 170

X

Xavier, Francis, 186, 188

Y

Yahweh, 19
Yale University, 216, 220, 225

Z

Ziegenbalg, Bartholomew, 243
Zurich, Switzerland, 148, 150
Zwickau, Germany, 142
Zwingli, Ulrich, 144, 148-52, 163, 174
    on Lord's supper, 149, 150

Credits

Grand Rapids Public Library: 93
Religious News Service: 43, 141, 142, 143, 149, 154, 160, 162, 217, 245, 281, 283
Three Lions, Inc.: 94, 106, 117, 131, 173, 218

Map, page 93: Reprinted from *Augsburg Historical Atlas* by Charles, S. Anderson, copyright 1967,
by permission of Augsburg Publishing House.